"Wilderness into Civilized Shapes"

"Wilderness into Civilized Shapes"

Reading the Postcolonial Environment

LAURA WRIGHT

The University of Georgia Press

Athens & London

© 2010 by the University of Georgia Press

Athens, Georgia 30602

www.ugapress.org

All rights reserved

Designed by Walton Harris

Set in 10.5 on 14 ITC New Baskerville Std

Printed digitally in the United States of America

Library of Congress Cataloging-in-Publication Data

Wright, Laura, 1970–

"Wilderness into civilized shapes" : reading the
postcolonial environment / Laura Wright.

     p.   cm.

Includes bibliographical references and index.

ISBN-13: 978-0-8203-3396-0 (hardcover : alk. paper)

ISBN-10: 0-8203-3396-4 (hardcover : alk. paper)

ISBN-13: 978-0-8203-3568-1 (pbk. : alk. paper)

ISBN-10: 0-8203-3568-1 (pbk. : alk. paper)

1. Commonwealth fiction (English) — History and
criticism. 2. Colonies in literature. 3. Ecology in
literature. 4. Imperialism — Environmental aspects.
5. Globalization — Environmental aspects. 6. Africa —
In literature. 7. India — In literature. 8. Ecocriticism.
I. Title.

PR9084.W75 2010

820.9'36 — dc22   2009039765

British Library Cataloging-in-Publication Data available

CONTENTS

ACKNOWLEDGMENTS

I would, as always, like to thank my family and friends for their support during the writing of this book. Thanks in particular to Jason, who has stood by me and understood both my need to do this work and has also helped me escape from it on occasion. Thanks as well to the faculty of the English Department at Western Carolina University for encouraging and supporting me during the writing of this work, and thanks also to Joseph Telegen and Colin Christopher, whose assistance with my research has proved invaluable.

Thanks to my fellow scholars who are doing work in this area, in particular, Bonnie Roos, Alex Hunt, and Andrea Campbell, whose acceptance of excerpts from chapter 4 of this study for their forthcoming collections has helped me to polish and refine that aspect of the work. Thanks also to Hans-Georg Erney for his acceptance, in 2006 and 2008, of two works in progress from this book for presentation at the British Commonwealth and Postcolonial Studies Conference, and thanks to Byron Caminero-Santangelo for organizing a colloquium on postcolonial environmentalism at the University of Kansas and for inviting me to present my work on Ngugi wa Thiong'o and Zakes Mda at that venue.

Finally, the animal rights theorist in me requires that I say thanks to Zeus, who was with me at the beginning, but not at the end, of this project. I miss you immensely.

"Wilderness into Civilized Shapes"

If one is engaged with the image and takes up toward
the elemental a bearing that draws the elements around
the expanse of things, then the force of imagination can
bring about the spacing of this expanse: it is there that
things show themselves.

—JOHN SALLIS, Force of Imagination: The Sense of the Elemental

Introduction

Imagining the Postcolonial Environment

"Wilderness into Civilized Shapes": Reading the Postcolonial Environment,
in that it examines the ways that authors of fiction *represent* postcolonial landscapes and environmental issues, positions the discourse
about both postcolonialism and environmentalism within the realm
of the imaginary. With this assertion in mind, my examination of the
texts included in this study is foregrounded by an analysis of the ways
that both postcolonial and ecocritical worldviews, while informed by
scientific and philosophical inquiry, are explicitly manifest through
fictional representations that are neither works of science nor philosophy. Issues relating to the environments depicted in the various works of fiction discussed in this text are multiple and complex
(comprising, to name a few, the creation of wildlife preserves and the
concurrent displacement of indigenous peoples, the privatization of
water, indigenous versus settler conceptions of the environment and
its appropriate treatment and uses, and so-called ecotourism and its
impact on indigenous communities), as are the various cultures—in
South Africa, Kenya, Nigeria, India, Canada, New Zealand, and the
United States—about which those works are written and from which
those works originate. My aim in writing this study is to look at the
way writers represent, through their fictions, various postcolonial environments; therefore, I do not intend to assert, beyond my incorpo-

1

ration of past and current issues that affect those environments, any scientific prowess with regard to environmentalism. Thus, I explicitly situate this work as a set of literary analyses that are centered on fictional representations of varied, compromised, and real postcolonial environments. I am, first and foremost, a student of imaginative literature whose primary mode of inquiry is postcolonial studies.

SITUATING POSTCOLONIALISM

As a field of critical inquiry informed by Edward Said's *Orientalism* (1978), postcolonial studies traces its beginnings to the Subaltern Studies Group of the early 1980s, a collective primarily of South Asian scholars—of which Said was a member—headed by Ranajit Guha. As a theoretical framework, postcolonial inquiry has sought to bring into focus the voices of marginalized peoples through sustained analysis of the mechanisms of colonial silencing, and such a project has proven immensely successful in certain ways and controversial in others. One of the primary goals of postcolonial inquiry, a discourse that has always primarily focused on literature, is to reclaim a precolonial history, to "elaborate the forgotten memories" of a "self-willed historical amnesia" (Gandhi 8). Furthermore, Nicholas Harrison situates another seminal moment "at the literary end of postcolonial studies" as occurring "when Chinua Achebe, lecturing at the University of Massachusetts in 1975, declared that Joseph Conrad was a bloody racist" (2),[1] but he notes that more recently postcolonial studies has tended to be informed by "the accusation of continued academic Eurocentricity even within postcolonial studies" (4).[2] As these perspectives illustrate, one of postcolonial studies' cornerstones, its attention to literature in general and fiction in particular, also proves to be one of its most contentious aspects. In that postcolonial theorizing has been primarily concerned with literary representation and an imaginary reclamation of lost history, it has, its detractors claim, failed to garner any impact beyond the rarified world of academia. Similar assertions are made about the field of ecocriticism despite its status as "an avowedly political mode of analysis" (Garrard 3). As Dominic Head suggests in his essay "The (Im)Possibility of Ecocriticism," "the process of developing specialized thinking about language and literature may be self-serving, channeled in the direction of a contained professionalism" (29). Postcolonialism, therefore, has much in common with the field of ecocriticism in that both modes of inquiry find themselves facing challenges based on the decidedly political and potentially activist nature of their foci.

SITUATING ECOCRITICISM

Ecocriticism's presence and prominence within the academy as "the study of the relationship between literature and the physical environment" (Glotfelty xviii)[3] is marked by the Association for the Study of Literature and the Environment (ASLE), which was founded in 1992 and is at the forefront of an ecocritical movement that has focused on analyses of North American texts (Garrard 4). Lawrence Buell notes that as a social movement environmentalism took shape in the 1960s and 1970s, but remained ununified and uncodified as a mode of textual analysis until very recently.[4] Buell is the "godfather" of Western ecocriticism, and his *Environmental Imagination*, along with Cheryll Glotfelty and Harold Fromm's edited collection *The Ecocriticism Reader: Landmarks in Literary Ecology*—both published in 1996—were seminal texts in terms of establishing a field of inquiry that had been taking shape since the 1960s, with the advent of the American environmental movement. According to Glotfelty, despite the fact that there had been no apparent "greening" of literary studies since the 1970s, "appearances can be deceiving. In actual fact, . . . individual and cultural scholars have been developing ecologically informed criticism and theory since the seventies; however, unlike their disciplinary cousins [history, philosophy, law, sociology, and religion] . . . [until the 1990s], they did not organize themselves into an identifiable group" (xvi–xvii). In his evocation of the importance of the imagination, particularly imaginative literature, in the perpetuation of change, Buell has done productive work to disempower the nature/culture binary that has been foundational to Western understandings of the nonhuman world, claiming "by 'environment(al),' I refer both to 'natural' and 'human-built' dimensions of the palpable world" and noting that "human transformations of physical nature have made the two increasingly indistinguishable" (*Writing* 3). Buell, whose studies focus by and large on the environmental import of writers from the United States from the 1700s to the present, invokes the concept of the "environmental unconscious" as an inherent aspect of *all* human psychophysiological makeup (*Writing* 25), and such a stance points to the need for all humans—not just those in the West—to protect the environments to which they feel an innate sensitivity.

As an academic practice in the West—and Garrard, Glotfelty, Fromm, and Buell examine ecocriticism predominantly in terms of its Western manifestations—ecocriticism as a theoretical model first manifested in 1990s-era studies of eighteenth- and nineteenth-century writers like Emerson, Wordsworth, Ruskin, Morris, and Carpenter, and Ramachandra Guha reads environmentalism, as a social movement, as a product of the 1960s that took hold most visibly in the United States (*Environmentalism* 1). Buell similarly notes the newness of the field, at least in terms of its academic manifestation, and he notes that the movement is gaining visibility because during the "last third of the twentieth century, 'the environment' became front page news" (*Future* 4).[5] Similarly, Guha reads environmentalism as a response to industrialization and, as such, sees the intellectual response of ecocritics as similar to that of socialists and feminists in that these movements were also defined in opposition to extant social constructions—capitalism and patriarchy (*Environmentalism* 5). Furthermore, in their foundational theoretical studies cited above, Garrard, Glotfelty, Fromm, and Buell gesture beyond the first world in terms of the future of ecocriticism, but none of these critics fully undertakes a postcolonial ecocritical project. Garrard recognizes globalization as an important variable in future studies, and Buell notes that while ecocriticism "has not yet achieved the standing accorded (say) to gender studies or postcolonial or critical race studies" (*Future* 1), he acknowledges the increasingly "worldwide" reach of ecocriticism (28) in his brief discussion of such "post-national" (81) writers as Irish playwright Brian Friel and West Indian poet Derek Walcott. And Glotfelty notes that "in the future we can expect to see ecocritical scholarship becoming even more interdisciplinary, multicultural, and international" (xxv).

INTERSECTING ENVIRONMENTALISM
AND POSTCOLONIALISM

In his 2005 essay "Environmentalism and Postcolonialism," Rob Nixon questions why these two fields of inquiry so seldom seem to intersect, given that "one might have expected environmentalism to be more, not less, transnational than other fields of literary inquiry" (716). Indeed, despite an increasing scholarly focus on the conjuncture of these fields of study, precious little has been published that links the two. Nixon posits several reasons for the dearth of scholarship in this area and concludes that postcolonial critics traditionally have shown little concern for environmental issues, viewing them, perhaps, as "irrelevant and elitist" (716) as compared to the plight of oppressed peoples, while the environmentalist "advocacy of an ethics of place" (718) has often resulted in hostility toward displaced human populations. In order to see and theorize the connections between these two fields, Nixon suggests, critics must "rethink oppositions between bioregionalism and cosmopolitanism, between transcendentalism and transnationalism, between the ethics of place and the experience of displacement" (721).[6] I cite Nixon's important discussion of the need and relevance of postcolonial environmentalism because of its attention to the problematic nature of such theorizing, and to point to Nixon's assertion that a failure of the environmental movement, in terms of its lack of exploration of non-Western environments is, in part, based on a lack of geographical imagination (718) that would allow for an examination of the relationships between cultural traditions, ecosystems, and social justice as these entities are affected by foreign powers. In essence, the very idea of what constitutes "nature" is an imaginary Western construction based on an Aristotelian system of binary thinking that differentiates humans from and privileges them above the so-called natural world.

Many foundational environmental theorists have worked to disempower the various binaries that underscore our thinking about nature, but in their attempts to give equal footing to the concepts of "nature" and "culture," they often utilize the rhetoric of colonial domination in order to demonstrate the ways that such dualistic constructions privilege one aspect of the binary at the expense of the other. Kate Soper asserts that the dualistic worldview in which nature and humanity are oppositionally situated is "axiomatic to Western thought, and remains a presupposition in all its philosophical, scientific, moral and aesthetic discourse" (38). Such a worldview always privileges one aspect of the binary and, as a seminal aspect of Western thought, is dependent on notions of self and other that underscore and justify the West's intrusion into non-Western cultures.[7] Similarly, Val Plumwood critiques the ways that the hierarchical nature of dualistic thought makes "equality and mutuality literally unthinkable" (*Feminism* 47), and she gestures toward a colonial framework when she discusses binarism in terms of its imperialistic import: "the logic of colonization creates complementary and . . . complicit subordinated identities. . . . The reclamation and affirmation of subordinated identity is one of the key problems of the colonized" (61). Plumwood's commentary about colonization in her discussion of nature is rhetorical and serves to illustrate her claim that the affirmation of women and femininity is a similar issue, that women and nature, like colonized individuals, are subordinated in the discourse of civilization. Such studies as those listed above point to the ways that, at least in terms of the language that Western scholars use to discuss the concepts of environment, nature, and culture, the "third-world" figures as a trope for discussions of the way that nature is a subjugated entity. Another telling example of the intrusion of the rhetoric of postcolonial studies into the realm of ecocriticsm is David Mazel's 1996 essay "American Literary Environmentalism as Domestic Orientalism," in which Mazel suggests "approaching the environment as a construct, not as the prediscursive origin and cause of environmental discourses" (143).[8]

Mazel's claim that "American literary environmentalism be approached as a form of domestic Orientalism as the latter has been formulated by Edward Said" ("American Literary" 144) provides another lens through which to examine the concept of universalism; in this reading, the environment is "Orientalized," rendered pure and in need of protection, the locus of intellectual inquiry, and object of scholarly exploration. Mazel uses Edward Said's foundational postcolonial critical study *Orientalism*—a text that was published the same year that the term "ecocriticsm" was coined by William Rueckert in his essay "Literature and Ecology: An Experiment in Ecocriticism"[9]—to make his argument. *Orientalism,* "commonly regarded as the catalyst and reference point for postcolonialism" (Gandhi 64), critiques representations of the non-Western world by Western writers.[10] In *Orientalism* Said evokes the Western-authored imaginary Orient, a locus crafted from fragments of texts, which reduces multifaceted cultures and peoples to one overarching construct. Such positioning situates the Orient as object of Western study and subject to Western disciplinary action (41). In his usage of Said's *Orientalism* to characterize an American environmental literary tradition, Mazell notes that such a comparison "might be disputed on the grounds that it concerns one's *own* territory rather than foreign lands upon which one has some evil imperial design" (144), but he continues by situating the late-nineteenth-century American West as a locus of imperial conquest. The rhetoric of postcolonialism is, therefore, evoked to critique a literary tradition in the United States as a colonizing or orientalizing agent.

In the examples above, Soper, Plumwood, and Mazell utilize the rhetoric of colonial domination to illustrate the ways that these dualistic constructions privilege one aspect of the binary—maleness, culture, colonizer—at the expense of the other—femaleness, nature, the colonized. In Soper's analysis, along with her critique of a kind of cross-purpose approach with regard to the Western view of nature, "one concerned with the limits of nature, and with our need to value, conserve, and recognize our dependency on it," and the other aware of "the cultural 'construction' of nature [and] its role in policing social and sexual divisions" (7), she evokes the culture/nature binary as ethnocentric, stating that the human/nature distinction is a "Western discourse" that has developed "in tandem with the development of Western culture or 'civilization' itself" (61). Plumwood evokes colonial discourse in describing nature as culture's other, explaining that "the contemporary form of globalization is a centric colonizing system" (*Environmental Culture* 29) and references "colonized identity" (*Feminism* 61) in order to describe the ways that women, like nature, are "othered" within this dualistic paradigm. While the acknowledgment of this binarism is useful in terms of an exploration of the interconnectedness of the nature/culture and colonized/colonizing schema, the studies cited above tend to pay lip service to the third world by using binary rhetoric to point out the similarities between the othering of nature and the othering of non-Western peoples without examining conceptions of nature that do not originate in the West and without examining environmental issues that are unique to populations in formerly colonized cultures. My acknowledgment of this circumstance is not meant to criticize unjustly these incredibly important and foundational scholars' studies but to demonstrate the ways that the utilization—and even deconstruction—of various dualisms via the employment of postcolonial rhetoric without an informed exploration of literal non-Western loci and issues can, essentially, render the postcolonial/third world metaphorical, a floating signifier for all that is "othered" within this schema: landscapes, women, and nonhuman beings. Such rhetorical explorations continue to consider Western notions of nature without discussing the environmental issues that are unique to formerly colonized cultures.

MOVING FORWARD

In his 2004 text *Ecocriticism: The New Critical Idiom*, Greg Garrard examines the rhetorical import of environmental issues and situates environmentalism's seminal moment—in the West—within the 1962 publication of Rachel Carson's *Silent Spring*.[11] Furthermore, while Carson's text is a scientific work that explains and quantifies the dangers of DDT, Garrard notes Carson's reliance, in her introductory chapter "A Fable for Tomorrow," on speculative fiction and her use of "the literary genres of pastoral and apocalypse" (2) to "turn a (scientific) problem in ecology into a widely perceived ecological problem that was then contested politically, legally and in the media and popular culture" (6). Carson's utilization of literary strategies generally associated with fiction allowed her to imagine an amalgam town in which all the plant and animal life has died as a result of pesticide toxicity and to represent a possible imaginary future, one devastated by the impact of DDT. She notes, "this town does not actually exist, but it might easily have a thousand counterparts in America or elsewhere in the world. I know of no community that has experienced all the misfortunes I describe. Yet every one of these disasters has actually happened somewhere, and many real communities have already suffered a substantial number of them. A grim specter has crept upon us almost unnoticed, and this *imagined* tragedy may easily become a stark reality we all shall know" (3, my emphasis). Carson's discussion of a composite town enables residents of any town in the United States to identify with the potential environmental apocalypse that her text presents. While such positioning proved, in the case of Carson's text, to be environmentally beneficial, in that it generated awareness that facilitated the 1972 banning of DDT in the United States, studies of the imaginings of environmental landscapes "elsewhere in the world" (3) must be careful to avoid rendering the postcolonial environment and environmental issues as analogous to those of the West; as Garrard notes, ecological problems are culturally relative: "a 'weed' is not a kind of plant, only the wrong kind in the wrong place" (6).

A body of contemporary literary critics has recently begun more closely to generate literary analyses that rely on both the postcolonial and the ecocritical. For example, both Susie O'Brien, in "'Back to the World': Reading Ecocriticism in a Postcolonial Context," and Norbert H. Platz, in "Rediscovering the Forgotten Space of Nature: A Plea for Ecocriticism in the New Literatures in English," urge students of literature to turn toward ecocriticism when examining postcolonial texts. O'Brien argues for a return to theory and away from ecocriticism's attempts to solve problems in the "real world," claiming that "ecocriticism needs to get back to theory if it is to negotiate the difficult cultural place in which it now finds itself. It is here, perhaps, that postcolonialism can help" (194), in that the "concerns and limitations of ecocriticism are shaped by its affiliation with the postcolonial science of ecology" (178). Similarly, Platz claims that "the New Literatures in English [from Canada, New Zealand, and Australia] not only reflect the aftermath of political and cultural imperialism but also increasingly manifest an awareness of the fact that during the period of colonialism many parts of the world fell victim to ecological imperialism" (176). Because of the obvious connections between the two fields of inquiry, these authors suggest—as does Rob Nixon, whose study I discussed earlier in this introduction—examining postcolonial texts via an ecocritical lens makes theoretical, as well as practical, sense.

In terms of utilizing an ecocritical approach in looking at post-colonial texts, however, it is necessary to examine the ways that environmentalism, as the social movement that gave birth to the kinds of ecocritical analyses codified by Buell and other scholars, is a Western concept. According to Thomas R. Dunlap, "in the twentieth century, ecology developed as a discipline in academic centers in Britain and the United States, and went from there to others" (3), and Ramachandra Guha points out some of the many problems associated with transporting environmentalist models from the West to non-Western loci. For example, Guha comments on the ways that the principles of European forestry did not translate in the colonies: "in Northern Europe, a single species of pine might dominate large areas of forest; a situation far removed from the tropical humid forests of Asia and Africa" (*Environmentalism* 39). Furthermore, because of monsoons, "in India . . . 130 years of state forest management have left the forests in much poorer condition than they were when scientific forestry first made an appearance" (41). Guha also notes that the topic of the first international environmental conference, which took place in 1900 in London, was wildlife protection in Africa (45). But he asks, "where did the African fit into all this? To be precise, nowhere" (46). Finally, Guha discusses the "environmentalism of the poor," in terms of a third-world dynamic that forces poor peoples to become environmental activists in the face of development that often results in their displacement (102).[12] From these various examples, it becomes clear that in postcolonial cultures, the factors that shape environmental concerns, strategies for dealing with environmental issues, and, in fact, the very reasons for an individual's environmentalist identification are vastly different from those in the West.

The reasons to acknowledge the non-correspondence between postcolonial and Western—particularly North American—environmental issues are various. First, "nature" in North American environmental thinking has been constructed as "wilderness," and the idea of wilderness, according to Garrard, "is the most potent construction of nature available to New World environmentalism" (59). However, according to Deane Curtin in *Environmental Ethics for a*

Postcolonial World, the North American concept of wilderness is the product of "the urban elite imagination" (5) that, when exported to postcolonial contexts, has contributed to national parks and wildlife protection areas that have benefited some endangered species while simultaneously displacing human beings. Conservation strategies operate in part by providing an attractive option, according to William Beinart and Peter Coates, "for white environmental concern because they furnish a route out of the central conservationist mentality: how to enjoy the advantage of urban-industrial society while salvaging a modicum of nature" (93), but the truth of the matter is that that modicum is relegated to an area behind a fence, a place that approximates a Western understanding of wilderness.[13] Furthermore, reading postcolonial landscapes through a Western lens that views the concept of environmentalism as preservation of some generality known as "wilderness" ignores an examination of the myth of an uninhabited, North American landscape as something other than the product of a colonially produced genocide. In actuality, for wilderness to exist, the native peoples that cluttered the imaginary North American landscape first had to be eradicated.

Because the genocide that shaped the demographics of the North American population has been largely absent from most formerly colonized countries, Western ideas about the postcolonial environment often focus on population control of non-Western peoples and on the role of third-world women in the maintenance of a sustainable population. According to Curtin, at the current political moment, strategies for third-world population control constitute another form of gender-specific colonization: "our thinking about population and the environment often assumes that we must adopt coercive and undemocratic means to stem the tide of the 'unreasoning masses.' Since gender is a subtext of these approaches, coercive means are often thought of as especially applicable to women: effective control of population in the 'real world' requires control of women's bodies, against their wills if that's what it takes" (75). While such a stance arises primarily from the reality that people in the third world are reproducing at rates that seem outrageous in terms of cultures that have achieved zero population growth (a group of cultures that does not include the United States)[14]—for example, the fertility rate in Nigeria is between six and seven children per mother (Curtin 95) —at least in part, such a position also arises from a strain of Eurocentric feminist thinking dependent on the premise that, in order for women to be fulfilled, they must be doing something other than raising children. Such a stance completely ignores the various cultural contexts in which, both traditionally and postcolonially, large families make economic and social sense. And perhaps most significantly, the rhetoric of population control tends to focus on numbers, not on resources, and more often than not projects the blame for the depletion of resources away from the West. Betsy Hartmann notes that an insistence on the third world's perpetuation of overpopulation is a myth that "breeds racism and turns women's bodies into a political battlefield" (4). She points a finger, instead, at industrialized nations for their disproportionate consumption of natural resources despite the fact that population growth in these loci is less rapid than in Africa and India: "currently, the industrialized nations, with 22 percent of the world's population, consume 70 percent of the world's energy, 75 percent of its metals, 85 percent of its wood, and 60 percent of its food" (23). In the context of the largely Western environmental debate surrounding resources, reproduction, and consumption, the concept of non-Western motherhood is often rhetorically synonymous with ignorance and environmental destruction.

In terms of scholars who have begun to venture into the field of postcolonial ecocriticism — or ecocritical postcolonialism — the above issues are of prime importance, and literary critics who engage with these convergent discourses have been careful to acknowledge the problems that an ecocritical approach may engender when applied to postcolonial cultures and texts. For example, William Slaymaker notes that "for some black African critics, ecoliterature and ecocriticism are another attempt to 'white out' black Africa by coloring it green" (132), and he states that "there is good cause to worry that environmentalism and ecologism are new forms of dominating discourses from Western or First World centers" (133), perpetuated by predominantly white scholars. Similarly, Graham Huggan, whose foundational 2004 essay "Greening Postcolonialism" examines Indian author Arundhati Roy's "The Greater Common Good," South

African author J. M. Coetzee's *The Lives of Animals,* and Canadian author Barbara Gowdy's *The White Bone,* asserts that "ecocriticism, at present, is a predominantly white movement, arguably lacking the institutional support-base to engage fully with multicultural and cross cultural concerns" (703). But the academic landscape is shifting, and other critics note the positive combination of the postcolonial and the ecocritical as a productive tool for literary analysis. For example, in her essay "The Greening of African-American Landscapes," Christine Gerhardt discusses the ways that these points of convergence inform readings of African American literature. Aside from the fact that both theoretical models are concerned with specific mechanisms of exploitation, "in their radical consequence, ecological criticism and post-colonial studies are deeply political endeavors that entail a large-scale critique of Western power structures," and "both are concerned with the complex relationships between the social and political center and its margins" (517). In "Toward an African Ecocriticism," Anthony Vital argues that in developing a postcolonial focus, "an African ecocriticism would differentiate itself from ecocriticism in the North, which has (for whatever reasons) . . . not felt compelled to engage with the consequences of European colonialism" (88). Such an assertion, of course, holds true for other postcolonial ecocriticisms as well, and it is my hope that this work provides a model for reading these various postcolonial texts and environments. Additionally, over the past decade, there has been increased attention to the role of environmentalism in the postcolonial world, as evidenced by such socio-historical texts as aforementioned William Beinart and Peter Coates's *Environment and History: The Taming of Nature in the* USA *and South Africa* and, more recently, Deane Curtin's *Environmental Ethics for a Postcolonial World.*[15]

Given the histories of both postcolonialism and ecocriticism as outlined above, my task in this study is twofold. First, I intend to work against the aforementioned imaginative failure discussed by Rob Nixon in order to provide an analysis of the ways that the authors considered herein have critically imagined the geography and ecosystems of the postcolonial world in ways that implicate colonialism—as well as globalization—in the degradation of "nature." Such an assertion does not, however, presuppose that, prior to colonization, there existed an overarching indigenous environmentally correct ethos that was altered and compromised by contact with colonial forces (despite the fact that certain authors featured in this text imagine and represent such a scenario), nor does it maintain that struggles against colonization and struggles against the environmental degradation resulting from or independent of the colonial paradigm are one and the same. Furthermore, the texts that I have chosen for inclusion in this study treat the relationship between colonization and environmental degradation in various, nuanced, and often contradictory ways that illustrate the ambiguous and fraught nature of that relationship as it has been influenced by historic and geographic factors. The second goal arises from the first, to critique, through analyses of imaginative literature, representations of non-Western understandings of the nonhuman world. It is important that I make clear that in this exploration I am interested in *representations* created by authors of fictional works as these authors attempt to situate issues of environmental import within postcolonial narratives. As such, these texts engage with both the productive possibilities for and the essentializing dangers of suggesting that Western and non-Western environmental knowledge systems differ. I will, therefore, analyze these depictions in terms of their imaginative import, not as evidence of anthropological truths about various peoples and cultures.

The chapters that make up this study focus on works that have become a part of the postcolonial literary "canon," including those of authors like Kenyan Ngugi wa Thiong'o and Flora Nwapa, whose novel *Efuru* (1966) was the first novel written in English by a Nigerian woman. But the text also examines other works—like Yann Martel's *Life of Pi* (2001) and Joy Williams's *The Quick & the Dead* (2000), which are not generally discussed in terms of their postcolonial relevance—and the ways that the terms "environment" and "postcolonial" are being reenvisioned and reconceptualized within the context of globalization and cultural (as opposed to land-based) imperialism. Instead of arranging my analyses in terms of chronology or culture, for the most part I have grouped texts together around a specific theme of environmental significance. For example, the first chapter, "Inventing Tradition and Colonizing the Plants: Ngugi wa Thiong'o's *Petals of Blood* and Zakes Mda's *Heart of Redness*," examines the ways that two traditional oral histories—one about an environmentally devastating event, the historical Xhosa Cattle Killing of 1856–57 in South African Zakes Mda's novel *Heart of Redness* (2000), and the other about a traditional Kenyan plant-based medicinal drink, Theng'eta, in Kenyan author Ngugi wa Thiong'o's novel *Petals of Blood* (1977)—are commodified and marketed in the modern Kenya and South Africa depicted in these works. These traditions, the consumption of a drink made from indigenous millet and the Theng'eta flower in Ngugi's novel, and the staged performance of reimagined Xhosa customs in Mda's, become items of capitalist exchange that are intimately linked with environmentally devastating Western developments: a casino in Mda's novel and the Trans-Africa highway in Ngugi's. Furthermore, both the ritual of Theng'eta and the performance of "traditional" Xhosa customs rely on imagined identification with a now inaccessible and uninhabitable past while simultaneously subverting and parodying that past in an attempt to monetarily benefit from its value as a marketable commodity. Both novels deal very explicitly with the displacements of peoples in the wake of corporate-driven land development, and with issues of deforestation and the replacing of native flora with European varieties of plants. In both works, plants function as metaphors for colonizers and colonized peoples, and the invasive species that characters seek to eradicate generate no hybrid entities.

The second chapter, "Safari, Zoo, and Dog Pound: Vegetarianism, Extinction and the Place of Animals in the Postcolonial Environment," explores South African J. M. Coetzee's *Disgrace* (1999), Canadian Yann Martel's *Life of Pi* (2002), and United States author Joy Williams's *The Quick & the Dead* (2000). The use of the animal as metaphor for subjected groups of individuals is prevalent in literature that explicates the plight of the oppressed, a fact that supports a reading of the animal body as the locus of oppositional thinking, the foundational example of all subsequent forms of human othering. In such narratives, shared racial or ethnic pain, pain produced by relationships between masters and slaves, turns everyone into animals, but to draw such a correlation is to rely on a system of thought that refuses to ac-knowledge the animal as deserving of the same kinds of respect hu-man beings *should* grant to other humans. In this chapter, I examine the role of the animal as metaphor for oppressed or colonized hu-mans (in the case of Coetzee's novel about a disgraced white South African academic who lives with his lesbian, vegetarian daughter and the dogs she kennels), and as beings fetishized and commodified as "other," as is the case in Williams's novel, which focuses, at least in part, on North American wildlife museums that preserve "exotic" African animals as stuffed corpses. In Martel's *Life of Pi*, the narrator, the son of an Indian zookeeper, advocates keeping animals in zoos and claims that "we commonly say in the trade that the most dan-gerous animal in a zoo is Man. In a general way we mean how our species' excessive predatoriness has made the entire planet our prey" (29). Furthermore, all three novels examine the concept of vegetari-anism as either a highly privileged dietary choice or, conversely, a moral obligation in the service of an environmentalist ethos.

The third chapter, "'Swimming in the River of Life' but Caught in 'the Stream of Justice': India's Water Woes and Arundhati Roy," examines India's water crisis as discussed by environmental activist Vandana Shiva in *Water Wars: Privatization, Pollution and Profit* (2002) and the role that water as resource plays in the life and literature of Indian author Arundhati Roy, particularly in her Booker Prize–winning novel *The God of Small Things* (1997), in which Sophie Mol drowns in the river in Ayemenem in 1969. This once-beautiful river is described by the narrator in 1992 as smelling "of shit and pes-ticides bought with World Bank loans. Most of the fish had died. The ones that survived suffered from fin-rot and had broken out in boils" (14). Furthermore, this chapter examines the role of the post-colonial author as environmental activist, specifically in Aradhana Seth's film *Dam/Age* (2002), which documents Roy's fight against the Narmada dam project in India. I examine Roy's fictional treatment of, and her lived public position with regard to, India's literal water woes, particularly the damming of rivers and subsequent privatiza-tion of water, as well as her activist performance in Seth's film in order to explore the performativity of Roy's public persona and the ways that performance is read by the media, literary critics, and environmental activists. Finally, I read Roy's activist performance in *Dam/ Age* through the lens of her construction of three fictional and linked performances in *The God of Small Things* as they illustrate the tenuous distinction between nature and culture.

In the fourth and final chapter, "Prophecy, Motherhood, and the Land: An Exploration of Postcolonial Ecofeminism," I examine Nigerian novelist Flora Nwapa's *Efuru* (1966), New Zealand novelist Keri Hulme's *the bone people* (1985), and South African novelist Sindiwe Magona's *Mother to Mother* (2000), all three of which contain environmentally significant prophecies that allow their three female protagonists to connect with and productively treat the land from which they, as colonial subjects, have been dispossessed. In *Efuru*, the Igbo lake goddess Uhamiri invites Efuru to worship her, and this worship requires that Efuru remain childless within a culture that values motherhood as a primary role for women. In *the bone people*, the protagonist Kerewin is implicated in the prophecy of the digger, stranger, and broken man, a prophecy that requires her to care for the landscape and people of New Zealand. Mandisa, the protagonist of *Mother to Mother*, listens to her grandfather's telling of the prophecy of Nongqawuse and the cattle killing that arose from it. In the present moment of the novel, set in 1993, Mandisa's son murders an American woman who, like the cattle who were killed a century and a half earlier, becomes a sacrificial offering to the failed prophecy. This final chapter examines the complications of applying ecofeminist readings to texts from non-Western cultures.

Wilderness into Civilized Shapes, which takes its title from a passage in Kenyan author Ngugi wa Thiong'o's 1977 novel *Petals of Blood*, seeks to give voice to the emergent field of postcolonial environmental literary theory that I have foregrounded above and to respond to the overwhelming call for work that examines the intersections between the fields of postcolonial and environmental theory as they are used to examine works written by and about formerly colonized peoples. It is not, however, meant to be an exhaustive cataloguing of environmental postcolonial texts, nor is it an attempt to provide an exhaustive scientific discussion of the environmental crises that affect the milieus from which those works emanate. As I stated early in this introduction, I am a postcolonial literary scholar, and my scholarship has tended to focus primarily on literature from southern and western Africa. This text is, first and foremost, a literary analysis. In terms of the debates surrounding the social and cultural impact of ecocritical and postcolonial literary studies, I find that my hope for this work is that it generates both literary and social awareness of the works examined herein and of the environmental histories and crises that have influenced those works. My sincere wish is that providing specific examples and explicating specific issues will inspire scholars to engage in reading and writing about the postcolonial environment in other cultural contexts and will encourage readers to pose solutions, to become activists in their personal lives, and, in their academic practice, to more carefully examine the connections between colonialism and environmental imperialism.

To grasp the ambivalence of hybridity, it must be
distinguished from an inversion that would suggest that
the originary is, really, only an "effect." Hybridity has no
such perspective of depth or truth to provide: it is not a
third term that resolves the tension between two cultures.
—HOMI K. BHABHA, *The Location of Culture*

Hybrid: A. *n.* 1. The offspring of two animals or plants of
different species, or (less strictly) varieties; a half-breed,
cross-breed, or mongrel. (1788 J. Lee *Introd. Bot.* [ed. 4]
Gloss., *Hybrida*, a Bastard, a monstrous Production of two
Plants of different Species.)
— *OED*

CHAPTER ONE

Inventing Tradition and Colonizing the Plants

Ngugi wa Thiong'o's *Petals of Blood* and Zakes Mda's *Heart of Redness*

In his famous coedited study *The Invention of Tradition*, historian Eric
Hobsbawm argues that "'traditions' which appear or claim to be old
are often quite recent in origin and sometimes invented" (1). He
continues: "'Invented tradition' is taken to mean a set of practices,
normally governed by overtly or tacitly accepted rules and of a ritual
or symbolic nature, which seek to inculcate certain values and norms
of behavior by repetition, which automatically implies continuity with
the past" (1). Through repetition and lack of variation, Hobsbawm
asserts, ritual becomes codified as tradition in that it ultimately becomes linked with past action, even if only because the action is re-

peatedly performed over a short period of time. Such a claim is clearly informed by Ernest Renan's theoretical stance on the importance of forgetting in the construction of nations,[1] as is Benedict Anderson's assertion, published the same year as Hobsbawm's, that the nation "is an imagined political community—and imagined as both inherently limited and sovereign" (6). I invoke these three well-known views of the importance of forgetting, invention, and imagination in the creation of tradition and national identity because of their theoretical relevance with regard to the two texts that I will examine in this chapter, Kenyan author Ngugi wa Thiong'o's *Petals of Blood* (1977) and South African author Zakes Mda's *Heart of Redness* (2000).[2] As colonial powers imagined narratives of their own national prominence, they subsequently invented a counter-mythology—dependent on a discourse of indigenous primitivism, spiritual vacuousness, and intellectual inferiority—that justified their takeover of African lands and the subordination of African peoples. Both Ngugi, who situates his narrative in recently independent Kenya, and Mda, who situates his immediately after the fall of apartheid in South Africa, write novels that imagine and mythologize the impact of precolonial pasts on the postcolonial present.

Like the characters who imagine and reinterpret tradition in his work, Ngugi, as the first Kenyan author to write a novel in English— *Weep Not, Child* (1964) —neither invented history nor set out to reinstate some "authentic" version of the past, but instead invented a literary tradition that, while undoubtedly influenced by a Western model, had no precedent. Therefore, in a very real sense Ngugi's imagined narratives became Kenya's national story[3]; Ngugi's novels invent a literary tradition based on an oral culture's colonization by Western forces and subsequent neocolonial identity as shaped by black African greed. Mda's project in *Heart of Redness* is, in many ways, similar to Ngugi's. While Mda was not the first black South African writer to write a novel in English, he does note that the end of apartheid played a significant role in his transformation from a playwright to a novelist. Mda, who initially wrote in his native Xhosa, notes in an interview with Elly Williams that during apartheid, "we needed work that would directly talk to the people—like poetry. Our poetry is not written on the page for a solitary reader, but for performance. You go out and perform it. We needed plays because plays are immediate . . . we did not have the luxury to sit down for months on end working on one piece of work, such as a novel" (qtd. in E. Williams 69). White writers—like J. M. Coetzee, Nadine Gordimer, and Andre Brink—wrote novels during apartheid because, Mda claims, they had the time to do so. In an interview in *Africultures*, Mda says that the end of apartheid freed his imagination: "I see stories everywhere." Mda's transition from playwright to novelist is significant in terms of the way that he, like Ngugi, has shaped the trajectory of indigenous African imagination, mythology, and history. In researching the Xhosa Cattle Killing in order to write *Heart of Redness*, Mda gave equal footing to "written history as it exists in books and in the archives, but also history as it exists in the *imagination* of the people" (qtd. in E. Williams 74, emphasis added). By codifying this cultural imagination, Mda generates a counternarrative about the Xhosa prophet Nongqawuse, one that subverts her reviled status as the destroyer of the Xhosa nation; in Mda's novel, it is Nongqawuse's historical significance that saves Xhosa land from environmentally destructive development.

Such narrative positioning is worth noting in examining the ways that characters in both Ngugi's and Mda's works attempt to come to terms with past historical events that lead up to and result from two seminal moments in the construction of national, anticolonial consciousness—the Xhosa Cattle Killing of 1856–57 in *Heart of Redness* and the Mau Mau emergency of the 1950s in *Petals of Blood*—through contradictory acts of collective forgetting, nationalist mythologizing, and, most important to my study, the invention of specific indigenous, environmentally significant cultural traditions. These traditions—the consumption of Theng'eta, a drink made from fermented millet and the indigenous Theng'eta flower in Ngugi's novel, and John Dalton's attempts to create a Xhosa "cultural village" in Mda's—are treated critically as they become items of capitalist exchange that are intimately linked with environmental devastation and the potential development of two Western, environmentally destructive entities, a proposed casino in Mda's novel and the Trans-Africa highway in Ngugi's. Furthermore, both the ritual of Theng'eta and the performance of "traditional" Xhosa customs rely on imagined identification with a now inaccessible and uninhabitable past, while simultaneously subverting and parodying that past in an attempt to monetarily benefit from its value as a marketable commodity. Such utilization of tradition in this way invokes notions of colonial mimicry in Homi Bhabha's sense and ultimately results in a reluctant hegemony among the characters in Ngugi's work, a hegemony that Mda's characters, through their resistance to the development of the casino and their insistence, instead, on ecotourism, are able to resist, according to Mda's narrator, "at least for now" (277).[4]

Both novels deal very explicitly with the potentially devastating effects of capitalist-driven development of the land, particularly as a result of deforestation and the replacing of native flora with European varieties of plants. Characters in both works seek either a return to an imagined traditional identity or struggle to define and occupy a hybrid space, and the presentation of the mortality and vulnerability of plant life functions in both texts as a mirror for nationalist survival. The destruction of indigenous plants and their displacement by alien species can be read on a very literal level as indicative of the decrease in biodiversity that results from the introduction of nonnative species, but such an instance can also be read as a cultural metaphor. Indigenous history, a connection to an authentic past, has been erased by an often appealing but insidious European presence in Africa, and in both works, tellingly, there are no hybrid plants, only nonnative species that crowd out and starve the native flora. Cultural hybridization is equally problematic, as is symbolically manifest in indigenous characters' attempts to eradicate invasive plant species. As Qukezwa says about the European inkberry bush in Mda's novel, "it kills other plants. These flowers that you like so much will eventually become berries. Each berry is a prospective plant that will kill the plant of my forefathers" (90). Similarly, Ngugi's narrator claims that an early white colonist, Lord Freeze-Kilby, planted wheat as a means of changing "Ilmorog wilderness into civilised shapes and forms" (68) that would yield European trees and crops. The search for an authentic or "traditional" identity that is somehow uncorrupted by the imposition of colonial culture in both works, then, is played out in part through attempted eradication of these invasive plant species: in the case of Freeze-Kilby, for example, the Ilmorog leaders "met and reached a decision. They set fire to the whole [wheat] field" (69), an instance that foreshadows the death by fire of three prominent neocolonial businessmen later in the narrative. Similarly, in *Heart of Redness,* Qukezwa is brought before the Xhosa leaders for cutting down trees that are "foreign," the lantana and the wattle that have "come from other countries . . . to suffocate our trees" (216). Such actions, however, are ineffective as attempts at establishing various prelapsarian—and imaginary—African Edens, impossible landscapes that are somehow uncompromised by their postcolonial status.

Kenyan author Ngugi wa Thiong'o's *Petals of Blood* was the last fictional work that Ngugi wrote in English before renouncing that language in favor of writing in his native Gikuyu.[5] In *Decolonising the Mind* (1986), Ngugi claims that "language carries culture, and culture carries, particularly through orature and literature, the entire body of values by which we perceive ourselves and our place in the world. . . . Language is thus inseparable from ourselves as a community of human beings with a specific form and character, a specific history, a specific relationship to the world" (15–16). Ngugi's decision to write in Gikuyu (and then translate his work into English for wider distribution) is at once a testament to his commitment to the belief that culture can only be transmitted through that culture's indigenous and, therefore, precolonial language, as well as a tentative acceptance of the hybridized medium of oral literature (or orature) as a means of preserving that cultural experience in the Western medium of the novel. Such a medium is problematic, however, if one considers the fact that in order to "write" Gikuyu—an oral language without a written component—Ngugi must utilize a phonetic system based on English. The tensions between Ngugi's Fanonist Marxist ideology, which explicates and critiques the culturally colonizing forces of Christianity, Western education, and the English language, and which is initially apparent in his 1967 novel *A Grain of Wheat,* and his so-called nativism have been addressed consistently and rigorously in many critical analyses of his works.[6] But in the context of my examination of Ngugi's presentation of a particular native practice, the production and consumption of Theng'eta in *Petals of Blood,* a work that clearly advocates Marxism as a remedy for neocolonial corruption, it is necessary to foreground some of the seeming contradictions that appear in these two philosophies.

Ngugi's decision to write in Gikuyu and his 1986 treatise on this decision, *Decolonising the Mind*—which was written for a Western audience—have been at the forefront of Western academic discussions of Ngugi's so-called nativism. In this text, Ngugi argues against the "literature of the [African] petty-bourgeoisie born of the colonial schools and universities," claiming that "this literature by Africans in European languages was specifically that of the nationalistic bourgeoisie in its creators, its thematic concerns and its consumption" (20). As recently as 2000 Ngugi has perpetuated this assertion, claiming that, historically, African literature has had "two contradictory tendencies. It was often motivated and driven by . . . nationalistic and racial pride . . . and yet its models were often the English authors read in class" ("Europhonism" 6). In a 2004 interview with Ângela Lamas Rodrigues, Ngugi discusses language in the context of globalization: "as we know, globalization is conveyed mainly through European languages, English more so than anything else." Furthermore, this means that people "are defined or define themselves through a European memory and, in the process, their own memory becomes barred" (162). Ngugi's decision to write in Gikuyu is based on his insistence that African literature be returned to the people, to the struggling peasant class, whose stories are oral, spoken in their native languages. This stance has drawn much criticism, particularly with regard to Ngugi's position as an intellectual who has lived in self-imposed exile in Britain and the United States since his release from prison in 1978.[7]

Anthony Arnove, for example, examines both Ngugi and Chinua Achebe's "misrecognition of their positions" (278) as members of the educated elite within the fields of language and African literature, and he criticizes Ngugi's project in *Decolonising the Mind* as resting on a "confusion between the categories of hegemonization (or incorporation), domination, and exploitation and on a generalization from Ngugi's experience as a member of the educated elite"

(283). Furthermore, Arnove points out that Ngugi works to allow the peasant classes to appropriate only elite forms of writing—like the novel—rather than explore non-elite forms, and he notes that while Ngugi writes in a Kenyan language, Gikuyu is a minority language, less accessible to the masses than Kiswahili. The concept of "the people," therefore, becomes a generalization for which Ngugi, as public intellectual, speaks as a perceived "authentic spokesperson for the dominated classes" (287). Simon Gikandi notes that in terms of Ngugi's decision to write in Gikuyu, "one could not help noticing that his work was being haunted by the pressures of producing knowledge in an African language within the limits and demands of Western institutions of knowledge" and that the Gikuyu language journal *Mutiiri*, created and edited by Ngugi in 1994 while he was teaching at New York University, "was being driven not so much by the concerns of Kenyan writers and peasants, but by the rhetoric of American identity politics and postcolonial nostalgia" ("Traveling Theory" 195).

Despite this stance with regard to the fraught nature of Ngugi's choice to write in his native language, Rodrigues asserts that labeling Ngugi's decision to write in Gikuyu as "nativist" represents "a profound misunderstanding" of his proposals (165). Similarly, Gikandi notes that "in spite of what has been misinterpreted as nativism . . . , Ngugi has never been comfortable with the role of the native informant," and that his "literary oeuvre is remarkable for its impatience with colonial and postcolonial theories of Africans and romantic attempts to recuperate an essential and unanimous African culture" (199). Indeed, in terms of the resurrection of the native past in *Petals of Blood*, the narrative is deeply suspicious. While the novel notes that indigenous cultural knowledge and practices, particularly in terms of the natural world, have been altered and shaped by colonial and neocolonial pressures, the work critically demonstrates the impossibility of resurrecting—or inventing—an "authentic" African past and posits, instead, a Marxist framework informed by that past as a potentially viable option for the future. Of his decision to write in Gikuyu, Ngugi asserts that he had an epistemological break with regard to language, and he notes that his decision to write in his native language functions as a kind of compromise between the recovery of a precolonial past and a historically informed present. He says, "but, of course, once you make that choice, it does not mean that you are going to *invent* your own history or new world, so to speak. You still have to write from your social perspective" (qtd. in Rodrigues 163, my emphasis). In *Decolonising the Mind*, Ngugi is careful to note that his decision to write in Gikuyu is not an attempt to reclaim a pre-colonial past but to create a new medium for the dissemination of Gikuyu culture in the present political moment. Furthermore, he is astutely aware that "writing in our languages . . . will not itself bring about the renaissance in African cultures if that literature does not carry the content of our people's anti-imperialist struggles to liberate their productive forces from foreign control" (29).

In terms of Ngugi's shift from English to Gikuyu, even though he was still writing in English in *Petals of Blood*, the text itself is, accord-ing to Evan Mwangi, a hybrid and "contains numerous non-English expressions that are left either untranslated or loosely hanging in the sentence structure in a way that would suggest that the narrative's ideal reader . . . is competent in both English and Gikuyu" (66). The novel is very explicit in its support of Marxism and, therefore, works to "carry the content of our people's anti-imperialist struggles" against colonial domination, presented in this case as three direc-tors of the Theng'eta Breweries and Enterprises, Chui, Kimeria, and Mzigo, members of the neocolonial elite. Furthermore, as Bonnie Roos notes, Ngugi's Marxist and nativist ideologies are closely bound to Frantz Fanon's idealization of the "revolution of the agricultural working masses as the people of the nation" (155). Ngugi's cham-pioning of the agrarian African multitude over the emergent and urban African middle class implies that a connection to the land is an essential element in the process of decolonization, and according to Simon Gikandi, during the 1970s Ngugi's writing was strongly in-fluenced by his belief that literary expression generated "representa-tions of a people's consciousness . . . that emerged out of their strug-gles with the environment and their efforts to create social life out of nature" (263). In that Ngugi believed that colonial rule not only destroyed culture through its imposition of the English language but also "alienated [Africans] from their environment" and "colonized their minds" (Gikandi, *Ngugi* 266), his Marxist vision is informed by an environmental ethos dependent on a connection between colonized individuals and the land from which they have been alienated. In *Petals of Blood*, this ethos is manifest most explicitly through the character of Wanja, who, through her organization of a women's farming collective, "brings life back to the very soil of Ilmorog" (Roos 156). Alternately, the neocolonial businessmen turn the land and its people's traditional connections to it into a commodity dependent on the sale of corrupted indigenous cultural practices.

W. R. Ochieng' and E. S. Atieno-Odhiambo claim, in their prologue to *Decolonization and Independence in Kenya: 1940–93*, that despite the fact that the term "neocolonial" is generally regarded in Kenya as offensive, "it is, nevertheless, important to recapitulate the salient features of the colonial state, for independent Kenya has borrowed substantially from it" (xiii). In *Petals of Blood*, Ngugi indicts Kenya's neocolonial status through his depiction of three black post-independence Kenyans who, through their capitalist interests, specifically with regard to the co-opting of Theng'eta for monetary gain, perpetuate the colonial paradigm. *Petals of Blood* is set in post-independence Kenya in the rural but developing village of Ilmorog and consists of the interwoven narratives of four characters: a school teacher named Munira, a crippled shop owner and former Mau Mau revolutionary named Abdulla, a businesswoman turned prostitute named Wanja, and Karega, a former school teacher turned trade union activist. The narrative begins in the present of the 1970s, with the arrests of the four main characters under suspicion of the murders of millionaire businessmen Chui, Kimeria, and Mzigo, who have burned to death in Wanja's home. The novel then flashes back to a period twelve years earlier when the four initially meet and become friends. The narrative perspective shifts from character to character (and is often intruded upon by Ngugi's own narrative didacticism)[8] and from past to present to reveal the ways that the four primary characters become entangled with and then estranged from one another, in part because of the sale of Theng'eta, a drink with precolonial ceremonial significance that, in the context of the neocolonial present, becomes corrupted as a capitalist commodity.

Theng'eta, literally "the spirit," the recipe for which is passed from Wanja's grandmother Nyakinyua to her granddaughter, turns from a libation once drunk in moderation and on specific celebratory occasions to an object of vice that is marketed to a disillusioned populace, the majority of whom have not benefited from Kenya's 1963 independence. The drink, a liquor distilled from an indigenous grain, fermented millet, is nothing more than an alcoholic beverage that, according to Nyakinyua, "can only poison your heads and intestines" (210). Only when another indigenous plant, the flower Theng'eta, is combined with the liquor does it gain a spiritual significance that can give its drinker second sight, but only if it is drunk "with faith and purity" (210) in one's heart. The drink in its contemporary manifestation is a symbol of the ways that the three aspects of cultural colonization of which Ngugi is the most critical—Christianity, Western education, and the English language—sever the connection between the material, environmental, and spiritual aspects of Kenyan culture. The drink combines traditional environmental and cultural elements, but its consumption is shaped by the neocolonial present in which the drinkers exist. In the present moment of the novel, therefore, the contemporary and postcolonial tradition of Theng'eta drinking is invented. During the colonial period, the drinking of Theng'eta was banned, according to Nyakinyua, by the colonizers for its tendency, they believed, to encourage insubordination (205); therefore, the revival of the practice of drinking Theng'eta in post-independence Kenya is as much an attempt to celebrate the harvest in Ilmorog and reclaim a precolonial tradition as it is an affront to the colonial government that once banned it. But the purity and faith that Nyakinyua claims are requisite for one to experience the full spiritual benefit of Theng'eta are impossible to reclaim from the past and impossible to maintain in the Kenya depicted in Ngugi's text, a place where the country's wealth lies in the hands of a relative few and where the natural environment is being exploited. The corruption of both the Theng'eta flower and the drink that is derived from it function symbolically in *Petals of Blood* to demonstrate the ways that, in the face of capitalist-driven development, one can become drunk on the sale of the natural world, particularly its indigenous plants, despite the dangers—both to the self and to the environment—of such intoxication.

Much criticism of Ngugi's novel has focused on the unwieldy nature of the narrative, the didacticism of its Marxist message, and the implausibility of its characters. For example, James A. Ogude criticizes Ngugi's "romantic portrayal of working class leaders" ("Imagining" 4) and claims that Karega's "coming to consciousness, his apparent transformation from a black nationalist to a trade union leader embracing a socialist vision, remains unconvincing" (5). Ogude excuses these and other flaws, however, by citing Ngugi's extremely difficult and impractical task of attempting to write a coherent call for change "in the face of fragmentation, displacement and a basic absence of models to inspire his writing" (6). Glenn Hooper similarly defends Ngugi's ambitious project: "sometimes regarded as . . . too structurally complex, *Petals of Blood* is nevertheless a milestone in African and postcolonial literature, a text noted for its excoriating attacks on neocolonial corruption, as well as for its ambitions for a dignified, proletarian-led future" (48). What critics like Ogude and Hooper tacitly recognize, I believe, is Ngugi's attempt to construct a coherent narrative from historical fragmentation in order to write a more positive (read Marxist) vision of post-independence Kenya into being. It seems worth noting that in terms of Ngugi's use of Theng'eta as a symbol for the corruption of tradition in the face of capitalist modernity, he, as the first Kenyan author to write a novel in English, is uniquely situated to demonstrate the malleability of national narrative; the cultural meaning attached to Theng'eta changes over the course of the novel because Ngugi, as creator of a Kenyan nationalist and Marxist mythology, changes it. The mythology at the center of the novel, then, is not the mythology of precolonial Kenya but is the mythology of the present as it attempts to come to terms with a profound sense of cultural loss. The changed status of the drink in this context demonstrates how the bastardization of the drinking of Theng'eta resonates with the corruption of other Gikuyu traditional practices, particularly the oath and the drinking of tea—which is presented earlier in *Petals of Blood* and which the drinking of Theng'eta explicitly mirrors. Both practices were reconceptualized in the context of the Mau Mau emergency of the 1950s, an event that immediately precedes the narrative action, as anticolonial symbols.

According to Brendan Nicholls, "militarily, Mau Mau failed. Psychologically, Mau Mau was an incontestable force that continues to occupy an unsettling or disturbing place in the European . . . imagination" (177). In reality, however, the number of native Kenyans considered "loyal" to the colonial government who were killed during the emergency far outnumbered white murders,[9] but as a perceived and imagined threat, the Mau Mau insurgency maintained a pervasive hold on the European psyche. Prior to the movement, within the context of Gikuyu culture, major and minor oaths, expressions of loyalty and service, were regularly taken by men.[10] According to R. Mugo Gatheru, "after one had taken an oath, it was impossible to be de-oathed; there was no concept of de-oathing in the traditional Kikuyu system" (149). Despite the mythology surrounding the forced oath-taking that took place during the Mau Mau emergency—during which by 1951, "the youth had imposed forced oathing for the achievement of unity on all Gikuyu" (Atieno-Odhiambo 35)—the corruption of the concept of the oath has its precedent in 1891 at the hands of Europeans with the establishment of the first mission station in Kenya between Captain Frederick Lugard of the British East Africa Company and the Gikuyu chief Waiyaki. Lugard betrayed an oath he took with Waiyaki, and in retaliation for the broken oath, the chief burned down Lugard's fortress. British forces subsequently abducted and murdered the chief. According to Gatheru, "Lugard had taken their traditional oath that neither he nor his people would interfere with the Kikuyu people and their property. They had agreed to administer the oath to him, an honor rarely granted to anyone outside the tribe. The sacrifice was a terrible omen" (19). This historical act of retribution, the burning of Lugard's fortress as a result of a broken oath, foreshadows Ngugi's fictional depictions of similar retributive burnings: Freeze-Kilby's invasive wheat is burned by Gikuyu villagers, and the three neocolonial businessmen—whose betrayal is their mimicry of European business practices—burn to death as well.

In the context of the mass oathings that began in 1950, in which "participants pledged to fight for the return of traditional lands" (Hall 290), the oath was taken often involuntarily and the colonial government made it possible to de-oath, particularly in terms of the

mbatuni oath that required murder of those loyal to that government. The oath tradition, therefore, even as it was utilized as an anticolonial agent, mutated as a result of and was shaped by European
colonization. Furthermore, the act of drinking tea is associated with
accepting the Mau Mau oath, and even after independence, taking
tea has ominous implications in Ngugi's novel; Munira is tricked into
a post-independence oath when he accepts an invitation to tea at
Gatundu (92). According to Joyce Johnson, in the novel, "just as
tea became caught up in the capitalist economy, so does Theng'eta"
(14). In his fictional reinterpretation of Theng'eta, Ngugi is able to
comment on the malleable nature of the oath during Kenya's colonial period and to critique the postcolonial tendency to invent tradition and construct an imagined past in the present moment. In
the narrative's ability to provide such a critique, Ngugi turns to an
external model, Marxism, in search of a more appropriate national
narrative.

In the service of the construction of such a national narrative, and
in terms of my ecocritical reading of that narrative, Ngugi's novel
also manifests a familiar tendency of first generation male African
writers of English, to depict female characters as symbolic and to rely
on the problematic metaphor of the nation and the land as a virginal
female, corrupted by outside interests—either of a colonial or neocolonial nature.[11] While such symbolic renderings can be read as testament to the ways that colonization has corrupted both the nation
and the environment, they nonetheless undermine real women's experience. For example, early in Ngugi's novel, the narrator describes
how Munira "was often thrilled by the sight of women scratching the
earth because they seemed at one with the green land" (24), and
Wanja, in particular, is closely elided with both the earth and the
nation just as she is forced to occupy both sides of various binary
constructions concerned with purity and corruption without ever
inhabiting any middle ground. She is depicted as both virgin and
whore, as both fecund and barren, and is like the Theng'eta flower
in her ability to alternately nurture and destroy the lives of her male
counterparts. Munira feels that he can "touch her only by deflower-
ing her by force and so himself flowering in blood. A virgin and a
prostitute" (76), and this description invokes Munira's young stu-

dent's earlier characterization of Theng'eta as a flower "with petals of blood" (21). Critics have taken Ngugi to task for the perpetuation of these nation-as-woman and earth-as-woman metaphors, which reduce female characters to merely symbolic status, in this and other of his works. For example, according to James Ogude, the character of Wanja "expresses Ngugi's ambivalent position on feminist discourses in Kenya. On the one hand, Ngugi portrays Wanja as a woman who transcends traditional limitations and, on the other hand, she is portrayed as the victim of colonial capitalist society" (*Ngugi's Novels* 115). According to Evan Mwangi, despite the fact that Wanja "is one of the earliest rounded [female] characters by a male writer in the history of African literature" (69), within the novel, "patriarchy and neocolonialism remain deeply entrenched in the narrative's use of . . . gendered tropes" (67). While Brendan Nicholls notes the way that landscape and ideology are closely bound in much of Ngugi's fiction, he is critical of Ngugi's tendency to present gendered views of both the land and the nation. He claims that "the gendering of the landscape and the nation in Ngugi's fiction works to domesticate female sexuality and to privilege male prerogatives" (194).

Nicholls's study is one of the only critical examinations of Ngugi's novel that explores environmental aspects of the work, despite what I feel to be an overt indictment of the environmental damage produced by colonialism and neocolonialism in *Petals of Blood*, a scenario that is presented by Ngugi in almost as didactic a manner as his Marxist agenda. In addition to its focus on the ways that Ngugi genders the landscape and the nation, Nicholls's essay also examines the role of the environment—particularly the forest—in terms of the protection it offered to Mau Mau resistance during the emergency period of 1952–60. He claims that the Mau Mau relationship with the land and its animals was "strategically canny" (184): "amongst the fighters, animals were a tactical resource. Elephant tracks guided them across rough terrain and showed the most direct route to water. By listening attentively to forest sounds, such as bird calls or the erratic movement of frightened animals, the insurgents produced a sympathetic sensory landscape on which the dangers of attack or discovery were signaled long before they became imminent" (185). Nicholls also notes the network of historical taboos associated, among the

Gikuyu, with the needless slaughter of animals or of cutting down trees; such actions could result in dire military, meteorological, or cosmic circumstances (185). It is clear from these readings that the significance of "nature," like the meaning of the oath and the drinking of tea, changes in terms of its symbolic value over the course of Kenya's colonial history. In Ngugi's novel, both nation and nature are treated as feminine and are symbolically corrupted through a pervasive capitalist modernity that calls for the development and re-shaping of the landscape, a modernity that Ngugi presents as synonymous with the prostitution that Wanja is forced to undertake as a last resort after her right to brew Theng'eta is taken from her.

❧

Before looking explicitly at the ways that Ngugi depicts environmental devastation as the result of such symbolic prostitution, I want to take a brief and more historical look at Kenya's environmental ethos, particularly as it has evolved since the 1960s depicted in Ngugi's novel, and particularly in terms of the role that real women have played in the environmental movement in Kenya. According to J. R. McNeill, two phases of environmental policies mark the late twentieth century, the first of which began in the mid-1960s in rich Western countries like the United States, with support from the third world remaining weak (350). Despite the fact that the first international conference on the environment, held in Stockholm in 1972, led to the headquartering of the United Nations Environment Program in Nairobi, it was not until the second phase, which began around 1980, that grassroots efforts began to shape the political climate of poorer countries like Kenya (350). Perhaps the best-known example of such action is the tree planting effort of Kenya's Green Belt movement, organized by the National Council of Women of Kenya in 1977, the same year that *Petals of Blood* was published: "from 1981 to 1987 the movement was led by a woman, a former professor of veterinary anatomy, Wangari Maathai. . . . The Green Belt movement proved strong enough to make an impact on the land and provoke a backlash: it had planted 20 million trees in Kenya by 1993, but government spokesmen vilified Maathai" (McNeill 351–52). According to Juan Martinez-Alier, in his study *The Environmentalism of the Poor*, "in 1977, Maathai abandoned her university position to motivate other and less privileged women to protect and improve their environment" (121). Despite the fact that Maathai won the Nobel Peace Prize in 2004, according to Gloria Waggoner, such campaigns as the Green Belt and other movements that reached their peak in the late 1970s and early 1980s "were viewed by some as a narrow approach, avoiding a look at the impact of aggressive development activities" (76). The development during this period of numerous organizations that formed their own individualized policies has resulted in a fractured environmental protection program with no central mission or infrastructure. Hence, the state of the Kenyan environment, particularly with regard to water and air pollution, has declined over the past several decades; according to Waggoner, in addition to a lack of safe drinking water and garbage collection, "between .5–1.5% of the Gross National Product (GNP) is lost annually due to soil erosion and desertification"; "40% of the natural forest cover has been lost to lumbering and other economic development"; and "wetlands have been drained for agricultural purposes" (78). Furthermore, according to Timothy Armstrong, "protected areas like the national parks and preserves contain less than 30% of Kenya's wildlife, and wildlife populations outside the protected areas are declining rapidly" (90). This decline is directly attributable to the loss of habitat as a result of forest conversion for agricultural use (90).

The landscape that is depicted in Ngugi's novel reflects many of these environmental problems, and Wanja, as a literary precursor to women like Maathai, is positioned at the forefront of a perceived movement aimed at changing the environmental reality. The land is drought-stricken and over-farmed; the forests are in serious decline, and "polluted air had come to dominate" (*Petals* 100) the lives of the residents of Ilmorog. Ngugi's text firmly places the blame for such issues on the institution of colonization, and the narrative's omniscient voice, focalized through Karega, notes early in the novel that "the land seemed not to yield much and there was no virgin soil to escape to as in those days before colonialism" (9). Alongside the novel's presentation of Ilmorog as a place of natural beauty is the assertion that the area has, both throughout history and legend, "been threatened by the twin cruelties of unprepared-for vagaries of nature and the uncontrolled actions of men" (111). Those actions include the transformation of indigenous foot paths to railways and later roads—particularly the Trans-Africa highway—that led to the consumption of oil, the pollution of the air, and the transport of raw materials and people from one place to another. The role of such modes of traversing and ordering the land (on foot and then by railway and later by car) are apparent early in Kenya's colonial history: "in the ten years between 1895 and 1905 the land that we today call Kenya was transformed from a footpath 600 miles long . . . into a harshly politicized colonial state" (Ochieng' and Atieno-Odhiambo xiv). Ngugi's novel provides an environmental critique of this transformation in its exploration of the railroad and its role in destroying the forests during the colonial period. Of the railroad, the narrator says, "the line had carried wood and charcoal and wattle barks from Ilmorog forests to feed machines and men at Ruwa-ini. It had eaten the forests" (11), and later, the trains "ate our forest. . . . Then they sent for our young men. They went on swallowing our youth" (115). The railway is implicated in the drought as well. Before settlers came to Kenya, Muturi claims, "the land was . . . covered with forests. The trees called rain. They also cast a shadow on the land. But the forest was eaten by the railway. You remember they used to come for wood as far as here—to feed the iron thing. Aah, they only knew how to eat, how to take away everything. But then, those were Foreigners—white people" (82). This indictment of the railway as a hungry beast parallels the novel's consistent and scathing criticism of the Trans-Africa highway that "cleaved Ilmorog into two halves" (323) and that is responsible for the shape of the "New" Ilmorog in neocolonial Kenya; the highway is rendered as a living being, "animal of the earth" (263), and is indicted for its roles in alienating indigenous peoples from the land and transporting people from agricultural villages to urban centers.

Petals of Blood, in its parallel critiques of both railway and highway, also indicts the neocolonial state for its role in perpetuating these capitalist-originated projects that result in wanton environmental destruction. Like Freeze-Kilby's invasive wheat, the legacy of colonialism takes root in post-independence Kenya as black elite businessmen mimic the insidious capitalist interests of their white predecessors. Interestingly, just as Freeze-Kilby's wheat is set on fire by members of the indigenous population, the *Daily Mouthpiece* announces the deaths of Mzigo, Chui, and Kimeria as follows: "a man, believed to be a trade-union agitator, has been held after a leading industrialist and two educationalists, well known as the African directors of the internationally famous Theng'eta Breweries and Enterprises Ltd., were last night burnt to death in Ilmorog, only hours after taking a no-nonsense-no-pay-rise decision" (4–5). The highway, like the railway, is similarly depicted as a living creature that residents of the New Ilmorog helplessly observe, and is implicated in conjunction with the deforestation mentioned above in a new environmental nightmare, oil drilling. The narrator claims that people sit along the highway and "watch the cars whining and horning their way across the seven cities of Central Africa in an oil company sponsored race. . . . They watch too the heavy tankers squelching tar . . . to feed a thousand arteries of thirsty machines and motors" (263). It is little wonder that in the context of such pervasive environmental devastation that Karega desires a return to "a past when Ilmorog, or all Africa, controlled its own earth" (125) — an Ilmorog of precolonial and, therefore, imaginary status. Instead, the novel leaves us with Karega's persistent hope for something hybrid and new, and a belief that a better life on "a new earth, another world" (295) is possible through the people's willingness to embrace Marxism. Of course, Kenya's subsequent history and its present environmental circumstances indicate that such optimism is utopian at best, misguided at worst, and that a return to a precolonial model is unattainable.

In the context of such blatant destruction and "devouring" of the natural world, the drinking of Theng'eta is removed from its precolonial significance, as the environment that produces it is corrupted. The Theng'eta flower, once a source of communal peace and well-being, is described as a flower with "petals of blood" (21) by a schoolboy who, as a result of his Western-style education in the postcolonial moment, has no access to the plant's historical and cultural meaning; in this instance, Ngugi brilliantly indicts the role of English-language education in the loss of the natural world—both literally and culturally—for colonized Africans. The excessive environmental devastation that Ngugi chronicles throughout the novel is mirrored by the pervasive consumption of Theng'eta by characters in the novel, particularly Abdulla, who begins to drink "to get drunk" and so he will not "know anything about whatever was happening around him" (312). Karega claims that Kenya's neocolonial state, where the majority of the wealth that once belonged to the colonial infrastructure now rests in the hands of a few members of the Kenyan African elite, prostitutes all Kenyans, and the beginnings of that prostitution are rendered symbolically in the corruption of Theng'eta. Karega says, "only two nights ago we all drank Theng'eta together to celebrate a harvest and the successful ending of what was certainly a difficult year in Ilmorog. It was a good harvest and you'll agree with me that such a sense of common destiny, a collective spirit, is rare. That is why the old woman rightly called it a drink of peace. Now it has turned out to be a drink of strife" (240). Because characters partake of the drink during a period of uncertainty, a historical moment during which the old colonial order has been mimicked by the neocolonial elite, the second sight its ingestion inspires is troubling, producing visions of familial loss and alienation, and visions of shadowy enemies encountered by Abdulla, who fought "in the forest" (228) during the Mau Mau emergency; furthermore, over the course of the evening, in the disclosures of their various visionary narratives, information that will generate rifts between the characters is revealed.

One such example is Abdulla's betrayal of a fellow Mau Mau fighter who, we learn during the course of the characters' intoxication, is Karega's murdered elder brother Nding'uri. From its reintroduction as an imaginary traditional practice, Theng'eta plays a primary role in the destruction of the bonds that have previously formed between Abdulla, Karega, Munira, and Wanja. Instead of bringing the community together in celebration of a successful harvest that should indicate a reclamation of the land, Theng'eta fractures the community and sends the four friends in different directions: Munira, initially the only one of the four who does not, at least at the onset of the Theng'eta drinking, feel a sense of communal unity and well-being, ultimately becomes jealous of the closeness that arises between Wanja and Karega during the ceremonial drinking and, in order to banish Karega from Wanja's presence, dismisses Karega from his teaching post. Abdulla and Wanja go into business selling the drink, but the County Council ultimately takes away, Wanja claims, "our right to brew" (279), essentially allowing the business to be overtaken by the more powerful capitalist interests of Chui, Kimeria, and Mzigo. For Munira and Abdulla, drinking Theng'eta becomes a way to obliterate the pain of the past and present. Just as Abdulla drinks to lose contact with reality (312), for Munira, the flower becomes a "deadly lotus. And only friend. Constant companion" (270).

At the end of the novel, Theng'eta's traditional significance has been so altered and its meaning so corrupted that the flower and drink become items for both capitalistic and literal consumption: rather than inspiring unity and second sight, the drink becomes a divisive hindrance to any "traditional" vision of Kenyan unity and peace. This corruption arises as well from the capitalist-driven devastation of a natural world that once offered shelter to the Mau Mau revolutionaries and with which characters in Ngugi's novel have lost both contact and cultural understanding. As I stated earlier, when Munira first comes to Ilmorog, he takes the school children "out into the field to study nature, as he put it" (21). While in the field, one child cries out, "look. A flower with petals of blood" (21), and when Munira first approaches what the reader later realizes is Theng'eta, his eyes fool him into seeing blood flowing from the flower. The indigenous plant is symbolically blood-soaked, and the recreation of its traditional purpose later in the novel inspires murder. Subsequently, when the children begin to ask him difficult questions about the natural world and the place of humanity within that world, Munira becomes uneasy, and swears "that he would never again take the children to the fields" (22). The image of the bleeding flower is, on the one hand, an image Munira ascribes to Wanja just as it is an image of the corruption and devastation of nature as a result of deforestation and the construction of Trans-Africa highway, and his lack of knowledge about Theng'eta illustrates that Munira and his student — as well as the other characters — have distanced themselves and been distanced, particularly by Western education, from the natural world as it had been implicated in their precolonial traditions. Furthermore, it is an image of the corruption and commodification of reimagined or invented tradition of Theng'eta drinking in the neocolonial moment. Theng'eta, just like the land that is now covered with asphalt and railways, can never be, either literally or symbolically, what it was before colonial forces intruded upon the landscape. Ngugi's narrative, having found no way to return to a precolonial past, turns instead to a vision of how to imagine Kenya's future, a hybrid model of Fanonist Marxism. It is Karega's socialist vision of cultural hybridity through the overthrow of "imperialism: capitalism: landlords" (344): "the system and its gods and its angels had to be fought consciously, consistently and resolutely by all the working people! . . . Tomorrow it would be the workers and the peasants leading the struggle and seizing power to overturn the system and all its prying bloodthirsty gods and gnomic angels, bringing to an end the foreign reign of the few over the many" (344). The novel ends with Karega's hope for "tomorrow . . . tomorrow" (345), a day when Africans can create "a new earth, another world" (295) from the earth that has been taken from them and a day when neocolonial divisiveness will be a thing of the past; that vision, as yet, remains unrealized.

Near the end of *Petals of Blood*, Wanja offers a perspective about the appropriate treatment of the past. She says that the past is important, "but only as a living lesson to the present. I mean we must not preserve our past in a museum: rather, we must study it critically, without illusions, and see what lessons we can draw from it" (323). This sentiment arises from Wanja's earlier encounter with the utamaduni village, a place where women "sing native songs and dance for white tourists" and a place "with huts built as they imagine our huts looked before the Europeans came. Our utamaduni . . . a museum . . . for them to look at" (292). Wanja's criticism of this kind of cultural preservation as imaginary performance is explicitly mirrored in South African author Zakes Mda's *Heart of Redness*, set some twenty years after the events chronicled in Ngugi's novel, when the protagonist Camagu is critical of white shop owner John Dalton's suggestion that there be a cultural village at Qolorha that will have "proper isiXhosa huts . . . [and] women will wear traditional costumes as their forebears used to wear. They will grind millet and polish the floors with cow dung. They will draw patterns on the walls with ochre of different colors. . . . Tourists will flock to watch young maidens dance and young men engage in stick fights. . . . They will learn how the amaXhosa of the wild coast live" (247). Camagu claims that such a display is dishonest and does not represent the way that "real people in today's South Africa" (247) live, and his comments about the village echo Hobsbawm's assertions about invented tradition: Camagu says, "I have a problem with your plans. It is an attempt . . . to reinvent culture. When you excavate a . . . precolonial identity that is lost . . . are you suggesting that they currently have no culture?" (248). In Mda's novel, characters search for a middle ground between an inauthentic presentation of an inaccessible Xhosa past that existed before the historical Cattle Killing of 1856–57 and a future shaped by the environmentally destructive development of a vacation resort and casino in Edenic Qolorha. By having Qolorha declared a National Heritage site because of its status as the place where Nongqawuse prophesied the salvation of the Xhosa over a century earlier, the development of the resort is averted and a proposed backpacker hostel for tourists who want to enjoy the natural beauty of Qolorha is planned instead. Therefore, Nongqawuse's prophecy, in its initial incarnation, led to mass starvation and loss of Xhosa land; however, in its contemporary context, Nongqawuse's legacy ironically saves Qolorha and its residents from a modern day white invasion that would similarly displace them. But while the ecotourist model advocated by Mda's narrative is, in many ways, preferable to the construction of the casino, it is still problematic, as I will illustrate later in this chapter, and, as Camagu recognizes, only temporary: "the whole country is ruled by greed," he thinks, and "sooner or later . . . the gambling complex shall come into being" (277) anyway. Like Ngugi's narrative, Mda's novel also situates the reader in a position of looking toward the future; however, Camagu's view of that future—perhaps because Mda wrote his narrative decades after Ngugi's and, therefore, has seen which way the social and environmental wind is blowing—is pessimistic, while Karega's is hopeful.

Just as Ngugi's Marxism is informed by an environmental ethos, in an interview with Elly Williams, Mda characterizes his work as "postmodern pastoralism," writing whose so-called magically realistic elements are dependent upon African oral tradition and rural environments in which "people do not have that border between what is magical and what might be referred to as objective reality" (qtd. in E. Williams 71). In *Heart of Redness,* the allegiances of the residents of rural Qolorha remain shaped by whether their ancestors were Believers or Unbelievers in the prophecy of the historical Nongqawuse, a young Xhosa girl who in 1856 convinced her people that in order to drive white settlers from South Africa, the Xhosa must slaughter all of their cattle and destroy their crops. The longevity of the division that resulted between these two groups during the Cattle Killing that followed the prophecy is manifest most explicitly in Mda's contemporary characters of Zim and Bhonco, two Xhosa elders who are diametrically oppositional, not only with regard to their beliefs about the validity of Nongqawuse's prophecy, but about everything else as well. Despite the fact that the two men "never see any issue with the same eye" (37), both are descendents of a common ancestor, Xikixa, who is beheaded in the 1830s by John Dalton, a magistrate in the British Army under Sir Harry Smith.

Mda's narrative is heavily influenced by the work of J. B. Peires, particularly his definitive work on the subject of the Cattle Killing, *The Dead Will Arise: Nongqawuse and the Great Xhosa Cattle-Killing Movement of 1856–7,* and the novel contains factual information that is taken almost verbatim from Peires's text,[12] particularly his presentation of Nongqawuse's prophecy.[13] According to Peires, the "new people"—ancestors of the living Xhosa—appeared before the young prophet and "told her that the dead were preparing to rise again, and wonderful new cattle too, but first the people must kill their cattle and destroy their corn" (311). Peires speculates that Nongqawuse and other prophets were able to convince so many of the Xhosa to follow this dictate because of the lung sickness epidemic, most likely introduced by European Friesland bulls in 1853, that had claimed the lives of their own animals; the Xhosa believed that their animals had been polluted and that a purification ritual was needed. Peires describes the devastation that resulted from the killing in terms of loss of six hundred thousand acres of Xhosa land to the British. In terms of loss of human life, Peires claims that "the only really reliable figure that we have is that the Xhosa population of British

Kaffraria dropped by two-thirds between January and December of 1857, from 105,000 to 37,500, then again by another third to read a low of 25,916 by the end of 1858" (319). While he utilizes written history about the killing, Mda's fictional retelling also complicates various readings of the event as resulting from either the delusions of a young girl or the machinations of a corrupt imperial mission to undermine the Xhosa.[14] Instead, in Mda's narrative, Nongqawuse is rendered as an imaginative child, the unwitting pawn in the battle between the British — as exemplified by Sir Harry Smith's assertion that "extermination is now the only principle that guides me. I loved these people and considered them my children. But now I say exterminate the savage beasts!" (Mda 19) — and the Xhosa, desperate to the extent that they were willing to do whatever was necessary (and believe any narrative that offered hope) to eradicate the white presence from their land.

That land, in the present moment of Mda's narrative, has been compromised by both indigenous and colonial factors. J. R. McNeill discusses one of South Africa's most significant environmental issues, soil erosion, in terms of "communal land tenure and cultural attachment to cattle" (40). He acknowledges that an indictment of Africa's indigenous peoples for environmental damage is controversial, but he asserts that "since cattle were the preferred store of wealth and sign of status, Africans had a general incentive to maximize their herds and overgraze unless societal rules discouraged it" (40). He is careful to point out, however, that, while social regulation might have worked in precolonial times, it became less effective given the ways that Africans were forced onto smaller and less fertile tracts of land as the result of "the various pressures of colonialism, marketization, and long-distance labor migration" (40), all of which had begun to affect the Xhosa prior to 1856. It is worth noting that, in the context of an environmental discussion about the role of cattle in African society and the dangers of overgrazing, the killing of 1856–57 was an attempt, both according to Peires and Mda, to purify the earth and rid it of psychic and physical pollution.[15] However, Robert Ross claims that despite the purification goal that underscored the killing, "Nongqawuse is now seen as having inaugurated, not the renewal, but the mass suicide of the amaXhosa" (53). Ross reads the

Cattle Killing as a historical metaphor: "the Cattle-Killing marks the end of the beginning of South African history. For the first time, an African society . . . had been broken" (53). It is not surprising then, given its profound significance both as a literal event and as a cultural metaphor, that the Xhosa Cattle Killing finds it way into literature, both from South Africa and elsewhere.[16] Through his incorporation of the killing in his novel, Mda challenges stereotypes of rural, cattle grazing Africans as destructive of nature even as he recasts the historical tensions between Believers and Unbelievers as a contemporary and fraught discourse between peoples who, in a very real sense, need the monetary benefits that the development of a casino would offer despite their desire to preserve their natural resources and landscapes.

Through multiple doublings and redoublings—as are immediately apparent in the binary of Cattle Killing–era characters of Twin and Twin-Twin, whose names indicate a doubled double, twins who initially are inseparable but later turn against each other—Mda's novel fractures and compounds individual perceptions of belief and unbelief in a way that exposes the dangers of dogma, liberal or conservative, in the face of development-driven environmental destruction as it affects post-apartheid South Africa. Various critics read the work as a polyphonic exercise in the destabilization of the binary oppositions that Mda's text makes manifest through its examination of the ways that the concepts of belief and unbelief—fixed and immobile as a result of their historical position within the context of the Cattle Killing—are emptied of any real meaning in the "new" South African Qolorha of the novel. J. U. Jacobs, for example, reads the text as performative and asserts that Mda's narrative structure functions as "the fictional equivalent of Xhosa overtone singing" (228) practiced by Qukezwa that, through its intertextual resonances (Peires's aforementioned history, the title's play on Conrad's *Heart of Darkness*, and nods to the magical realism of authors like Gabriel García Márquez), palimpsest structure (as alternating between 1856 and present day South Africa) and diglossic treatment of Xhosa words and phrases, contribute to the narrative's multiple voices. Similarly, Siphokazi Koyana reads the "multiple ways in which there is dialogue between Qolorha (place and physical landscape) and the varied meanings or interpretations of the events that occurred there in the past and those that are occurring in the present reality of the text" ("Qolorha" 52). In "Postcolonial Ecologies and the Gaze of Animals: Reading Some Contemporary Southern African Narratives," Wendy Woodward examines the way that Mda's presentation of Xhosa environmentalism within the text cannot be read as either unilaterally precolonial in nature or as purely the product of a postcolonial ethos: Mda "does not proffer an idealized or utopian record of ecocentric communication with the environment and animals, nor do the amaXhosa constitute a unifaceted community who foreground postcolonial ecologies either in the nineteenth or twentieth centuries" (308). Such readings point to the ways that Mda's text reaches beyond the various dualities—of belief/unbelief, environmentalism/development, and Xhosa/European—that underscore the narrative's engagement with Xhosa history.

This manipulation of such doubling is apparent at the beginning of the novel when Twin and his brother Twin-Twin, the sons of the "headless ancestor" Xikixa, turn against one another because Twin believes Nongqawuse's prophecies while his brother does not. Peires chronicles the ways that decisions about such beliefs affected families during the killing: "the hatred of believers for unbelievers ripped whole families apart. Fathers turned on their sons and wives deserted their husbands" (160), and the fictional disagreement between the two brothers illustrates such intrafamilial division. Initially the two are "like one person" (13), but their difference of opinion about Nongqawuse results in their estrangement from each other and, eventually, Twin's attack on his brother's farm. Zim and his daughter, Qukezwa, direct descendents of Twin, maintain the practice of belief that, in the absence of a prophet to support, manifests itself in Zim's adoption, late in the novel, of traditional Xhosa costume and Qukezwa's aforementioned attempts to eradicate all nonnative plant species from Qolorha. Mda's treatment of these believer characters, while both critical and amused, is often more sympathetic than his treatment of the Unbelievers, particularly Bhonco, the direct descendant of Twin-Twin who magically inherits "the scars that were inflicted on his great-grandfather . . . by men who flogged him" (13), and Bhonco's daughter, Xoliswa Ximiya, the secondary school principal who wants, as her father does, to do away with her people's "redness," the red ochre dye that she associates with primitive ignorance. The narrative's preference for the believer characters is most apparent in that Camagu, the character through which all of the action is focalized, chooses to marry the passionate and spontaneous Qukezwa over Xoliswa, who is depicted in the narrative as inflexible and icy. But the novel is critical of both belief and unbelief, which, through the characters of Zim and Bhonco, are taken to untenable extremes.

For example, the narrator discusses how Bhonco "laments the sufferings of the Middle Generations," those who lived and died during the time between the Cattle Killing and the present moment, but "he does not believe in not grieving anymore. We cannot say he believes in grieving, for as an Unbeliever he does not believe" (90). Such a negatively inflected analysis (he does not believe in not grieving) of Bhonco's feelings—as grief or lamentation devoid of belief—points to the difficulty and absurdity of discussing such concepts without reference to the concept of belief. Furthermore, Bhonco refuses to believe in anything, despite the fact that his decision to "bring the Cult of the Unbelievers back from the recesses of time" (13) clearly illustrates his steadfast—and ironic—belief in unbelief. Similarly, Zim's decisions to wrap himself in a red blanket, shave his eyebrows, and take "regular enemas and emetics to cleanse himself, as he comes into contact with Unbelievers like Bhonco on a regular basis" (166) render him laughable to the other residents of Qolorha. These practices, which Zim essentially creates and then invests with belief, constitute other examples of invented tradition in that they generate "a new set of rituals that combine the best from the two denominations" (166), the followers of Nongqawuse and the followers of her contemporary prophet, the eleven-year-old girl Nonkosi. Zim borrows from the dictates of various prophets in order to inject "new life into his belief" (166) while simultaneously heightening the historical divisions that turned brother against brother during the Cattle Killing.

Unlike Bhonco who, because of the ancestral scars that appear on his back, bears the weight of tradition directly on his skin, and Zim who, by shaving his head and eyebrows, inflicts tradition onto his body, Camagu has lived in exile in the United States, obtaining a doctorate in communications while South Africa gained its independence. As a result of his absence, he is unfamiliar with the invented and reinterpreted traditions that arose during this period, particularly the *toyi-toyi* or "freedom dance that the youth used to dance when people were fighting for liberation" (28). His inability to do the dance, to speak about his role during the fall of apartheid—and, as David Lloyd claims, his refusal to "yield to government sycophancy, nepotism and mendacity" (37)—keeps him from getting a job when he returns from the United States and sets him wandering, after a beautiful woman named NomaRussia, toward Qolorha. Women often function in Mda's text, as they do in Ngugi's, as symbols in the interest of the construction of a national narrative, but in Mda's novel, women also occupy literal and rhetorically significant positions; as the narrative asserts, "women were the leaders of the cattle-killing movement" (110), and it is through Camagu's interactions with women—NoManage and NoVangeli, for example, who teach him to harvest oysters and form a business cooperative with him, and Qukezwa who teaches him how to care for the environment—that Camagu formulates an ethos of what Woodward claims is an "ecological ethics linked with sound economics" (295) that shapes his trajectory in the novel. According to Ute Kauer, "contemporary South African literature is, far from being post-national, concerned with a redefinition of the national" (107) that he sees as feminine (109), and he reads *The Heart of Redness* as part of this emergent paradigm. After Camagu meets NomaRussia, he dreams that he is the river and NomaRussia is its water (60), but when he is propositioned by Zim's daughter Qukezwa, she takes the place of NomaRussia in the dream, embodying and displacing the overt sexual symbolism of the water that Camagu wants to flow "up his eager body" (60); Qukezwa, like water, becomes a sustaining force in Qolorha, protecting its environment and offering, through the birth of her and Camagu's son at the end of the narrative, hope for its future.

Mda's narrative further complicates various oppositions—Twin and Twin-Twin, Bhonco and Zim, Xoliswa and Qukezwa, and, in terms of Bhonco, Zim, and Camagu, one's inescapable implication in the thrust of history and the other's self-exile from it—through other kinds of doubling, particularly by ensuring that nearly every name in the text (with the notable exception of Camagu) identifies at least two characters, one in the past and one in the present. For example, Qukezwa is Zim's daughter in the present and the wife of Twin in the past; John Dalton is at once the enemy of the Xhosa who beheads Xikixa in the 1800s and the white shop owner and friend to the Xhosa in the present day. It is tempting to read Camagu—the only character whose name refers only to him, an outsider to the village of Qolorha, and a Western-educated African who nonetheless still believes in the power of his totem animal, the brown snake—as the hybrid mediator between the Believers and Unbelievers, but such a reading is in many ways too simplistic. Camagu's opinions change over the course of the narrative, and his connection to the Western ideology that results from his education is weakened; Camagu ultimately embraces the heart of redness, an understanding and reverence for his homeland, its people, and its plants and animals. To further ensure that the reader cannot make one-to-one correlations between or draw oppositional assumptions about identically named characters, Mda further fractures identity by dislocating the reader's position in a coherent and linear conception of time. For example, Heitsi is identified by Twin's wife, Qukezwa, as the earliest prophet of the Khoikhoi, a man invested with supernatural powers: "Heitsi Eibib prayed, 'O Tsiqwa! Father of fathers. Open yourself that I may pass through, and close yourself afterwards.' As soon as he had uttered these words, the Great River opened, and his people crossed. But when the enemies tried to pass through the opening . . . the Great River closed upon them, and they all perished in its waters" (23). Within the novel, however, "Heitsi" is also the name that Twin and Qukezwa give their son; and "Heitsi" is invoked a third time as the name that Camagu and the other Qukezwa give their son at the end of the novel. Through such multiplicity, a linear notion of time is disrupted and the mythic becomes the present reality. At the end of the novel, for example, the reader is uncertain whether the Qukezwa who "sings in soft pastel colors" and the Heitsi who "plays in the sand" (271) do so in the nineteenth or twentieth centuries, or in both simultaneously. The narrative ends—both in the past and the present—with the hope for salvation through a tenuous environmental preservation informed by historical prophecy. In the case of Nongqawuse, that prophecy resulted in the destruction of land and cattle; in the case of the prophet or child that Qukezwa feels must "carry out the business of saving his people" (277), Heitsi may not be able to have access to the sea, if the gambling complex is eventually built and the residents of Qolorha are restricted from using the beaches so that white tourists might have greater access to them.

Just as Ngugi critiques the role of neocolonialism for its reliance on white colonial models in Kenya, Mda satirizes the nature of Black Economic Empowerment (BEE), a South African government initiative aimed at generating black-owned businesses, which went into effect after apartheid ended. Michael MacDonald claims that such deals have done little to establish genuine businesses: "new businesses, like old businesses, recoil from competition, and competition threatens leveraged—that is, African-owned—businesses most of all, inviting collusive businesses to hide their anticompetitive interests behind the fig leaf of racial empowerment" (155). To highlight this reality, Mda places the casino development project in the hands of Lefa Leballo, the chief executive of the "black empowerment company that is going to develop village into a tourist heaven" (198), but Mda satirizes the black businessman by having him accompanied by two white men, consultants, who "were chief executive and chairman of the company before they sold the majority shares to black empowerment consortia" (198). When Camagu proposes an environmentally sound alternative to the complex, the white consultants, the generically named Mr. Smith and Mr. Jones, begin discussing other options, such as time-share units and a retirement village. It is clear that both men wield control of the project, and that neither is interested in the opinions of the Qolorha residents; in fact, both men "seem to have forgotten about the villagers," and "even Lefa Leballo is left out" (203) of their self-interested plans. David Lloyd points out Mda's satirical treatment of the black empowerment initiative and he notes the way that the proposed casino will affect the natural environment: "the indigenous vegetation will be destroyed when decorative exotics replace them and, as the beaches are privatized, [the villagers] will lose access to an important food source. In fact, they will effectively lose their land and be reduced to tourist curiosities" (37). Just as the neocolonial businessmen in Ngugi's novel perpetuate an exploitative colonial past, the BEE movement creates colonial mimics who, perhaps unwittingly, continue to place African land in the hands of white capitalist interests.

However, according to Siphokazi Koyana, in *The Heart of Redness*, "the people of Qolorha succeed in preserving their unique vegetation, the spiritual sanctuaries associated with Nongqawuse, as well as the sea in which they play and from which they feed both their bodies and their collective memories" ("Qolorha" 56). In Mda's telling of the killing, the nineteenth-century Xhosa are environmentally responsible, people who pass from one generation to the next "the art of working the soil and looking after animals" (Mda, *Heart* 74), and the conservationist mentality is rendered as African in origin. As the contemporary John Dalton claims, the Xhosa king Sarhili, who ruled during the killing, "was a very strong conservationist. He created Manyube, a conservation area where people were not allowed to hunt or chop trees. He wanted to preserve these things for future generations" (165). According to Wendy Woodward, "reconnecting with the land . . . and recalling precolonial knowledges is a postcolonial strategy in Mda's . . . texts" (294); this strategy is manifest in Mda's depiction of Nongqawuse as an uncertain and perhaps unwilling prophet who "in the manner of all great prophets . . . [seems] confused and disoriented most of the time" (Mda, *Heart* 54). The girl, who rarely speaks, is situated between competing interests, the expulsion of white settlers by the Xhosa and the acquisition of Xhosa lands by the whites, particularly Sir George Grey, the governor of the Cape colony. Instead of being the bringer of Xhosa downfall, Nongqawuse is depicted as a victim in a battle—over the land and its flora and fauna—between colonizing forces and the indigenous Xhosa. The battle that raged between the Believers and the Unbelievers over whether or not to listen to Nongqawuse and kill their cattle is played out in the present day between the Unbelievers who are in favor of the development of the resort complex and the Believers who oppose the environmental destruction that will accompany such a project. In *The Heart of Redness*, Camagu is drawn to the beauty and magical status of Nongqawuse's Qolorha, "a place rich in wonders." He says, "the river did not cease flowing, even when the rest of the country knells in drought" (7). In the context of this battle, Zim's daughter, Qukezwa, emerges as a kind of reverse Nongqawuse, an active environmental prophet, working to destroy invasive species and preserve the natural biota and beauty of Qolorha.

The debate that initially takes place between the Believers and Unbelievers during the killing plays out on a microcosmic scale between Bhonco and Zim; Camagu is cast as an innocent bystander, a man new to the community who aligns himself, at least at first, with John Dalton, who, despite his white skin, according to Zim, "is more of an umXhosa than most of us" (147). Bhonco asserts that the "Unbelievers stand for progress" and "want to get rid of this bush which is a sign of our uncivilization. We want developers to come and build the gambling city that will bring money to this community. That will bring modernity to our lives and will rid us of redness" (92). Zim counters that the tourists who come to Qolorha "steal our lizards and our birds" and "steal our aloes and our cycads and our usundu plants and our *ikhamanga* wild banana trees" (93). After he is visited by his totem, the brown snake, and after Qukezwa takes him to Nongqawuse's valley, Camagu's environmental activism begins to take shape and he takes a stand against the building of the gambling complex. He realizes that "a project of this magnitude cannot be built without cutting down the forest of indigenous trees, without disturbing the bird life, and without polluting the rivers, the sea, and its great lagoon" (119). At this point in the narrative, by opposing the building of the casino, Camagu seemingly enters into the fray between the Believers and Unbelievers, aligning himself with Zim and Qukezwa's camp. But Camagu argues against identification with any one ideology: "I do not belong to the Believers, in the same way that I belong to the Unbelievers. I am just a person. My ancestors were not here when these quarrels began with Prophetess Nongqawuse" (143). In fact, the way that Camagu opposes the casino places him in opposition with all of Qolorha's factions, including John Dalton, whose plan to create a cultural village, according to Camagu, is inauthentic and functions to deny the value of contemporary Xhosa culture.

A change in the relationship between Camagu and John Dalton is first apparent when Camagu criticizes Dalton's creation of communal water taps in the village. The people often do not pay for water, and Dalton is forced to close the taps. Camagu claims that "the water project is failing because it was opposed on the people" (179). Siphokazi Koyana reads Dalton's water scheme "as a clear example of the inadequacy of development strategies that aim to improve people's lives without giving them true ownership of the process of empowerment" ("Qolorha" 54). But as the people of Qolorha seek a solution that is both respectful of the environment and monetarily beneficial, via Camagu, Mda's narrative illustrates the shortcomings inherent in all options: the casino-based tourist complex is untenable because building it will destroy the environment and displace the people of Qolorha from their beaches; Dalton's cultural village will exploit the people who, Xoliswa Ximiya feels, "act like buffoons for these white tourists. . . . Her people are like monkeys in a zoo, observed with amusement by white foreigners with John Dalton's assistance" (96); and, most significantly, Qukezwa's attempts to eradicate invasive plants — like Nongqawuse's attempts to drive white settlers into the sea — is presented, near the end of the novel, as equally improbable. Qukezwa, who, like her father, is now shaving her head and wearing the traditional red of the Xhosa, is brought before the inkundla for chopping down trees that "are not the trees of our forefathers" (215). Such attempts to eradicate nonnative species, while informed by a conservationist mentality, nonetheless constitute an impossible undertaking in the current moment. Qukezwa, like Nongqawuse before her, offers a highly flawed and shortsighted solution to the problem of white intrusion; because the landscape has been altered as a result of European influence, removing all invasive plant species not only be would impossible, but also such an action can only operate on a metaphoric level, functioning as a symbolic displacement of a firmly entrenched capitalist developmental system. As Wendy Woodward claims, "any victory over globalizing capitalism in the form of developers at Qolorha is only tenuous and contingent" (308).

Through the various challenges that the novel offers to black empowerment and "new" South African status quo, Mda's narrative provides a sustained critique of the postcolonial tendency to recreate (as Qukewza attempts to do) and invent (as would Dalton's cultural village) tradition. The most pronounced example of such a critique is Mda's presentation of the "painful dance" (73) that the Unbelievers undertake to invoke sadness and visit the world of the ancestors. Camagu watches this dance and is saddened by what he sees: "they are going into a trance that takes them back to the past. To the world of the ancestors. Not the Otherworld where the ancestors live today. Not the world that lives parallel to our world. But to this world when it still belonged to them. When they were still people of flesh and blood like the people who walk the world today" (73). The dance frightens Camagu, who says that he has never seen anything like it. Bhonco's wife, NoPetticoat, explains that the dance did not exist during the time of Nongqawuse but "was invented by the Unbelievers of today" to "lament the folly of belief" (73). The invention of the ritual practiced by Bhonco and the other unbelieving elders is the result of the revival and celebration of unbelief in the present and has no past precedent in precolonial Xhosa culture; the subsequent trance visitation to the past is an impossibility, another attempt to connect with a now inaccessible and, therefore, imaginary history. Furthermore, NoPetticoat tells Camagu that the Unbelievers have borrowed the trance from the amaThwa, "the small people who were called Bushmen by the colonists of old" (187), and when the ama-Thwa elders appear late in the novel and demand the return of their dance, Bhonco concedes that he and the other Unbelievers must "invent" their own dance: "at first it will not have the power of the dance of the amaThwa. But it will gain strength the more we perform it" (189), or, as Hobsbawm asserts, it will "inculcate certain values and norms of behavior by repetition, which automatically implies continuity with the past" (1). Mda's presentation of this borrowed, returned, and invented ritual again illustrates the ironic nature of unbelief; the Unbelievers clearly believe in the power of the dance to provide them with access to a precolonial past. The invented tradition of the dance and its demise as the practice of a particular indigenous group—the amaThwa—performed by another—the Xhosa—who have no access to the amaThwa past, also foreshadows Camagu's later criticism of Dalton's proposed cultural village, another attempt by an outsider, the white Dalton, to "remember" Xhosa history, this time for monetary gain. Tellingly, the Unbelievers are unable to create their own dance, and Bhonco instead faces a sadness that results from the emptiness of unbelief, an emptiness that leads Bhonco physically to attack Dalton for his ancestor's misdeeds.

When Dalton explains his desire to open the cultural village and employ actors, Camagu argues with him, saying that such a plan is dishonest: "real people in today's South Africa don't lead the life that is seen in cultural villages. Some aspects of that life perhaps are true. But the bulk of what tourists see is the past . . . a lot of it an *imaginary past*" (247, my emphasis). Camagu proposes instead the building of a backpackers' hostel that caters to environmentally conscious tourists. He advocates "the promotion of the kind of tourism that will benefit the people, that will not destroy indigenous forests, that will not bring hordes of people who will pollute the rivers and drive away the birds" (201). The novel seemingly idealizes this option, but there are problems with this model as well, particularly with regard to ecotourism's perpetuation of another imagined national identity. According to Rosaleen Duffy, "one of the impacts that is created by ecotourism is the creation of a highly politicized image of national identity. The image of a pristine paradise . . . and exotic locals is designed to attract overseas visitors. . . . The difficulty is that this peculiar national identity is created for consumption by an external audience of ecotourists and the tour operators that deal with them" (158). While Camagu is able to convince many of the residents of Qolorha that the building of the casino will not benefit them and will damage their beautiful environment, it is John Dalton who brings the project to a halt by procuring "a letter from the government department of arts, culture, and heritage declaring the place a national heritage site" (269). Dalton's procurement and presentation of the letter, however environmentally beneficial, is also caught up in the politics of colonial manipulation: he applies for and receives the letter well in advance, but he saves it until the last possible minute, swooping in just as the builders are about to break ground, to save the Xhosa and in a dramatic attempt to "win his people back" (270) from what he perceives is their allegiance to Camagu. Such a move is indicative of the colonial mentality that indigenous peoples were not capable of caring for themselves, and reinforces the mentality that Camagu criticizes in Dalton's construction of the aforementioned communal water taps. Camagu chastises Dalton for his shortsightedness when Dalton complains that no one in the village pays to maintain the taps: "perhaps the first step would have been to discuss matters with the villagers, to find out what their priorities are. They should be part of the whole process. They should be active participants in the conception of the project, in raising the funds for it, in constructing it. Then it becomes their project. Then they will look after it" (179). Dalton's staged stunt to halt construction of the casino creates a rift that exists between Camagu and Dalton for years, until Bhonco attacks Dalton and demands the head of his ancestor Xikixa, avenging Twin-Twin who "never took the chance to strike out at John Dalton, to avenge his father's head" (272). At this point, the narrative places the past alongside the present and indicts the present day John Dalton for the actions of his ancestor; the bodies of long dead Xhosa, in Mda's text, refuse to stay buried and return to demand retribution, figuratively arising from the dead, just as Nongqawuse, over a hundred years earlier, claimed they would.

The novel ends with a chapter that similarly weaves past and present together in a seamless unity, with both Nongqawuse and Camagu seemingly existing simultaneously. Camagu appeals to John Dalton to end their feud, claiming that "there is room for both the holiday camp and the cultural village at Qolorha" (277). As he leaves the hospital, Camagu sees the "wattle trees along the road. Qukezwa taught him that these are enemy trees," and he feels glad that he lives in a place where "those who want to preserve indigenous plants and birds have won the day" (277). But Camagu also acknowledges that the day that has been won will pass, that sooner or later, "the gambling complex shall come into being" (277). If there is any hope to be had, the polyphonic and temporally simultaneous structure of the text seems to suggest, it is in the cyclical and nonlinear nature of history, wherein Nongqawuse can be read at once as the cause of a people's destruction in the past and, through her cultural cachet as such a figure, their salvation in the present, and the girl whose failed prophecy in 1856 is fulfilled late in the twentieth century. Nongqawuse "really sells the holiday camp" (276), Camagu claims, and such a statement indicates an uncomfortable verisimilitude between Camagu's ecotourism business venture and Dalton's invented, capitalistic model in terms of the cultural village; the only difference is the product being marketed—culture or nature. In the case of the holiday camp, the enigma of a dead teenage girl provides the draw to a beautiful, pristine, and untouched South African landscape, while in terms of the cultural village, the invocation and invention of traditional Xhosa life provides the entertainment for which tourists will pay. The final paragraph, in which Qukezwa wonders how "this Heitsi" (277) will save his people if he is afraid of the sea, forces the reader to consider which Heitsi and which Qukezwa are being depicted. Heitsi's assertion that "this boy does not belong in the sea! This boy belongs in the man village!" (277) indicates that this Heitsi exists in the present, a hybrid child who must inhabit the space of nature and culture—and negotiate the imposition of one upon the other—in order to imagine a future informed by, but perhaps not dependent upon, the past.

I *can* . . . imagine saying to a dominant white culture, which
has perfected the global food market and excelled at industrial
farming, that we have an obligation to be vegetarian. In fact,
the vastness of food choices available to white people . . .
results in a particularly strong argument for the conclusion that
the "winners" in the colonial struggle for power are morally
compelled to be vegetarian.

—DEANE CURTIN, Environmental Ethics for a Postcolonial World

In response to our collective guilt about eliminating so many
species, efforts are now being made to rescue animals from the
brink of extinction. In those cases where domestic husbandry is
not an option, we must consider the environment in which the
threatened species lives (or lived), and try to rescue that.

—RICHARD ELLIS, No Turning Back: The Life and Death
   of Animal Species

CHAPTER TWO

Safari, Zoo, and Dog Pound

Vegetarianism, Extinction, and the Place of
Animals in the Postcolonial Environment

I want to begin this chapter with background information about
issues of extinction, the often imperialist and human-centric rhetoric of species conservation and preservation, and the postcolonial
politics of vegetarianism, because these issues are central to an
explanation of how the three authors I examine in this chapter, Yann
Martel, Joy Williams, and J. M. Coetzee, portray the place of animals
in various postcolonial environments. The novels discussed herein,
Martel's *Life of Pi* (2001), Williams's *The Quick & the Dead* (2000),

and Coetzee's *Disgrace* (1999), differ from the novels I discussed in the preceding chapter in that are all written by white, Western—and in Coetzee's case, influenced by a Western postmodernist tradition—authors, who, through a nuanced exploration of animal/human relationships within postcolonial settings (India, Kenya, and South Africa), disrupt the monolithic imperial authority of the white, often sentimental and anthropomorphic narrative of animal "otherness." I have chosen these three texts in part because the national status of their authors complicates our understandings of what constitutes postcolonial writing. For example, Martel is Canadian and Williams is from the United States. Coetzee is South African, but it has always been difficult to characterize him as an "African" writer; indeed, in 2003, he moved to Australia. But my choice of these three authors and works is based on their depictions of animals within postcolonial environments, and the way that their texts work against what Rob Nixon asserts is a failure of geographic imagination, ironically by presenting characters whose views about animal/human relationships are, at least initially, quite simplistic and informed by positions of privilege, sentimentality, and entitlement. Furthermore, reading these texts in terms of how they depict various postcolonial environments, I believe, furthers that imagination as well. While all three narratives contain animals that can be read symbolically, often as metaphors for displaced and colonized peoples, more significantly, all three contain animals that function as literal animals, as characters, and as beings who, like their human counterparts, have suffered twofold as a result of the colonial project of empire and one of its omnipresent consequences, environmental devastation. Ultimately, these narratives render the bodies and consciousness of living and dead animals in ways that illustrate a respect for animal alterity and a sense of responsibility for the other—both animal and human—that is not dependent on receiving anything in return. The three texts listed above engage with several important debates with regard to the role of animals in the postcolonial environment, including the culling of elephants and the highly fraught role of the safari—both as sports junket for Western hunters in the 1970s and as "ecotourist" friendly photography tour of the late twentieth and early twenty-first centuries—in the perpetuation of various imaginary Africas.

Furthermore, vegetarianism, as an ethical imperative and dietary choice, is an explicit theme in all three works and is treated alternately with skepticism and respect; because the protagonists in all three works battle with the largely privileging politics of a vegetarian ethos, the novels provide a problematic dietary discourse that seeks to communicate the conflicting ways that animals are rendered, as both endangered species in the postcolonial world and infinitely consumable in the West, within a period of heretofore unseen, human influenced decline in biodiversity. Within the realm of the popular media, issues of environmental concern are prevalent, particularly issues relating to species extinction. For example, the text on the cover of the May/June 2007 issue of *Mother Jones* magazine proclaims that in ninety-three years, 50 percent of all extant species will be extinct. In the edition's lead story, "Gone: Mass Extinction and the Hazards of the Earth's Vanishing Biodiversity," Julia Whitty claims, "it's a fact little known to the population at large. By the end of the century, half of all species may be extinct due to global warming and other causes." According to Whitty and others, including historian J. R. McNeill, we are currently experiencing the sixth great extinction — often referred to as the Holocene extinction event — in the Earth's history; the last such event occurred 65 million years ago (McNeill 262). Despite the fact that there have been five other mass extinction incidents, the Holocene event is vastly different from its predecessors in terms of its causes, speed, and scope. McNeill claims that unlike the preceding five extinction spasms, the cause of the current extinction epidemic is known. He attributes it to human agency, the product of "a rogue mammal's economic activity" (263), and McNeill describes the magnitude of this current wave of extinction as follows: "since A.D. 1600, at least 484 animals and 654 plants have gone extinct. Most extinctions have happened on islands and in freshwater lakes and rivers: isolated habitats. The twentieth century extinction rate for mammals was about 40 times the background rate; for birds about 1,000 times background. Roughly 1 percent of the birds and mammals extant in 1900 went extinct by 1995" (262–63). From the historical viewpoint of McNeill, the twentieth century constitutes a mere "blip of geological time" (263) and speculation about the consequences of such mass extinction belong in the future: "the erosion of biodiversity certainly happened in the twentieth century, but its societal impact as yet remained small" (263). His view is on the impact that this extinction event will have on one species, human beings. Furthermore, while numerous species have become extinct, human agency, according to McNeill, has actually "improved the prospects" for certain species, the domesticated plants and animals that constitute our "minion biota," to thrive (263).

Despite the rampant disappearance of various plant and animal species, human beings remain prolific in their procreation. In one of her many nonfictional essays, "The Case against Babies," Joy Williams's often scathing, often hilarious take on population control, human agency—particularly the agency of the white upper- to middle-class United States citizen—is rendered in a critical light, and Williams takes on both the rhetorical neutrality of historians like McNeill and the euphemistic rhetoric of ecologists: "Earth's human population has more than tripled in the last century. Ninety-seven million of them each year. While legions of other biological life forms go extinct (or, in the creepy phrase of ecologists, 'wink out'), human life bustles self-importantly on" (*Ill Nature* 93). Williams recasts the population control argument to take the proverbial blame off of third-world women and calls for a recognition of the fact that in terms of resource and energy consumption, "when an American couple stops spawning at two babies, it's the same as . . . an Ethiopian couple drawing the line at one thousand" (104). Like Williams's invocation of the African couple, at the end of her article in *Mother Jones*, Julia Whitty also invokes subjugated and formerly colonized peoples in her discussion of the ways that national borders problematize issues of species survival. Whitty claims that the proposed seven-hundred-mile border fence between the United States and Mexico will have devastating ecological consequences in terms of species migration: "from an ecological perspective, it will sever the spine at the lumbar, paralyzing the lower continent." As support, she points to the case of the border fence between India and Pakistan, which often "forces starving bears and leopards, which can no longer traverse their feeding territories, to attack villagers." From Whitty's, McNeill's, and Williams's texts emerge three very different takes on issues of extinction, but there are explicit similarities between the arguments.

First, all three assert that there will be consequences, either now or in the very near future, for the current decimation of biodiversity on planet Earth. And all three hold accountable, albeit to varying degrees, human beings for both the destruction of certain flora and fauna and the persistence of others. Finally, the rhetorical strategies employed by Whitty, Williams, and McNeill rely on the language of imperial domination (the "minion biota" in McNeill's book) and on examples from postcolonial cultures (the "spawning" Ethiopians in Williams's piece, and Indians and Pakistanis that constitute bear and leopard food in Whitty's) to make their cases.

None of these arguments, however, deals with issues of ethics in terms of species preservation, choosing instead to examine the ways that loss of biodiversity might ultimately harm and even endanger human life. And, clearly, the species that we human beings allow to thrive are those plants and animals that are primarily cultivated for human consumption.[1] More often than not, the question of who or what has an inherent right to existence is only ever brought to the forefront of discussions about species decimation when an animal rights perspective enters the narrative frame, and in terms of trying to convince human beings that the preservation of biodiversity is critical, an often more effective and persuasive argument is to focus, as Williams, Whitty, and McNeill do, on the potential loss of human life that, logic would dictate, will ultimately result from the extinction of other species. In many ways, the politics associated with the privileging of certain species over others, particularly sentient nonhuman species, are deeply engaged with an imperialist and Western-centric discourse that undercuts both the non-Western cultural milieu to which these species are indigenous and the supposed "rights" of animals, whether endangered or mass-produced objects of consumption. First, as I illustrated above with examples from Williams's and Whitty's arguments, third-world peoples are invoked as victims of colonial domination who will suffer disproportionately during this sixth wave of extinction. Furthermore, they are cast rhetorically *as* animals, speechless, and unable to act on their own behalf. For example, even as she makes the case that building a fence on the United States/ Mexico border will result in an ecological disaster, Whitty places Mexican immigrants and endangered animals on the same rhetorical plane, caught on one side of that fence, unable to voice their need to migrate and unable to reach sustenance.

The ways that Western environmentalists speak for voiceless endangered species often result in their speaking for non-Western peoples as well, or in assumptions that the needs and beliefs of non-Western cultures with regard to issues of extinction either mirror Western views or, if they do not, are in need of revision. For example, overfishing and the loss of tropical rainforest and jungle-based habitats as human development and industry encroach on these loci has led to the decline of numerous species associated, particularly in the minds of Westerners, with postcolonial exoticism (lions, tigers, elephants, and so forth) and indigenous sustenance (whales and other marine life). The passage of the Endangered Species Act of 1973 represented, according to Deane Curtin, "an extension of liberal concern for the welfare of sentient beings" (39) that paralleled liberal concern for the rights of women and minorities in the United States, but often the protection of endangered nonhuman species has come with the consequence of infringing on the welfare and traditions of non-Western humans. Perhaps nowhere is the conflicting nature of the Western rhetoric of species preservation more apparent than in much of the current debate surrounding vegetarianism. In seeming conjunction with the twentieth- and twenty-first-century extinction spasm has also occurred the rise and commercialization in the West of a vegetarian diet as an ethical imperative and as a presumed reaction to and proposed remedy for environmental destruction—including species decimation. Arguments in favor of such an ideology often cite, among other factors, the environmental damage done by factory farms and the depletion of arable land as a result of overgrazing. For example, according to Bruce Friedrich, the amount of land used to satisfy the food requirements of a vegan for one year is one-sixteenth acre; for a meat eater, the figure is twenty times as high. Similarly, "it requires about 300 gallons of water to feed a vegan for a day. It requires about four times as much to feed a vegetarian, and 14 times as much to feed a meat-eater."

In terms of a postcolonial dynamic, the vegetarian argument is made by theorists like Carol J. Adams, who claims that the meat-based diet of the United States is not only an anomaly, but is also patriarchal and racist. In *The Sexual Politics of Meat*, Adams links increased meat eating with capitalism and patriarchy in the West and with racism toward plant-based cultures: "into the twentieth century the notion was that meat eating contributed to the Western world's prominence" (31). As support, she quotes nineteenth-century English physician George Beard's analysis of the superiority of "civilized" meat-eating peoples over the "rice-eating Hindoo and Chinese and the potato-eating Irish peasant," who were all kept in subjugation to the English, to whom he refers as a "nation of beef-eaters" (qtd. in Adams 31). The flip side of this stance, however, is the contention that a vegetarian diet is, particularly in its current Western incarnation, an elitist endeavor, dependent on a certain degree of privilege and access to resources not available to the general population. Also, just as Adams argues that a meat-based diet is a racist imposition on traditionally vegetarian cultures, the opposite can also be said to hold true for indigenous cultures whose diets are animal-based. In his discussion of the Makah Indian Nation of Washington State, for example, Deane Curtin cites the Nation's assertion that it has a right to hunt gray whales, a species that was removed from the Endangered Species List in 1994 (137). For the Makah, whaling is culturally significant and has become a key aspect of their cultural renaissance.[2] Despite the United States government's allocation of twenty gray whales to the Makah over a four-year period, however, animal rights and environmental activists have protested Makah whaling and denounced the practice. In response to such culturally specific instances, Curtin advocates a position he calls "Contextual Moral Vegetarianism" (143), which, while pro-vegetarian from an ethical and environmental perspective, allows for contextual arguments to the contrary.

❧

Yann Martel's 2001 Booker Prize–winning novel *Life of Pi* is the first-person narrative of another contextual moral vegetarian, Piscine Molitor Patel, a native of Pondicherry, once the capital of French India. "Pi," as he renames himself after schoolmates and teachers continually refer to him, both by accident and on purpose, as "Pissing," recounts a story of the shipwreck that claims the lives of his family members and of his subsequent months drifting at sea in a lifeboat, alone except for a Bengal tiger named Richard Parker. The tiger and Pi form a relationship based on a hierarchy established by Pi, who learns from his zookeeper father that "the animal in front of you must know where it stands, whether above or below you" (44). Pi's first-person narrative is framed by and interspersed with the narrative of the "author," a metafictional device that allows Martel to position the white Western voice as "other" in relation to the Indian character whose story of respect for animal alterity can be read as an indictment of the Western tendency to either anthropomorphize or demonize animals. Pi claims that "an animal is an animal, essentially and practically removed from us" (31), neither the mirror reflection of "Animalus anthropomorphicus, the animal as seen through human eyes" nor its reverse, the "'vicious', 'bloodthirsty', 'depraved' animals that inflame[s] the ire of [human] maniacs" (31). By disrupting the white authorial voice in this manner, Martel is able to let Pi's narrative of his alternating areas of expertise, zoology and religious studies, present the reader with two compelling arguments. First, by writing back to the tradition of the shipwreck narrative in a way that allows for the disruption of the animal/human binary, Martel has written a postcolonial econarrative that makes a case for the maintenance of biodiversity through the persistence of zoos. Alternately, Martel's frame story allows the author character to make the case for the truth of fiction and the power of narrative in the formation and maintenance of belief, particularly belief that may lead to positive environmental action. In *Life of Pi*, when Mr. Okamoto claims at the end of the novel that "the story with animals is the better story" (317), he is speaking comparatively about Pi's two narratives of shipwreck and survival, the one with animals—which Mr. Okamoto does not believe—and the more believable one without. But such sentiment holds true for reality as well: the world with animals is the better world, and a belief in that "truth" may lead to positive environmentally conscious actions for the readers of Martel's "better story."

The novel begins with an "Author's Note" and is subsequently divided into one hundred chapters and three parts, the first of which is Pi's present-tense narrative of a childhood lived predominantly in his father's zoo in Pondicherry. Of the genesis of this zoo, Pi states, "our good old nation was just seven years old as a republic when it became bigger by one small territory. Pondicherry entered the Union of India on November 1, 1954. One civic achievement called for another. A portion of the grounds of the Pondicherry Botanical Garden was made available rent-free for an exciting new business opportunity and—lo and behold—India had a brand new zoo" (12). The first part of the novel also focuses on Pi's encounters with Hinduism, Islam, and Christianity, and his adoption of all three belief systems because he "just want[s] to love God" (69), despite the protestations of his spiritual guides, a Catholic priest, a Hindu pandit, and a Muslim imam. The second part of the novel constitutes the longest section of the work and details Pi's experiences at sea after his family sells the zoo and departs for Toronto on the Japanese cargo ship *Tsimtsum*. Also on board are various animals from the Pondicherry Zoo that Pi's father has sold to men who own a zoo in the United States. Pi, who heretofore "has never seen real live Americans," describes these men as if he is viewing animals in a zoo, as "pink" and "fat"; he claims that they sweat "profusely," smile broadly, and offer "bone-crushing handshakes" (90) after procuring the deal. The depiction of these American zookeepers is significant primarily because this incident manifests Pi's difference, both in terms of appearance and philosophy about animals, from the American businessmen. Furthermore, the American zookeepers treat the animals in a very scientific fashion, sedating them, drawing blood, and observing "feces as if horoscopes" (90). As a result of all the examination, Pi comments that the animals must feel as if they have been drafted into the "U.S. Army" (90). Such clinical treatment of the animals is at odds with Pi's father's more nuanced approach: "my father was a natural. . . . He had a knack for looking at an animal and guessing what was on its mind" (40). Immediately, a binary is put forth and illustrated: the methodical and scientific nature of the American zookeepers versus the intuition of the Indian. Furthermore, both the Western and Japanese characters in the novel insist on factual data, while the Indian Pi and his father are consistently willing to take various leaps of faith.

When the ship sinks, Pi is initially on board the lifeboat with several of these transatlantic animals—a zebra, a hyena, an orangutan, and the aforementioned Richard Parker—but, in typical Darwinian fashion, the hyena kills the zebra and the orangutan and is, in turn, killed by the tiger, thereby leaving only Pi and the tiger adrift for 227 days. The final short section of the narrative takes place after Pi's lifeboat washes ashore in Mexico and is Pi's recollection of part 2 to the Japanese investigators Mr. Okamoto and Mr. Chiba. The men declare that they do not believe Pi's story and ask that he tell them the truth. Pi defends this original narrative, claiming that "tigers exist, lifeboats exist, oceans exist. Because the three have never come together in your narrow, limited experience, you refuse to believe that they might. Yet the plain fact is that the *Tsimtsum* brought them together and then sank" (299). Despite his defense of the veracity of his seemingly impossible narrative, Pi acquiesces and recounts another more believable story, one that consists of "dry, yeastless factuality" (302), a story without animals in which the lifeboat is occupied by Pi's mother, an injured sailor, and the ship's chef. In this second narrative, which accounts for only eight pages of the total novel, the chef kills both Pi's mother and the sailor, and Pi, in turn, kills the chef. While the men admit that the second story is more plausible, when Pi tells them that they will never know the truth or falsity of either story and asks which story they prefer, Mr. Chiba says, "the story with animals," and Mr. Okamoto concurs, "yes. The story with animals is the better story" (317). Therefore, the novel asserts that one's ability to recognize the better story is what allows for a broader understanding of truth as encompassing more than mere facts.

The voice of the author that frames Pi's stories of life in Pondicherry, exile on the lifeboat, and subsequent rescue, creates an illusion of interviewer and interviewee, and this metafictional device allows Martel, through the guise of the author as character, or "author character," in my reading, to establish the voice of Pi as authority, particularly Indian authority, while critiquing his own status as a white, Western outsider who is writing about a postcolonial locale. The author's note at the beginning of the novel functions to establish both setting and author as necessarily fictional in the construction of the narrative of belief in the "better story" that lies at the heart of the novel. The author as character in the author's note claims that in 1996, after his second book is met with "faint praise," he goes to Bombay to write a novel about Portugal in 1939. He claims, "this is not so illogical if you realize . . . that a novel set in Portugal in 1939 may have very little to do with Portugal in 1939" (vii). While certain factual aspects of this note correspond to certain aspects of Martel's life—his second work, *Self*, was published in 1996, for example—the philosophical aspects of the note establish the writer's complicity in the tenuous relationship between the better story (Pi's story about animals, for example) and truth. Says the author character, "that's what fiction is about, isn't it? The selective transforming of reality? The twisting of it to bring out its essence?" (viii). Mr. Adirubasamy, the elderly man who tells the author that Pi's story will "make [him] believe in God" (x), sets the author's search for Pi in motion, and the story that the author claims to find in India is, despite the seeming authenticity of the author's note, contrafactual: there never has been, for example, a zoo in Pondicherry.[3] Establishing a distinction between the author who finds the story and Pi who tells it provides Martel (or the author character if we assume, as I do, that the two are not the same person) a position from which to abdicate authority and give it, instead, to Pi, a character who, for the purposes of Martel's novel, must be non-Western.

But the reader might easily ask why Martel's protagonist *needs* to be non-Western in general and Indian in particular. What about Pi's story and about the *Life of Pi* makes it necessary for Martel to undertake the complicated task of writing and narrating a postcolonial other? Why not, in other words, have the protagonist be Canadian? Before attempting to answer this question, I want to look briefly at the subject positions of both Canada and Yann Martel. In an interview titled "The Empathetic Imagination," Sabine Sielke asks Martel if he considers himself a "citizen of the world" (30). Such a question is not surprising given Martel's transnational identity: he was born in Spain to Canadian parents and has lived, among other places, in Alaska, British Columbia, Costa Rica, France, and Mexico. The brief author bio on the back of Harcourt's trade edition of *Life of Pi* proclaims that "when he's not living somewhere else, he lives in Montreal." Martel has indeed been marketed as a citizen of the world, an author whose identity defies clear national affiliation. Martel, however, answered Sielke's question as follows: "no. I'm Canadian. I don't believe there are citizens of the world. Everyone is from somewhere, rooted in a particular culture. We're also citizens of the languages we speak. Some people speak many languages—I speak three, I'm a citizen of English, French and Spanish—but no one speaks World. World is not a language" (30). This answer clearly illustrates the complexity of claiming a national allegiance in an increasingly global world; on the one hand, Martel is a "citizen" of various languages, and on the other, a citizen of Canada. Everyone may in fact "be from somewhere," but, at least in Martel's estimation, one may also be a part of language communities that defy easy national categorization. In the context of this discussion of language-based citizenship, it is worth noting that on the lifeboat, Pi and Richard Parker create their own nonverbal language community, based primarily on each character's ability to translate the sounds and actions of the other and secondarily on a shared diet. Martel may not consider himself a global citizen, but his various historical "homelands" position him, whether he agrees to this categorization or not, as a transnational writer who claims allegiance to a questionably postcolonial site, Canada.

Canada's postcolonial status has been widely debated over the past two decades,[1] particularly with regard to Canada's position as part of the British Commonwealth and with regard to the plight of indigenous peoples. According to Laura Moss, "a clear divide in the postcolonial paradigm is often perceived between the 'invader-settler' nations of Australia, New Zealand, and Canada . . . and those parts of the world where colonization was more predominantly a process of displacement . . . and even annihilation" (2). In trying to make a case for the postcolonial status of Canadian literature, Moss goes on to say,

> Depending on the focus of postcolonial studies, Canada may or may not be included in the list of postcolonial locations. In addition to referring to the results of the interaction between imperial culture and indigenous cultural practices, the term "postcolonial" may also refer to the location of production of the text. . . . Or, postcolonialism may be roughly defined as a concern with a series of issues including: cultural imperialism; emergent nationalisms within a nation and between nations; negotiating history and the process of decolonization; hierarchies of power, violence, and op-

pression; censorship; race and ethnicity; multiculturalism; appropriation of voice; revising the canon and "writing back" to colonial education; and Indigenous languages and "englishes" versus standard English. All of these issues are at play, to a greater or lesser degree in Canadian literature. (4)

Furthermore, according to Frank Birbalsingh, Canada's national self-concept has evolved and shifted since Canada peacefully achieved self-government from the British in 1867 after nearly a century of colonial domination. Canada's colonial history is unique, then, because "unlike most former colonies which established nationality by resisting imperial rule, Canada steered a middle course that generally avoided resistance" (vii). Such complicit interaction with British rule has made Canada's national position difficult to identify, but its identity has evolved over three main stages since its colonization in the eighteenth century: Canada was first viewed as a colonial or provincial outpost of empire; second as a colonial nation; and third, "by the middle of [the twentieth] century, there is scarcely any consistent image at all" (5). Within the context of *Life of Pi*, Yann Martel as author and his alter-ego author character maintain and perform Canada's lack of unified identity, particularly when both culture and author are read alongside the seemingly "authentic" Indian character of Pi.

The answer to why Pi must be Indian in Martel's narrative, then, can be found through an examination of the way various dualisms are employed and disrupted within Martel's text, including the colonizing/colonized dualism that marks the relationship between the author character and Pi and the human/animal binary that marks the assumed distinction between culture and nature. Martel establishes and disrupts this assumed duality early in the novel, within the context of a vegetarian dietary metaphor. The author character claims that whenever he visits Pi, "[Pi] prepares a South Indian vegetarian feast. I told him I like spicy food. I don't know why I said such a stupid thing. It's a complete lie. I add dollop of yogurt after dollop of yogurt. Nothing doing. Each time it's the same: my taste buds shrivel up and die, my skin goes beet red, my eyes well up with tears, my head feels like a house on fire, and my digestive tract starts to twist and groan in agony like a boa constrictor that has swallowed a lawn mower" (42–43).

The Canadian author character is no match for the dietary prowess of the Indian, and the analogy that the author character uses to describe his experience is particularly telling in terms of Martel's project in *Life of Pi*. That his stomach churns "like a boa constrictor that has swallowed a lawn mower" indicates a conflict between the natural and technological worlds (the snake versus the lawn mower), between the exotic and the mundane (a South American reptile versus a mechanical—and environmentally destructive—implement used in the maintenance of the Western bourgeois yard), between, most likely, the vegetarian and meat eater, and, perhaps most significantly, between animal and human. But the snake has swallowed the lawnmower, nonetheless; this example of blending, the mixing of these various binary components in an uneasy unity, is indicative of the search for a third place of identification that emerges during the shipwreck section of the work when Pi compromises his own ethical vegetarianism in order to survive and during which his relationship with the animal in his midst, namely Richard Parker, changes from one of master/servant to a more symbiotic arrangement dependent on a shared language and diet. In terms of the metaphor of the boa and the lawnmower, the survivor is the animal, albeit an animal invested in (and ingesting) the technology of modernity, at an uneasy stasis—like Canada's identification as postcolonial, or Martel's as Canadian.

Critics have commented on the various aforementioned dualisms that shape the novel; Stewart Cole, for example, points to a similarity between the binary of fiction and religion as these elements are critiqued in the novel: "disbelief is anathema to both" (26). June Dwyer claims that "Pi understands animals' otherness, but at the same time he feels affinity with them. His story reflects this duality, as does his choice as an adult to pursue careers in both religious studies and zoology" (18). Similarly, Florence Stratton claims that at the core of the narrative lies a debate about the various binaries that shape modern thought. She claims, "*Life of Pi* is organized around a philosophical debate about the modern world's privileging of reason over imagination, science over religion, materialism over idealism, fact over fiction or story" (6). Within the context of the narrative, Pi represents, at least in theory, one side of various binary pairs that shape the focus of the novel: he is Indian as opposed to Canadian, vegetarian as opposed to carnivorous, Hindu (by history) as opposed to Christian, religious as opposed to secular. Furthermore, his story is oral as opposed to written; the author does the transcription of the tale, claiming, "it seemed natural that Mr. Patel's story should be told mostly in the first person—in his voice and through his eyes. But any inaccuracies or mistakes are mine" (xii). With regard to his feelings about animals, Pi is practical as opposed to sentimental or malicious—qualities he associates predominantly with Westerners (30). He claims, "animals in the wild lead lives of compulsion and necessity within an unforgiving social hierarchy in an environment where the supply of fear is high and the supply of food low" (16), and goes on to state that "one might even argue that if an animal could choose with intelligence, it would opt for living in a zoo" (18). Finally, however, Pi states that he does not mean to defend zoos, but this assertion is merely a vehicle for Pi to comment on the environmental destruction that endangers animals outside of zoos: "close them all down if you want (and let us hope that what wildlife remains can survive in what is left of the natural world)" (19). But despite Pi's rhetorical placement on one side of a set of binary oppositions, Martel's novel, with its attention to trinities and its title character's ability to explore in-between and taboo spaces, disrupts such easy correspondences.

For example, as I already mentioned, even at an early age, Pi becomes a "practicing Hindu, Christian and Muslim" (64), as is humorously evidenced when he later cries out "Jesus, Mary, Muhammad and Vishnu!" (150) when Richard Parker attacks the hyena on the lifeboat. His ability to believe many things at once is in direct contrast with the author character's inability to believe anything at all, as evidenced by his claim that hearing a narrative that will make him believe in God is a "tall order" (x). Pi's affinity for this kind of multiplicity increases, both by philosophical imperative and out of necessity, after the shipwreck as Pi, now a self proclaimed "Indo-Canadian" (165), must negotiate a relationship with a nonhuman animal—a tiger — that has always been on the other side of various fences, both literal (in the zoo) and metaphorical (in terms of Pi's assumed difference from him). Over the course of the novel as Pi tells the author character the story of negotiating the species boundary between human and tiger, the author character negotiates the cultural boundary that initially characterizes Pi as the postcolonial other whose story he seeks to ascertain. For example, once when the author character arrives at Pi's house earlier than usual, he encounters Pi's two children as well as a dog and cat that he did not realize existed (92). He notes that the story of Pi's interaction with his children, an instance characterized by universality, "has a happy ending" (93).

Pi's status as Indian is again significant, particularly since early on he evokes the partition of India, the division of one nation into two, that was marked not only by mass violence, death, and the codification of one's national identity as either Indian or Pakistani, but also by the construction of the kinds of fences that Whitty describes in her *Mother Jones* article as resulting in species-specific decimation. On the boat, however, there are no such divisions, and Pi is only able to maintain a perceived dominance over Richard Parker by controlling the tiger's access to food, blowing a whistle, and positioning the boat so that it will rock and make the tiger seasick should Richard Parker attempt to assert dominance over Pi. But despite Pi's earlier assertion that animals are animals, a lesson he learns definitively when his father forces the entire family to watch a tiger attack and kill a goat early in the novel, the relationship that Pi maintains with Richard Parker is a delicate combination of dominance, respect for the alterity of the tiger, and, at times, love. Pi is well aware of the dangers of dressing "wild animals in tame costumes" (34), but he is also able to negotiate the divide between animal and human in order to interact and speak with the tiger in ways that defy both extreme sentimentalism and abject fear. For example, Pi responds to Richard Parker's "speech," the prusten snort that tigers make to "express friendliness and harmless intentions," initially with "fearful wonder" and a sincere hope that the tiger will not die, thereby leaving Pi alone with "despair, a foe more formidable than a tiger" (164). The example of prusten as communication allows the reader to see Pi's ability to read the tiger's actions as species-specific gestures that have no human equivalents. Pi, therefore, cannot respond in kind, but, over the course of the narrative, he and Richard Parker are able to establish a kind of lingua franca of sound and gesture. Just as Martel claims to be a citizen of certain languages, so too can we read Pi and Richard Parker as citizens of the same self-created language nation, that of the lifeboat and the rules that hold true for it.

In terms of his diet, Pi also expresses a multiplicity of facets, interests, and compromises, and these are particularly important within the context of a novel about animals as both predators and objects of human and animal consumption. The author character comments that when Pi cooks, "we are in India. But he handles Western dishes equally well. . . . And his vegetarian tacos would be the envy of all Mexico" (25). When Pi's father forces him to watch the lion kill the goat, he claims that the experience is "enough to scare the living vegetarian daylights out of me" (36). Pi repeatedly points to his vegetarianism as evidence of his pacifism, but on the boat with the tiger, he realizes that "a person can get used to anything, even to killing" (185). The diet of which he and Richard Parker partake is identical, consisting primarily of fish and turtles, and eating animals causes Pi a great deal of stress, particularly early in the journey. He says, "to think that I'm a strict vegetarian. To think that when I was a child I always shuddered when I snapped open a banana because it sounded to me like the breaking of an animal's neck. I descended to a level of savagery I never imagined possible" (197). Later in the novel, after Richard Parker kills the unknown man that Pi encounters while at sea, Pi admits, "I ate some of his flesh" (256). This incident is significant for two reasons, first because it situates Pi and the tiger in the same rhetorical dietary space, and second because it illustrates the conflict between ethical belief and physical necessity while simultaneously illustrating the false dichotomy between human and animal. Pi may believe that eating animal flesh is unethical, but in the context of a lifeboat adrift at sea, his ethics give way to his will to survive. More telling, however, is the leap that Pi is able to make from eating animals to eating human flesh. Pi must battle his ethics in order to kill, and he weeps for the first fish he kills, claiming, "I never forget to include this fish in my prayers" (183). But the ethical struggle that characterizes Pi's killing of this first fish is entirely absent in his eating of the dead man; despite the fact that Pi claims that he also prays daily for this man's soul, he says that the man's flesh "slipped into [his] mouth nearly unnoticed" (256). In the wild, as Pi claims earlier in the novel, animals struggle to survive, eating what they can find. The choice of ethical consumption is rendered as an impossible fantasy on the lifeboat; Pi must, in this instance, contextualize his decision to eat meat.

Through the various binary constructions that it disrupts, *Life of Pi* allows us to view a third place of signification in a postcolonial narrative about the importance of animal and human relationships, about relationships between and as amalgams of cultures in the twenty-first century, and about the need to believe in the "better story" (64), alternately the story with animals that Pi tells the author character and the story that allows animals to continue to exist in the environmentally devastated world, in "biologically sound" zoos (17). If we accept Laura Moss's assertion that a trait of the postcolonial is its tendency to "write back" to extant and canonical traditions, then Martel's narrative is postcolonial not only because its animal and human protagonists are Indian, but because it writes back to and interprets in an environmentally conscious way an extant literary tradition, the shipwreck narrative, the best known of which is Defoe's 1719 novel *Robinson Crusoe*. In Defoe's telling, the shipwrecked European Crusoe orders the natural world—and its other inhabitant, Friday—around him. Conversely, according to June Dwyer, Martel's novel "can be read as the twenty-first century convergence of both developmental and historical shipwreck narratives, a text where a young shipwrecked human grows up—so to speak—and takes his place in the circle of nature, rather than at the top of the heap" (10). Dwyer also reads Martel's novel as disrupting a domination paradigm that "is replaced with a more ecologically acceptable one of respect" (10). Pi's relationships with animals in general and with Richard Parker in particular offer a possibility for the way that this respect may be manifest. First, Pi's claim at the beginning of the novel that he is not a defender of zoos is negated by his subsequent comment that if there are no zoos, "let us hope that what wildlife remains can survive in what is left of the natural world" (19), as well as by his analysis of the various ways that zoos benefit animals. The novel itself, through its initial presentation of the Pondicherry Zoo and its later explanation of Richard Parker's adaptation to life within the small confines of the lifeboat, makes a compelling case for the role that zoos can and should play in the maintenance of species diversity during the Holocene extinction event that I discussed at the beginning of this chapter.

The ethics of keeping wild animals in captivity have long been debated, and Pi mentions this debate early in the narrative: "Well-meaning but misinformed people think animals in the wild are 'happy' because they are 'free.' . . . They imagine this wild animal roaming about the savannah on digestive walks after eating a prey that accepted its lot piously, or going for callisthenic runs to stay slim after overindulging. They imagine this animal overseeing its offspring proudly and tenderly, the whole family watching the setting of the sun from the limbs of trees with sighs of pleasure. The life of the wild animal is simple, noble and meaningful, they imagine" (15–16). Pi then systematically disproves this fantasy image, citing the extreme hardships that animals face in the wild, and he asserts, in an aforementioned quote, that both "wildlife" and "nature" are becoming things of the past. In *A Different Nature: The Paradoxical World of Zoos and Their Uncertain Future*, David Hancocks echoes Pi's defense of zoos by showing the evolution of the zoo from mere "collections of animals, like jewels, for the wealthy," to places that are now "facsimiles of wild environments that resemble their models in appearance, mood, and content" (159). Verisimilitude with "reality" is important, Hancocks claims, as is the "growing awareness that zoos must become directly involved in wildlife habitat protection" (160). Conversely, in *Savages and Beasts: The Birth of the Modern Zoo*, Nigel Rothfels argues that "zoos are for people and not for animals" (7) and that while people now tend to prefer "exhibits in which animals appear to be living in 'nature,'" new "immersion exhibits are not 'nature.' They are not even replicas of 'nature.' They are fantasies now reinforced by nature television" (202). But the case that Pi makes for keeping animals in zoos—and the zoos that he advocates are those that provide animals with their needs in terms of space, food, and companionship—has more to do with the preservation of species as opposed to some idea of how a zoo should replicate nature. In fact, in the context of *Life of Pi* and in the context of the "real" world, what constitutes nature and what is "natural" or authentic is problematic, as can be seen both in Martel's creation of the Indian Pi and Pi's admission that he and the tiger both eat human flesh on the lifeboat. Both beings, driven by hunger and a will to survive, do what, within the context of their experience, is entirely natural.

Furthermore, in part 1 of the novel, Pi cites the example of a black leopard that escapes from the Zurich Zoo in 1933 and is not found for ten weeks. Pi asserts that the tropical cat survived outside of its natural habitat in the Swiss winter "without being seen by anyone, let alone attacking anyone" because "zoo animals are not dangerous absconding criminals but simply wild creatures seeking to fit in" (42), and the concept of "fitting in" indicates an adaptability on the part of animals—human and nonhuman—that Pi and Richard Parker both illustrate later in the novel. That the two survive together on a lifeboat for the better part of a year provides evidence of the malleable nature of sentient life, both human and tiger. That Richard Parker disappears into a Mexican jungle never to be seen again is another such example, as is Pi's story of a polar bear that escapes the Calcutta Zoo and is believed to be living "freely on the banks of the Hugli River" (297). That animals do sometimes seek to escape from zoos would seem to negate an argument for a zoo's ability to provide animals with what they need, but Pi counters this assertion by claiming that animals do not flee in order to find a specific place, to some abstraction known as freedom, but because something has startled them. According to Pi, animals flee, both in captivity and in the wild, to escape "from something" (41). And the thing that scares animals more than anything else, Pi asserts, is humanity. Most animals, he claims, "cannot get over their fear" (296) of human beings. Dealing with animals in the postcolonial environment depicted in *Life of Pi* requires the reader to examine a relationship in which both animal and human negotiate their respective fear of one another and interact in ways that defy more traditional anthropomorphic readings. When Pi tells Richard Parker "I love you!" (236), he does not expect the tiger to answer in kind, just as he could not answer the tiger's prusten snort, but the sentiment is based on a shared history, one in which both beings have been at the mercy of their environment, and one in which they have enabled each other to survive.

While the novel is not an allegory for the current environmental situation, the reinvention of the animal/human relationship within it provides a firm case for the fact that "the story with animals is the better story" (317), just as a planet where animals are considered beings worthy of respect and care is better than a planet without them. Yann Martel has commented on the danger of writing the animal out of the story of human life on planet Earth. He says, "I am concerned about the destruction of the environment. I do believe that it's good that we have zoos because if we don't, children will never see animals in the flesh. An animal becoming extinct will have no more impact on them than a TV show that's been discontinued. Children won't really feel for an animal the way they would if giraffes were being pushed to extinction and they had seen giraffes" (qtd. in Sielke 22). Such an assertion again speaks to the psychic and spiritual costs that humans will incur as biodiversity decreases, as does Hancocks's claim that there is yet another reason to support zoos: "the value of biological diversity for our emotional, intellectual, and spiritual well-being" (162). But Martel's narrative is also about the power of belief, particularly the belief that perhaps species of various kinds need each other not only in order to survive but also in order to be our best selves. Pi Patel believes that the animals with which he shares his existence do not speak his language or share his emotions, but they do have an inherent right to share his world. As Martel has said of his writing, "the self-involved, the *angst* of the solitary does not interest me. I'd rather look at the other, whether it's the animal other, the cultural other, the religious other" (Sielke 20). Mr. Okamoto's report at the end of *Life of Pi* is filled with the language of uncertainty: the ship "appears" to have sunk quickly; the precise reason for why is "impossible to determine"; and all possible reasons are "speculation" and "conjecture" (319). The only aspects that he treats as facts are those components that he initially doubted, those that constitute the better story: "very few castaways can claim to have survived so long at sea as Mr. Patel, and none in the company of an adult Bengal tiger" (319). In the battle between the boa constrictor and the lawn mower, at least in Martel's novel, it seems that the animal has won.

A scenario similar to Martel's author character's dietary metaphor of the boa constrictor and lawn mower is present in Joy Williams's most recent novel, *The Quick & the Dead*. The novel's protagonist, Alice, overhears two women talking about Tarzan Zambini, a former circus lion tamer who retires and moves into a desert house in Arizona with his lions. All share the house together, but when a highway cuts through the property, Zambini sells the house, which becomes a lawn equipment store. According to one of the women, the lions "lived on one side of the house and Tarzan lived on the other and there was a swimming pool between them . . . but Tarzan had to move out and give up his lions when the highway came through. There he was out in the middle of nowhere with his lions, and comes progress's inexorable wheel to slice his spread in half, and now there are these stupid lawn mowers where the lions used to play" (161). As is the case with much of Williams's novel, this scenario is both absurd and utterly plausible, a brief narrative moment in which various levels of artifice are revealed: Tarzan Zambini is a double fiction, a character created by Williams who takes the name of another fictional character created by Edgar Rice Burroughs in his 1912 novel, *Tarzan of the Apes*. Similarly, Zambini's lions are multiply displaced, first in that they are removed from their native habitat and trained to perform in a circus in the United States, and second because they are rendered oversized house cats when Zambini retires. We know only that the former lion trainer has to "give up" his lions when a highway is built, but what happens to them, like the fate of Richard Parker, remains unknown; the highway divides the desert from itself, and the lions are sacrificed, yet again, to the destruction of the environment that heralds the intrusion of modernity. Like the zoo of Martel's novel, the circus mentioned only fleetingly in Williams's provides one of many examples in the text of the ways that postcolonial animals are commodified and presented to various human audiences in the West.

Despite the fact that United States author Williams's novel was a finalist for the 2001 Pulitzer Prize and her collection of essays *Ill Nature: Rants and Reflections on Humans and Other Animals* (2001) was a finalist for the National Book Critics Circle Award for criticism,[5] to date, no literary scholar has given her work the theoretical attention that it deserves,[6] particularly in terms of its ecocritical relevance. The reasons for this lack of scholarly attention with regard to Williams are based, I feel, on several factors, primarily the assertion posited by various reviewers that while Williams is an adept and skilled writer of short stories, she lacks the ability to remain focused for the duration of a novel—and she has written four total, two of which, *The Changeling* (1978) and *Breaking and Entering* (1988), are now out of print. According to Carson Brown's *January Magazine* review of *The Quick & the Dead*, "at times it feels as though Williams cannot contain the giant idea of power behind the novel, that her vision crosses the line that separates far-reaching from unwieldy." Secondly, Williams's harsh worldview, penchant for black humor (Gail Caldwell says of her style, "imagine Cormac McCarthy bumping into Flannery O'Connor"), and her uncompromising, unrelenting criticism of Western excess and ethical hypocrisy—particularly with regard to the destruction of the environment—forces readers to acknowledge their complicity in that destruction and, therefore, to occupy an uncomfortable position. According to Jennifer Schuessler in her *New York Times* review of *The Quick & the Dead*, "for Williams, seeing the universe whole seems to demand a kind of radically refocused compassion that can sometimes look, well, like heartlessness." Furthermore, Gail Caldwell's *Boston Globe* review of the novel asserts that "the beauty of this novel is without mercy and the mercy without beauty." While critics applaud Williams's skill as a writer—the novel is "a death trip writ large in gorgeous calligraphy" (Caldwell)—they often take issue with the relentlessness of her project and with the seeming lack of unity and resolution offered by the work.

The things that make *The Quick & the Dead* so problematic for reviewers, however, are also the things that make it such a valuable text in terms of its experimental style, its examination of animal and human relationships, and its bleakly probable view of the future of life, both animal and human, on planet Earth. Reviewers have read Williams's novel as "unwieldy" because they have tried to read the work, unsuccessfully, as a linear narrative. I contend instead that the novel, which consistently employs images of weaving, of mirrors, and of motherless offspring, is structured as a web that is at once circular and unending, a point that Williams alludes to early in the narrative when the character of Corvus discusses a Native American blanket that belonged to her recently deceased parents. Corvus points "to a Navajo Black Design blanket that hung on the wall. 'See the way it is in the center, like the center of a spider's web? That's so the weaver's thoughts can escape the weaving when it's finished. So the mind won't get trapped in there'" (18). Williams's narrative structure reflects this "natural" phenomenon, a spider spinning a web, and allows Williams to pick up and drop threads pertaining to animal rights, human materialism, and environmental destruction that illustrate the ways that inhabitants of the late twentieth-century world depicted in her work are "trapped" in a space wherein they often fail to realize that "nothing we do is inevitable, but everything we do is irreversible" (4). In *The Quick & the Dead* Williams offers a critique of two manifestations of that irreversibility as they pertain to the endangerment of certain animals: the wildlife museum wherein all the animals are dead, stuffed, and positioned as if they are alive, and the big game safari, the vehicle that allows these animals to be killed in the first place. The web that makes up Williams's novel allows the narrative to contain the world it creates—as the character of Sherwin says, "God's the net. We are the creatures within the net" (73)—and it also demonstrates how issues of life and death, particularly in the late twentieth-century world, double back on and are, at times, indistinguishable from each other.

The character at the center of Williams's web is Alice, the extroverted and militant vegetarian and animal rights advocate who turns a critical eye outward, blaming and judging others without ever becoming particularly cognizant of her own contradictions; not surprisingly, Alice "hated mirrors" (11). She is also Williams's funniest creation in *The Quick & the Dead*, a parody or heightened version of the views that Williams herself presents in her aforementioned essay collection *Ill Nature*, a text in which Williams pontificates on animal rights, population control, and environmental destruction. The dramatically inclined Alice, whose favorite childhood book is *Charlotte's Web* (207), is a teenager who talks to her six-year-old babysitting charges about "animals and excess packaging" (6). Alice wants a scar (7), plans to stage "puke-ins" at restaurants that serve veal (17), and wears T-shirts that say things like "Thank you for not breeding" (109). The two other central characters are the materialistic Annabel and the introverted and wise Corvus, two girls who, along with Alice, are "motherless" (70) and who, in the eyes of Annabel's father, Carter, are like the Fates: "one spun, one measured, one cut" (199). Together, the three "spin" the web of a story that contains seeming multitudes of minor characters who exist at varying distances from these primary three; therefore, certain characters—like Carter, a bisexual piano player named Sherwin, and Annabel's dead mother, Ginger—are more fully developed than others. These others, like nineteen-year-old stroke survivor Ray Webb, enigmatic Nurse Daisy, fourth grade visionary Emily Bliss Pickless, and big game hunter Stumpp, are linked to the primary three by various degrees of separation. These characters exist at various boundary points on the web that mark, as Corvus says, "this life, the next life, and the life between" (149). In Williams's novel, characters live and die, and the distinction between these two states is tentative at best, a point illustrated by the fact, for example, that Ginger is a major character in the novel, regularly appearing to make Carter feel guilty about his repressed homosexuality.

Like *Life of Pi*, *The Quick & the Dead* is divided into three sections and is particularly preoccupied with various trinities, a structural feature emblematic of the novel's consistent ability to negotiate the taboo space between the binary oppositions of human/animal, culture/nature, and life/death—the "life between" (149) mentioned by Corvus.[7] Each section begins with a brief narrative sketch in which a narrator (or perhaps the author as narrator) presents a kind of "riddle" (197) directly to the reader, addressing him or her as "you." All three sketches discuss the place in which the reader will find her or himself in the proceeding section—the narrator asserts at the beginning of book 1, "so. You don't believe in a future life. Then do we have a place for you!" (3)—but until one has read the section, the introductory material remains enigmatic; in order to locate the "place" in question, one must go back and reread the sketches after reading the entire section, a reading strategy that again reinforces the nonlinear web structure of the book while simultaneously reinforcing a major point within the text, the difficulty of finding a place or home where one, animal or human, might be received in the late twentieth-century world depicted in the novel. In the first such section, the narrative is set at the homes of the three girls. The primary setting of book 2 is Green Palms, a nursing home where Corvus volunteers once a week, and book 3 is situated in "Eden turned hex backwards" (197), Stumpp's Wildlife Museum. The novel's central motif, the mirror images of life and death and the blurring of the divide between both, is present on nearly every page of the work. Early in the novel, for example, Alice tells Annabel about a woman named Candy: "When she was seven months pregnant, there wasn't a heartbeat anymore, but the doctors didn't want to do a cesarean or induce labor so she has to carry it around stillborn full-term and she's trying to make a new world cataclysmic situation out of it. The cycle has been broken, the *web of life* torn, dead world coming, et cetera" (49, my emphasis). Later, Corvus suggests that "Alice and Annabel think of the people [at Green Palms] as already being dead" (115), and in Stumpp's museum, "the dead of other species" look "beautiful" (220). The text is also replete with the inverse, life coming out of death; at one point, for example, the narrator comments on Stumpp's business venture in genetic research: "eggs were being harvested from aborted fetuses" (221). Within all of this death in life and vice versa, there lies a kind of karmic justice gone awry, a perpetuation of destruction and resurrection dependent upon, as Alice says, the fact that "evil must be repaid, and not necessarily to the one who'd done the deed" (148). Those who suffer the most in Williams's text are animals, but, then again, everyone in this work suffers in particularly poignant and poetically just ways for the damages they inflict, directly and indirectly, on the natural world.

While *The Quick & the Dead* is set in the United States, specifically in Arizona, the third of the three sections that the novel comprises is situated in a wildlife museum owned by a former big game hunter named Stumpp. The museum is juxtaposed with Green Palms; both "had been built around the same time" (219), and both contain species, animal and human, who inhabit the uncertain space between life and death. The people at Green Palms exist in a space where it feels as if "salvation was being deliberately, cruelly withheld" (116) wherein people are "tenured to death . . . without being dead" (170); similarly, the animals in the Wildlife Museum are dead, stuffed, and positioned in lifelike poses, "reaching out for twigs" (223). These animals are the choicest specimens of the over one thousand animals that Stumpp killed on many safaris in Africa and Alaska. The narrator describes Stumpp's feelings about Africa in its current condition: "Africa at this point in time particularly broke Stumpp's heart, crawling with people as it was. All those scrawny humans crouching in the dust. He wouldn't go to Africa anymore. Let them have what was left; he'd partaken of it when it was glorious. Stumpp wasn't one of those trophy hunters who went on and on anecdotally about the beasts he'd shot. He couldn't recall each and every incident, not even most of them, but he felt warmly toward all his animals. None of them had given him any problems" (219). While many of the animal-related issues that Williams tackles in this text are specific to the United States—the historic decimation of the buffalo population and the consequences of contemporary urban sprawl, a situation illustrated when a deer falls into Annabel's swimming pool and nearly drowns—a fair amount of the novel focuses on animals from postcolonial locations, particularly elephants from Africa, as this continent and its species are viewed by and marketed to Westerners via the medium of television and within such staged and artificial constructs as Stumpp's museum and Tarzan Zambini's aforementioned circus. Stumpp's assertion that he had partaken of Africa when it was "glorious" is based on an imaginary Africa wherein animals existed for the purpose of being hunted and is juxtaposed with his disappointment that Africa is now "crawling with people," a statement that marks not only the negligible status with which Stumpp views human Africans but also the decimation of nonhuman species due to historically unchecked hunting practices. Stumpp's memory of Africa's former glory is furthermore based on imaginary manifestations of Africa, particularly African countries like Tanzania and Kenya that marketed exotic adventure to the would-be Western big game hunter.

The history of big game hunting safaris in Africa and such safaris' current connections to contemporary notions of ecotourism, a model that promises, according to the Ecotourism Society, "responsible travel to natural areas that conserves the environment and improves the well-being of local people" (qtd. in Duffy 6), are issues that are deeply implicated in an imperialist model of colonial exploitation, one that persisted after many African nations had gained independence from their former colonizers. In fact, ecotourism in places like Kenya, South Africa, and Tanzania is based on a history of big game hunting that happened simultaneously alongside the establishment of colonial rule. According to Brian Herne in *White Hunters: The Golden Age of African Safaris*, the term "White Hunter" originated in British East Africa after the turn of the twentieth century, but "big game hunting was already popular in other parts of the 'Dark Continent,' notably in South Africa, where . . . [white] hunters . . . had been active long before Somaliland and East Africa came into vogue" (3). Herne's text examines the heyday of the White Hunter in Africa, beginning with the first safari business—started by R. J. Cunninghame, Bill Judd, George Outram, and Leslie Tarston around 1903 (7)—to the decades of the 1960s and 1970s, during which increased hunting regulations and conservation measures took hold. It is during these decades that Stumpp, "half a century old" (225) in Williams's novel, would have been hunting. While Herne's text focuses on, glorifies, and mythologizes the legacies of white hunters like Stumpp, Edward J. Steinhart's *Black Poachers, White Hunters: A Social History of Hunting in Colonial Kenya*, focuses on the ways that indigenous African peoples' hunting practices were literally and rhetorically criminalized in order for white safaris to thrive. Steinhart asserts that "the struggles over the definition and control of hunting and the politics and revenues which it yielded may be key to understanding the contests of power that went on for seven decades between settlers, officials, and Africans" (18). Furthermore, this Western demonstration of domination of nature paralleled "European racial and class domination over black Africans" (Duffy 294); therefore, colonized subjects and hunted animals occupy the same rhetorical space in the colonial milieu in which big game hunting came of age.

Equally problematic, at least in some cases, is what happens when animals are protected under the auspices of wilderness refuges, a more recent phenomenon that has occurred as a result of species decimation due to historically unchecked hunting practices. In recent decades, photographic safaris have replaced most hunting safaris, and animals are often protected—at least in theory—in wildlife preserves. But if the colonial philosophy described above traditionally equated indigenous human life with animal life and valued neither, then the wildlife refuge system has often benefited animals and corporations at the expense of indigenous human populations. For example, according to Martha Honey in *Ecotourism and Sustainable Development: Who Owns Paradise?*, when the Ndumo Game Reserve was established in 1924, the Tonga people of South Africa were forced to leave the area and were denied access to water within the reserve (367). In the late 1980s, when the Ndumo and Tembe reserves planned to merge so that the Tembe elephants could access water in Ndumo, the Tonga were once again threatened with the possibility of relocating, but "in the mid-1990s, the villagers, with the assistance of rural development workers, struck a deal whereby they agreed to move farther south" (367). Rosaleen Duffy, in her study *A Trip Too Far: Ecotourism, Politics and Exploitation*, comments that "in the developing world, there is an added layer to the politics of tourism because of memories of colonial control," and in places like Kenya, "conservation and tourism schemes have replicated the colonial system of separating people and the environment" (101). Furthermore, most of the income generated by such reserves benefits the private corporations that run the wilderness and photographic safaris, with minimal income being generated for indigenous populations that are often displaced and disenfranchised by these business ventures.[8]

At the current moment, according to Honey, Tanzania, Zimbabwe, and South Africa permit "trophy hunting only in designated 'blocks' in game controlled areas and reserves" (243). While Joy Williams's text never mentions the specific country of Stumpp's game hunting safaris, the "Africa" in which Stumpp hunted is a vastly different place from the more prohibitive contemporary continent that Stumpp bemoans in the preceding quote about Africa's former glory, a place where tighter hunting regulations and ecotourism have taken the place of the big game hunts of previous decades, but a place where "scrawny," no doubt, black, human beings continue to be treated dismissively by white conservationists. According to Duffy, ecotourism in Africa, like hunting, is dependent on the "politically laden image of the destination country" and, in the contemporary moment, "host societies are packaged and commodified for consumption by an external audience, promising the exotic, the unspoiled, the pristine and—even worse—the primitive" (xii). Many African countries have opted for a more conservationist form of tourism, given the rate at which indigenous species were being decimated by hunters. For example, Kenya outlawed hunting in 1977 and that country's tourism industry is now based primarily on (at least on the surface) a more environmentally conscious model. Critics like Duffy, however, claim that "ecotourism is firmly locked into notions of 'green capitalism,' and thus it cannot provide radical sustainable development, contrary to its supporters' claims. Ecotourism is a business . . . and it focuses on profit rather than conservation" (x). Furthermore, other African countries have banned hunting only to reopen the practice because of the financial benefits that it affords. Tanzania banned hunting in 1973, but reallowed the practice in 1978, and despite the fact that the elephant population dropped from six hundred thousand in the 1960s to around one hundred thousand in the 1990s, Tanzania still allows the culling of elephants to continue (Honey 247). Ecotourism has a problematic relationship with hunting, which is often seen as restraint on poaching. According to Honey, "sport hunting is . . . the ultimate paradox for ecotourism. Although most of those involved in conservation and nature tourism find hunting distasteful, cruel, and ethically reprehensible, many admit that if properly managed, trophy hunting helps curb poaching and does less environmental damage and brings in much more foreign exchange than do photographic safaris" (244).

Because fewer people hunt than take photos and because the cost of hunting expeditions is significantly higher than the cost of photographic safaris,[9] environmentally "friendly" photographic tours often result in more environmentally destructive issues, including more pollution, more garbage, and more destruction of terrain as photographers often drive off roads to get shots of animals stalking their prey (Honey 245).

In her fiction and nonfiction Williams is critical of both big game hunting and its seemingly ecofriendly counterpart, the photographic safari, because of the false images of animals and land that both practices sell to Westerners. In her essay "Safariland," Williams claims that the "desired illusion here is . . . Africa," a place that allows those on safari to feel that they "have entered a portion of the earth that wild animals have retained possession of. The illusion here is that wild animals exist" (*Ill Nature* 27). In this essay Williams critiques the lies of the photographic safari, particularly the lie that there exist any animal populations that have not been marked, sold, placed, trapped, fragmented, scattered, and positioned within the perimeters of the safari. To make this point, she provides numerous examples from a photographic safari in Botswana, a place that has been marketed as "*the* Africa for this type of tourist" (28), and the ways that animal movement and life have been historically restricted as a consequence of the colonial division of territory. She describes the 1,875 miles of fence that the government started erecting in 1954, "to segregate cattle from wild herds" (29). This fence, like those described by Whitty at the beginning of this chapter, has been an environmental nightmare: "hundreds of thousands of wild animals have died against it in their futile trek toward water in time of drought. The fence runs everywhere, and where the fence runs, the animals do not" (29), and this fence has caused the near extinction of zebra and buffalo populations in most of Botswana. Williams's analysis of the photographic safari is a critique of not only the historical treatment of wild animals in Africa but also of the idea that what one sees when one looks through the lens of a camera is legitimate and authentic, somehow the real Africa: "but this is Africa," the safari goers think; "this really feels like it could be Africa at last" (39). The Africa that is presented to them is, as Duffy claims, a "politically laden image" (xii), a marketing ploy, a lie packaged to lure the environmentally conscious tourist to a pristine, precolonial facsimile of "Africa." Furthermore, by pointing out the ways that the animals that fill their photographic frames are positioned as they are because of a long history of environmental exploitation that persists into the present moment, Williams's essay continually undercuts the illusion that people who go on such safaris are doing something positive for the environment.

In another of the essays that appears in *Ill Nature*, "The Killing Game," Williams also takes hunters to task, particularly the rhetoric of conservation and respect for the animal they employ to justify killing as sport. She claims, "instead of monitoring animals . . . wildlife managers should start hanging telemetry gear around hunters' necks to study their attitudes and record their conversations. It would be grisly listening, but it would tune out for good the suffering as sacrament and spiritual experience nonsense that some hunting apologists employ" (49–50). The tone in "The Killing Game" is decidedly harsher than that of "Safariland," perhaps because Williams is more sympathetic to the photographers, at least as far as their good intentions are concerned. But when it comes to hunters, she clearly has no patience; as for the subsistence arguments, she says, "please. . . . The subsistence line is such a cynical one" (51). For hunters, she asserts, "the animal becomes the property of the hunter. Alive, the beast belongs only to itself. This is unacceptable to the hunter" (51). By the end of the essay, Williams's tone is scathing. Hunters' arguments are "self-serving," sport hunting "immoral"; the practice is "grotesque," and it is time, she says, "to stop being conned and cowed by hunters." Killing animals in this fashion is unjustifiable, no matter what rhetoric is offered by the hunter; according to Williams, "hunters make wildlife *dead, dead, dead*" (70), and arguments about conservation, species population control, and subsistence are transparent excuses to justify the fact that hunters are sadists who enjoy both the infliction of pain and the annihilation of animals. Given her obvious feelings about animal exploitation, both by hunters and photographers, Williams's presentation of the big game hunter Stumpp in *The Quick & the Dead* is more nuanced than one might initially expect.

While Stumpp does reflect many of the qualities of hunters that Williams describes in "The Killing Game," particularly the need to kill in order to own, Stumpp is also haunted and troubled by his history as a hunter, and even though he is unable to identify the cause of his unease, the reader can discern that the guilt Stumpp feels as a result of killing animals is responsible. In terms of his business ventures, Stumpp is currently investing "in the arenas of gene research and embryo cryopreservation. Shooting megafauna had always been just for relaxation" (220). But Stumpp has become unable to relax, and feels that perhaps he should withdraw his funding from the research on human embryos, as he worries that this research is the cause of his symptoms: "investing in the future had its psychological draw-backs. . . . Eggs were being harvested from aborted fetuses" (221). Connected to Stumpp's concern about egg harvesting from aborted fetuses is the regret he experiences with regard to having killed one of the elephants on display, a matriarch. He thinks "matriarchs held the memory of the family, years and years of it in that small heav-ily convoluted brain. . . . The oldest cows knew time's history. They remembered Africa, the breadth of it, and were the sources of im-parted history. Once the guns erased them, the ones who remained could know only less, always less. . . . The youngsters now knew al-most nothing in their shrunken Africa" (224). This section reads almost verbatim like the section of "Safariland" in which Williams discusses elephant culling. In the heads of the young elephants of today, she asserts, "their Africa has vanished" (*Ill Nature* 40). The un-conscious connection that Stumpp makes between the harvesting of eggs from human embryos and the killing of matriarchal elephants is a connection dependent on the severing of the parent—specifi-cally the mother—from its offspring. Again, in this example as in so many throughout the book, Williams shows life emerging from death, but she also illustrates that the life that emerges in this man-ner is stunted, cut off from its past, its ancestry, and its homeland. The elephant is cut off from the "Africa" of its precolonial ancestors, and the fear that Williams establishes through Stumpp's anxiety over genetic research is a fear that the human race, in its ever increasing numbers and its penchant for wanton consumption, is enacting a similar violence against itself, irreparably damaging its chances for any kind of connection—between past, present, and future, between memory and responsibility for the other, between species, and be-tween individuals.

The elephants in Williams's novel are real elephants, animals whose numbers, through unchecked hunting practices, have been decimated and whose history, as a result, has been erased, but they also provide a frightening template for a possible human future, one influenced, as Stumpp realizes, by a past "replete with lost guides" (303). Stumpp decides to sell the museum after he befriends and ultimately kidnaps the "half-pint sutra" Emily Bliss Pickless, who tells him "you can become something you're not" (303). At the end of

Williams's novel, the three motherless girls, like the young elephants cut off from their matriarchal history, find themselves seeking guidance in unlikely places and from unlikely people. Annabel, who dissolves from the narrative earlier than the other two, attempts to contact her dead mother, only to have her mother refuse to materialize. Corvus, whose parents have recently been killed in a car wreck and whose dog Tommy is lynched by a particularly noxious character named John Crimmins (who is later emasculated by a mail bomb), sets the family house ablaze and moves into Green Palms. When Alice tries to rescue her, Nurse Daisy turns her away saying, "'*sit in your cell, and your cell will tell you everything.*' That's something she's learned that you never will" (301). Alice is left wandering, searching, but as "no place had yet received her" (297), she is unable to find the guide she needs.

She finds herself in the midst of a candlelight vigil where a character simply called the Candleman tells her that everyone must participate: "some, you know, their concerns are obscure, but they're all participating in a healthy outrage and sorrow. There's nothing like lighting your little candle when all around are lighting theirs. Nothing! Illumination. Extinguishment. Equilibrium. Then everybody goes home" (307). Such is the nature of the world depicted by Williams wherein "concern is the new consumerism" (306), a world in which reaction is removed from its impetus and gesture supplants action. A world without memory. But Alice refuses to "be someone who was in a place only because she wasn't anywhere else" (306). The narrative perspective shifts at the end of the novel, from third person back to second, from waking to dreaming world, from literal to mythic, this time in midsentence: "she would wake from the dream even the most reluctant and particular have but once, the one where four animals arrive to carry *you* off for the moment" (308, my emphasis). The dream in which both reader and characters are now implicated is one in which "you have never seen such animals as these" and one that "you long for . . . not to end" (308). When you wake, you realize that the animals "indeed . . . have not brought you back" (308). The hope, after all, is that one may escape the web to find a new place of belonging, a place where memory is reconstituted, and a place where the animal is the guide.

Like the girls in Williams's novel who seek guidance in a world filled with lost guides, disgraced college professor David Lurie, the protagonist of South African author J. M. Coetzee's *Disgrace*, is the former guide—professor and father—who is now lost in the here and now of the "new" South Africa. David references his status as a failure by apologizing to his daughter, Lucy, for "not turning out to be a better guide" (79) and thinks of her again later as the daughter "whom it has fallen to [him] to guide. Who one day will guide [him]" (156). In turn, Lucy rebuffs David's actions in this capacity claiming, "you are not the guide I need, not at this time" (161). While Williams's work references an imaginary Africa that is marketed to Western audiences via hunting and photographic safaris, Coetzee's work is firmly situated *in* an Africa that is undergoing pronounced social and environmental change, and the text repeatedly posits its location firmly "in this place, at this time" (112), South Africa at the late 1990s post-apartheid moment. The narrative centers around the disgrace of David Lurie, a white South African academic who is forced to resign from his university teaching position after he engages in a questionably consensual sexual relationship with a young female student named Melanie. After his resignation, Lurie leaves Cape Town to live with his daughter, Lucy, in the Eastern Cape and eventually to work at the Animal Welfare League with Bev Shaw, a middle-aged woman who euthanizes some of South Africa's superfluous pet and livestock population. Lucy cultivates a smallholding—she refuses to allow David to romanticize it by calling it a farm—and shares her land with Petrus, a black man who helps her care for the dogs she kennels. Lucy's status as a landowner, gardener, and animal advocate is complex and uncertain, and when three black men rape Lucy, she proclaims her decision not to report the crime a "private matter" (112), an experience about which she will share no confession, just as David refuses to confess—despite an admission of guilt—to any wrongdoing in terms of his interactions with Melanie. The novel ends with Lucy's decision to keep the baby that results from this rape and David's decision to "give up" to Bev's needle a dog with whom he has formed a particularly strong bond.

There are numerous references to the shifting times that shape the lives of characters in *Disgrace,* and the attention to time is significant; the novel is set soon after 1994, the year that saw the end of apartheid in South Africa. The shift is marked by David's resignation and his leaving the city to go to the country, a point that Derek Attridge discusses at some length in his recent book, *J. M. Coetzee and the Ethics of Reading:* "Although much of the discomfort Lurie experiences on the smallholding arises from traditional African farming practices that have been unaffected by the politics of transformation . . . the story of post-apartheid South Africa we are being told is emphatically *not* the story of the technologically advanced but oppressive state sliding into backwardness under majority rule" (172). While the term "backwardness" is problematically associated with "traditional African farming," Attridge is using the above example and others to argue against the outcry of racism that heralded the novel's release in South Africa. But I want to take issue with Attridge's claim that Lurie's discomfort arises from "traditional" farming practices; the space that Lucy occupies in terms of the crops she grows and the animals she tends is a vastly different space from that occupied by either traditional indigenous African or colonial Boer farmers. Unlike either of these groups, Lucy's farming practice is dependent on the safeguarding of dogs (as opposed to the slaughter of livestock) and the cultivation of flowers (instead of subsistence crops). The narrator even claims, "this is how she makes a living: from the kennels, and from selling flowers" (61). I am interested, instead of presentations of the "new" South Africa—the moniker generally ascribed to South Africa's post-apartheid incarnation—Coetzee's depiction of a "new age" South Africa in which "dogs and daffodils" have replaced "cattle and maize" (62) and his construction of the character of Lucy, a woman that David feels is the product of "history" (61). Lucy is a woman who both embodies and eschews a kind of earth-motherliness dependent on interactions with our "minion biota," the animals—particularly our companion species, the dog—and plants we cultivate at the expense of the extinction of others. Despite Lucy's obvious connections to both land and animals, however, she remains disconnected from humans, and it is ironically David, initially self-centered and anti-animal welfare (at one point he claims, "animal-welfare people are a bit like Christians of a certain kind. Everyone is so cheerful and well-intentioned that after a while you itch to go off and do some raping and pillaging. Or to kick a cat" [73]) who, through a learned ability to empathize with both companion and subsistence animals, offers the novel's best hope for future human connection as well.[10]

Both *Life of Pi* and *The Quick & the Dead* feature companion species, often in direct opposition to the wild animals that garner more ethical considerations in both texts. When the author character interviews him, Pi has a dog named Tata and a cat named Moccasin (92); in *The Quick & the Dead*, Tommy, Corvus's mother's dog, dreams, mourns, and is killed, and Alice professes an intense dislike for cats, claiming "cats are false figures. People have them around so they don't have to address real animals" (43). The "real" animals in Alice's schema are those animals that are endangered. The wild and exotic animals that populate, as both living and dead beings, Martel and Williams's narratives are completely absent from *Disgrace*, except as metaphors for David's predatory behavior (for example, the narrator describes Melanie's reaction to David's "seduction" as follows: "she had decided to go slack, die within herself for the duration, like a rabbit when the jaws of the fox close on its neck" [25]), and the animals that are most prevalent in the postcolonial environment depicted by Coetzee are the dogs that Lucy kennels and that Bev euthanizes and the sheep that Petrus slaughters for a celebration feast. By focusing the narrative on the plight of dogs and livestock animals, *Disgrace* raises questions about the distinctions we make between "real" and "false" animals, endangered animals that deserve ecological consideration and companion and livestock animals that we cultivate and protect for our own self-interests. These categorizations of "real" and "false" (and fact/fiction, truth/lie) deserve attention in terms of the metafictive aspects of *Disgrace*, despite the fact that Coetzee's novel, unlike Martel and Williams's, never explicitly raises these issues.

Both *Life of Pi* and *The Quick & the Dead* fully acknowledge the fictiveness of the narratives that they contain, as can be seen through the various ways each employs metafictive devices — the author character in Martel's novel and the preliminary sketches at the beginning of each of the three sections of Williams's that address the reader directly as "you." Conversely, Coetzee, an author whose previous novels are often steeped in a metafictive tradition that works to undermine the "master narrative" of history,[11] has chosen in *Disgrace* to depict certain "real" aspects of contemporary South African culture, particularly rape. Such a choice is interesting for an author whose novels have tended to avoid aligning themselves with a particular location and time, like *Waiting for the Barbarians* (1980); have been situated outside of South Africa, like *Foe* (1986), *The Master of Petersburg* (1994), and *Slow Man* (2005); or have been situated in fictive, often apocalyptic South Africas, like *Life & Times of Michael K* (1983) and *Age of Iron* (1990). The depiction of a very specifically situated South Africa ("this place at this time") and a specific historical occurrence, rape,[12] not surprisingly, resulted in condemnation of his novel, especially from inside of South Africa. Rosemary Jolly notes that "within the African National Congress, *Disgrace* was rejected outright as racist. The ANC, in its 1999 submission to the Human Rights Commission's investigation into racism in the media, names *Disgrace* as a novel that exploits racist stereotypes" (149). Derek Attridge, who claims that there should never have been any doubt about Coetzee's "strong opposition to the policies and practices of the Nationalist government in power between 1948 and 1994, and the older traditions on which they were built" (163), nonetheless recognizes that "even readers whose view of the artist's responsibility is less tied to notions of instrumentalism and political efficacy . . . may find the bleak image of the 'new South Africa' in this work hard to take" (164). Such criticism is indicative of larger issues pertaining to authenticity and race, particularly within the postcolonial context: it seems that as white writers, Martel and Williams can write *about* postcolonial contexts in large part because they are not writing from *within* them and because both narratives admit, through various acts of metafiction, their own fictional status.

As a white South African, however, Coetzee's subject position complicates his ability to write *about* certain circumstances from *within* the culture about which he writes. In many of his earlier narratives, particularly *Dusklands* (1974) and *In the Heart of the Country* (1977), Coetzee played with such notions of authenticity, history, and authority by creating characters who tell contradictory stories, know impossible and anachronistic facts, and implicate themselves directly as fictional, writerly creations. In some of his more recent works, *The Lives of Animals* (1999) as well as *Elizabeth Costello* (2003), Coetzee has dealt with issues of authority and authenticity in a different way, by creating a fictional author persona in the form of elderly Australian novelist and animal rights advocate Elizabeth Costello, a character who also appears in his more recent novel *Slow Man* (2005). Costello is the outspoken and often polarizing character about whom Coetzee tells stories when he is invited to give public lectures; the stories often involve Costello giving lectures and, therefore, Coetzee's stories of Costello function as metalectures wherein Costello can voice strong opinions — perhaps altogether different from her creator's — as a way of generating discussion. For example, in Coetzee's published 1997–98 Princeton Tanner Lectures, *The Lives of Animals*, Costello makes the dreaded comparison between the treatment of animals in industrialized countries and the Jews during the Holocaust: "we are surrounded by an enterprise of degradation, cruelty, and killing which rivals anything that the Third Reich was capable of, indeed dwarfs it, in that ours is an enterprise without end, self-regenerating, bringing rabbits, rats, poultry, livestock ceaselessly into the world for the purpose of killing them" (21). Such an assertion creates dialogic interaction between the characters and audience within the text, as well as between the text and the audiences who read it or who originally heard Coetzee giving the lecture. Judith Shulevitz asserts in her *New York Times Book Review* of *Elizabeth Costello*, "perhaps the way to look at Costello is as just one player in a series of narratives that in their very sparseness achieve the dramatic tension of philosophical dialogues" (15). Through Costello, Coetzee enacts what I have elsewhere called dialogic drag,[13] and such dialogism is also apparent in *Disgrace* in the form of questions asked by the third-person narrator whose perspective is focalized through David Lurie.

These questions, such as "does he have it in him to be the woman?" (160) and "if he is being led, then what god is doing the leading?" (192), remain unanswered and become more prevalent after Lucy's rape, and they force the audience to participate in a philosophical dialogue about ethical responsibility and imagined identification with the other, whether that other is black, female, or animal. Such questions, while not as overt a metafictive intrusion as Martel's author character's discourse and Williams's second-person narrator's riddles, also serve to undermine monologic narrative authority and alienate the audience from the willing suspension of disbelief that would grant the story status as a true depiction of the new South Africa; instead, readers must confront real ethical issues—rape, the treatment of animals, and the place of education, for example—in order to acknowledge a multitude of possible reactions, answers, and scenarios. Furthermore, unlike Williams and Martel, who willingly discuss, both in interviews and nonfiction, their politics, writing processes, and subject matter, Coetzee rarely grants interviews (and when he does, they are often, in his own words, "contentless"[14]); never discusses his personal life, political views, or writing; and often refuses to show up to collect prestigious awards, as was the case both times he won the Booker Prize.[15] Such resistant positioning—of a monologic authority, an accepted real or true narrative of history, and claims of literary authenticity—make Coetzee and his writing difficult to categorize and define. One thing that his work consistently does, however, is engage with ethics in terms of representation of and responsibility for human and animal "others."

In *Disgrace*, by focusing initially on a particular nonhuman species that has benefited—at least statistically—from the decline of biodiversity on planet Earth, Coetzee places the dog, the animal with which we have the most personal, human interactions, at the center of a narrative about South Africa's changing culture and environment. In *The Companion Animal Manifesto: Dogs, People, and Significant Otherness*, Donna Haraway explores the complex relationship between dogs and humans, particularly their rhetorical signification—as metaphors and theoretical entities—and their corporeality: "Dogs, in their historical complexity, matter here. Dogs are not an alibi for other themes; dogs are fleshly material-semiotic presences in the body of technoscience. Dogs are not surrogates for theory; they are not here just to think with. They are here to live with. Partners in the crime of human evolution, they are in the garden from the get-go, wily as Coyote" (5). Because of the prevalence of dogs within *Disgrace* and because of David Lurie's changing relationship with regard to the animals he helps euthanize and sees sacrificed for slaughter, many critics—myself included—have chosen to write about the linguistic and literal significance of animals in the novel.[16] For example, Mike Marais writes about the redemptive nature of dogs in the novel, claiming that "Lurie must give up the dog [at the end] because it is in the dog's interest that he does so. His own needs, desires, feelings, predilections and predispositions are totally immaterial" (78). Similarly, Tim Herron notes that the implication of "shared suffering" that exists between David Lurie and the animals he euthanizes may be transformative, but Herron also claims that "the lives of animals are routinely erased by human beings, not just through acts of physical violence but also by means of their exploitation in cliché, in pseudobioethical assertion, and in metaphor" (473). Rosemary Jolly asserts that "the novel interrogates what to be human might mean without recourse to the species boundary between human and nonhuman animals" (150), and she discusses the rhetorical power of the animal metaphor: "in his fiction Coetzee investigates the fact that our representation of animals is the locus of a language through which human beings measure their ethical worth as humans" (151). Finally, in his chapter on *Disgrace* in *J. M. Coetzee and the Ethics of Reading*, Derek Attridge claims that "there is much, too much for a single chapter, to be said about the animals in *Disgrace*, and about their relation to the animals in Coetzee's earlier fictions and other writings" (184).

The dog, as a companion species, is already once removed from the realm of "real" animals, those that Williams's Alice considers worthy of environmental concern. The dog occupies space in *Disgrace* in ways that are, again, both "real" and "false," as literal animals and metaphorical conceits. For example, Lucy claims of the dogs she kennels, "dogs still mean something. The more dogs, the more deterrence" (60). Lucy's reference to the deterrence that dogs offer is a statement about the role of white-owned guard dogs in both the old and new versions of South Africa as a means of deterring would-be black intruders. In this case, dogs are literal beings that exist in Lucy's kennel, but dogs have culturally specific "meaning"—they are readable—that provides the impetus for Lucy's black rapists to kill her dogs before leaving the premises. Dogs in South Africa, particularly the breeds that Lucy kennels—"Dobermanns, German Shepherds, ridgebacks, bull terriers, Rottweilers" (61)—are imbued with racist significance, and Lucy, despite her egalitarian tendencies, through the kenneling of these dogs participates in the white discourse of fear with regard to black South Africans. David worries for her safety, and she tells him that in addition to the dogs, she also owns a rifle. He thinks, "dogs and a gun; bread in the oven and a crop in the earth. Curious that he and her mother, cityfolk, intellectuals, should have produced this throwback, this sturdy young settler. But perhaps it was not they who produced her: perhaps history had the larger share" (61). As the offspring of her urban and academically inclined parents, Lucy's lifestyle can be read on the one hand as filial rebellion: to farm, to be a vegetarian, to eschew racism by sharing her land with Petrus and his family, but, as David is aware, she is also the product of South African history, a history of both institutionalized racism and agriculture. On the one hand, South Africa's history overrides her pacifism and independent-mindedness: she kennels guard dogs and owns a gun. But on the other, she is a "throwback," a woman who, according to Bev Shaw, "lives closer to the ground" (210) than her father. And Lucy is incredibly aware of the weight of her country's history and of the responsibility that comes with being a white citizen in the new South Africa, a place where she and those like her—for example, Bev, "not a veterinarian but a priestess, full of New Age mumbo Jumbo" (84), according to David—must attempt to guide their elders. There is no map to follow, and much of what the novel carefully explores is a trial and error model of education and becoming, for blacks and whites alike, as they struggle to find common ground in a country where the ground itself is fraught with a history of dispossession and fragmentation.

This ground, the land with which Lucy is intimately acquainted, is complicated by its contentious history of oppression and environmental destruction, and the exploitation of animals in South Africa's colonial and apartheid history has never been far removed from the degradation of the environment and the oppression of indigenous South African peoples by colonial forces; this legacy continues up to the present day world depicted in *Disgrace*. In the early twentieth century, for example, South African environmental problems were mainly the result of overgrazing of livestock (Beinart and Coates 63), and in the latter half, "deforestation and soil erosion have followed in the wake of the movement of refugees and displaced persons" (Ohlson and Stedman 297–98). The historical and symbolic role of livestock animals—particularly cattle and sheep—is omnipresent in South Africa, from the time that the agriculturally inclined Khoikhoi people broke with the more nomadic hunters the San, for whom "control over hunting for the distribution of meat, and particularly trade in ivory, were mechanisms for asserting power, stamping territorial authority, and defining gender roles" (Beinart and Coates 19). Sometime before the fifteenth century, the Khoikhoi began to cultivate livestock, and in the communal culture of the Khoikhoi people, "livestock was by far the most valued form of private property in a society where land was never divided among individuals" (Elphick 59). Currently, according to Michelè Pickover in her work *Animals Rights in South Africa*, "animals are legally classified as 'things,' 'goods' or 'agricultural products.' The Animal Protection Act [of 1962] excludes farmed animals" (145). With modernization has begun to emerge a Western-influenced, meat-based culture increasingly dependent on factory farming in which respect of the animal as being is in decline and the negative environmental consequences of such farming practices are on the rise.

As evidence of the value placed on livestock by the Khoikhoi, according to Richard Elphick, "neither sheep nor cattle were regularly slaughtered. Slaughter was undertaken chiefly to celebrate special occasions . . . or as a sacrifice to combat illness among humans or stock" (60); milk was a much more valued nutritional source, because it did not require depletion of an owner's livestock population. Again, in contemporary South Africa, the model is vastly different; from 1985 to 2005, according to Pickover, "meat production in 'developing' countries like South Africa increased by 27 percent" (142). Furthermore, the fact that animal sacrifice was practiced to save livestock as well as humans clearly indicates the value placed on livestock animals by the Khoikhoi, a value that, while it may have been predicated on the need for the subsistence that animals allotted, is at least structured on a sense of respect for the inherent value of the animal. By the late 1600s, however, the Khoikhoi lost their livestock in large part because of the Dutch East India Company's policies of robbery and military action, as well as by virtue of the Dutch colonizers' "spread of new diseases, interdiction of chiefly aggrandizement, expropriation of pastures, [and] demand for Khoikhoi labor" (Elphick 174). As the Cape settlers moved inland, they appropriated not only large tracts of land, but also any livestock that was on that land (Ohlson and Stedman 21). The contested role of cattle in South Africa was still apparent well into the twentieth century, when "voluntary" removals, like the Mogopa removal of 1984, for example, forced black South Africans to leave their farms and sell their cattle for mere pittance to Boer farmers. Because "cattle are a measure of a man's success in the villages" (Goodman 325), the loss of cattle that one had cared for and seen increase over generations was not only a devastating financial blow, but was also akin to the loss of a kind of ancestral memory, like that of the matriarch-less elephant herds described by Williams, the loss of a history dependent on human and animal codependency and interaction.

Disgrace situates a discourse about animal rights and vegetarianism within a context—the "new" South Africa—where, as Lucy claims, "there is no funding any longer. On the list of the nation's priorities, animals come nowhere" (73), and where human rights, particularly the rights of black South Africans, have historically been denied. Within the frame of both narrative and historical South Africa, the discourse of rights and ethics distinguishes between human and animal rights, privileging one and denying the other; both cannot exist at the same time. *Disgrace* not only examines the reasons why human rights necessarily occupy the dominant position in contemporary South Africa, but the narrative also posits an associative ethical framework in which animal and human rights might potentially inform and depend on each other. That South Africa—as exemplified by David Lurie—may not be capable, at the historical moment depicted in the text, to imagine such a possibility, is presented as neither surprising nor condemnable. The novel focuses on the rights of companion and livestock animals (as opposed to the more exotic and endangered species in Martel's and Williams's texts), and such a focus allows readers to examine relationships between humans and the animals with which we have the most direct contact, either through shared habitation or through ingestion. A particularly significant instance with regard to this discourse of rights takes place after Lucy's rape. The carnivorous David Lurie—unlike Lucy who "refuses to touch meat" (121)—feels an empathetic attachment to two slaughter-sheep that Petrus has tethered to a bare patch of earth. He examines his feelings for the sheep, but cannot understand why he feels a bond with them. He says, "in this case I am disturbed. I can't say why" (127). After the sheep are slaughtered, David is confronted with whether or not to eat the meat in celebration of Petrus's recent land acquisition. Ultimately, he thinks, "I am going to eat this. . . . I am going to eat it and ask forgiveness afterwards" (131).

The incident with the sheep, livestock animals, can be read as counterpoint to the novel's initial focus on the fates of dogs, companion animals, in the new South Africa, and the connection between animal slaughter, consumption, and the concept of forgiveness results in a human inability—at least at the current moment in which the work is situated—to articulate the significance of the connections that exist between human and nonhuman animal life. According to Pickover, in South Africa, "the way we treat animals has all the hallmarks of apartheid—prejudice, callous disregard for suffering and a misguided sense of supremacy" (141). That Petrus, who slaughters the sheep, and Lucy, who as a vegetarian would never consider eating them, miss this point is telling. That David is able, at least on a physical level, to feel empathy for the sheep (despite his inability to articulate why he feels as he does) is more so. David's feelings for and about the sheep combined with his decision to eat them and "ask forgiveness afterwards" underscores a complex set of rights-based circumstances that, at the present narrative moment, David is unable to fully comprehend. The fact that his feelings for the sheep emerge after his daughter's rape is indicative of David's visceral identification with Lucy's suffering, of being treated like a proverbial "piece of meat," with the suffering of the sheep that literally become meat after being slaughtered. To complicate matters, David's decision to eat the meat offered to him by Petrus indicates a willingness to engage in a celebration of black empowerment, an instance that is similar to Curtin's contextual moral vegetarianism; even though David is a meat eater, in the case of the sheep with whom he feels empathy he would rather not partake. He does, however, eat the meat in support of a culturally specific celebration, an event to which he has been invited, but at which he is, nonetheless, an outsider.

Finally, David's claim that he will ask forgiveness "afterwards" places the act of contrition in an unspecified future moment and indicates a cognitive leap, both in terms of vegetarianism and responsibility for the human other, that David is, at the current moment, unable to make. In terms of forgiveness, David can and does ask it of Lucy: "forgive me . . . for being one of the two mortals assigned to usher you into the world and for not turning out to be a better guide" (79), and he asks it of Melanie's father, saying "I ask for your pardon" (171); he even "gets to his knees and touches his forehead to the floor" (173) in a gesture of apology to Melanie's mother. He never, however, apologizes to Melanie herself, despite Lucy's assertion that "women can be surprisingly forgiving" (69). Finally, the forgiveness that may or may not be granted "afterwards," outside the scope of the narrative, is for the wrongs of apartheid, forgiveness that is not immediately forthcoming, and forgiveness for which David cannot yet ask. In connection with the concept of forgiveness, David also becomes acquainted with the concept of love, again through various interactions with animals. In terms of its animal focus, the nonhuman beings at the center of the novel are initially dogs, but the focus shifts to the sheep after Lucy's rape. At the end of the narrative, however, David has returned to help Bev euthanize variously discarded companion animals, primarily dogs. The narrator claims, "he and Bev do not speak. He has learned by now, from her, to concentrate all his attention on the animal they are killing, giving it what he no longer has difficulty in calling by its proper name, love" (219). That David has learned how to love a fellow creature, particularly from a woman he initially finds revolting, is indicative of the potential for greater change in David, a change that will occur (if it occurs at all) beyond the frame of the narrative.

The rhetorical significance of the literal dogs that Lucy kennels shifts after the rape and Lucy's decisions not to report the incident and to keep the baby that results from it. David argues with her, on both counts, and also tries to convince her not to marry Petrus, but Lucy says she wants to start again "at ground level. With nothing. Not with nothing but. With nothing. No cards, no weapons, no property, no rights, no dignity." David answers, "like a dog," to which Lucy responds, "yes, like a dog" (205). Lucy's desire to begin again from this subjected position also reflects a hope that perhaps the position of the dog in particular and animals in general that "come nowhere" (73) on the list of the nation's priorities, may also be reconceptualized. Lucy tells David early in the novel that animals "are not going to lead me to a higher life, and the reason is, there is no higher life. This is the only life there is. Which we share with animals" (74). Despite her status as "a frontier farmer of the need breed" (62), Lucy is a woman at once aware of and trapped by the weight of South African history. While she is able to reinvent the farmer/livestock paradigm responsible for much environmental devastation over the course of South Africa's past, she seems unable to connect her care for animals to any real feelings for the black South Africans with whom she shares a national affiliation. Conversely, Pickover claims, "I believe animal rights is the only perspective that can right two wrongs: the personal and institutionalized beliefs that make oppression and violence possible to both humans and animals" (15). If there is to be a "new age" in South Africa, it is, perhaps, more likely to be ushered in by David Lurie.

In India, every river is sacred.

—VANDANA SHIVA, *Water Wars*

Judicial process and institution cannot be permitted to be
scandalized or subjected to contumacious violation in such a
blatant manner in which it has been done by [Arundhati Roy]
. . . vicious stultification and vulgar debunking cannot
be permitted to pollute the stream of justice.

—Indian Supreme Court statement in reaction to Roy's essay
"The Greater Common Good"

CHAPTER THREE

"Swimming in the River of Life" but Caught in "the Stream of Justice"

India's Water Woes and Arundhati Roy

When the titular protagonist of Bharati Mukherjee's novel *Jasmine*
(1989) first arrives in the United States from her rural village in
India, she notes that "the first thing I saw were the two cones of a
nuclear plant, and smoke spreading from them in complicated but
seemingly purposeful patterns, edges lit by the rising sun, like a gray,
intricate map of an unexplored island continent, against the pale
unscratched blue of the sky. I waded through Eden's waste: plastic
bottles, floating oranges, boards, sodden boxes, white and green
plastic sacks tied shut but picked open by birds and pulled apart by
crabs" (107). Jasmine's description reveals the American "Eden" of
her imagination to be a fiction, a toxic "unexplored island continent"
surrounded by a polluted ocean.[1] In *The God of Small Things* (1997),
Arundhati Roy illustrates the ways that the environmental corruption depicted by Mukherjee as characteristic of the 1980s era United

States has traveled across the ocean to India by the 1990s. In Roy's novel, at the age of thirty-one, Rahel returns to India from the United States in 1992 to find that her beloved Meenachal River has shrunk as a result of a saltwater barrage that had been built "in exchange for votes from the influential paddy-farmer lobby," an alteration that generates two harvests a year instead of one and "more rice, for the price of a river" (118). Furthermore, early in the novel, the narrator describes how the river "smelled of shit and pesticides bought with World Bank loans. Most of the fish had died. The ones that survived suffered from fin-rot and had broken out in boils" (14). Both novels situate the causes of environmental damage squarely in the West, as does environmental activist Vandana Shiva, who claims that "it was in the mining camps of the American West that the cowboy notion of private property and the rule of appropriation . . . first emerged" (22). Furthermore, both texts focus on bodies of water and bodies of women as literal and figurative sites of pollution: Jasmine is raped almost as soon as she sets foot on American soil, and Ammu, Rahel's mother, like the Meenachal River, is "polluted" in the eyes of her family and community as a result of her affair with the untouchable Velutha. A key difference between Mukherjee's and Roy's treatment of both environmental and gender-based oppression is the fact that Roy explicitly, confrontationally, and vocally champions in her public life the causes she addresses in her fiction.

As Roy states in Aradhana Seth's documentary *Dam/Age* (2002), "I've written the book I wanted to write, and now I'm swimming in the river of life," protesting the Narmada Dam Project and writing various essays that focus on the evils of war, the dangers of globalization, and the threat of religious fundamentalism.[2] In *The Cost of Living*, Roy furthers her admonition of the West's role in India's environmental crisis, claiming that "the dam-building industry in the First world is in trouble and out of work. So it's exported to the Third world in the name of Development Aid" (15). In turn, the Indian government pays to receive the West's "gift wrapped garbage" (15). In this chapter, I want to examine Roy's fictional treatment of and public position with regard to India's literal water woes, particularly the damming of rivers and subsequent privatization of water, as well as her figurative "swimming" as a metaphor for activist performance in her own "river of life"—as well as the Narmada and, in *The God of Small Things*, the Meenachal. I am particularly interested in the performativity of Roy's public persona and the ways that that performance as well as her status as an upper-caste woman who, in many ways, speaks for lower-caste Indians has been and is read and critiqued by the media, literary critics, and environmental activists. In this chapter, I will read Roy's activist performance in *Dam/Age* through the lens of her construction of three fictional and linked performances in *The God of Small Things* as they illustrate the tenuous distinction between nature and culture. The first performance takes place when Sophie Mol arrives at Ayemenem and Rahel recognizes her cousin's reception as a "Play" (164); the second is the performance of the Kathakali Man who "hawks . . . the stories his body can tell" (219); and the third is the policemen's historically scripted beating of Velutha, "human history, masquerading as God's purpose" (293) as observed by Rahel and Estha. Roy's life and her characters' actions run up against another figurative body of water, the "stream of justice," in Roy's case the Indian Supreme Court when it charged her with contempt, and in the case of her characters, particularly Ammu, Velutha, Rahel, and Estha, the social constructions of the caste system, gender-based inequality, and law enforcement. What Roy's fictional performances illustrate is the way that history is scripted and how certain individuals, as a result of their caste, race, gender, or age are required to stay "offstage." In the context of *Dam/Age*, those who remain offstage or at least in the background—as is the case in *The God of Small Things*—are the lower-caste Indians who will be displaced when the river is dammed. Roy's performance in *Dam/Age*, conversely, situates her, as an upper-caste woman, as the unified and singular voice of environmental protest, precisely because, in what I will call its "third act," the film situates Roy offstage, marking her absence as the silencing of the voice that speaks for the dispossessed. Therefore, Roy establishes her voice as a resounding and necessary presence within the narrative of the river and its people's salvation.

The God of Small Things is nonlinear and tells two interwoven stories, the first of Rahel and Estha, fraternal twins who share a "single Siamese soul" (40) and are separated after the death of their English cousin Sophie, and the second of Ammu, the mother of the twins, and Velutha, the untouchable employee of Ammu's family's pickle factory with whom she has a sexual relationship. The third-person narrative voice alternates between 1969, when the twins are eight and their cousin dies, and 1992, when they are thirty-one and have returned to Ayemenem, the place where the tragedy occurred. The story focuses on seemingly "small things," ahistorical and personal moments, that lead to the accidental death of Sophie Mol, the murder of Velutha, and the shunning of Ammu, which in turn results in the twins' estrangement from each other in a culture where "personal despair could never be desperate enough" (20). But the narrator claims that the story "actually began thousands of years ago. Long before the Marxists came. Before the British took Malabar, before the Dutch Ascendancy, before Vasco da Gama arrived, before Zamorin's conquest of Calcut. . . . That it really began in the days when the Love Laws were made. The laws that lay down who should be loved, and how. And how much" (33). This examination of history, of time beyond a sense of the reader's ability to relate linearly, allows Roy to move about within the text, to drop hints about the narrative's resolution—allowing the reader access to the tragedy before it happens—and to, according to Madhu Benoit, superimpose time in layers: a "double-time pattern" that is "built into the novel from the very beginning: chronological time . . . and a-chronological time, or time pertaining to history, or the collective memory shared by a society" (99). Roy's attention to time in *The God of Small Things* (hereafter *Small Things*) is apparent very early in the novel when the twins' aunt, Baby Kochamma, is, according to Rahel, living her life "backwards" (23) and when the narrator claims that Rahel's childhood toy wristwatch "had the time painted on it. Ten to two. One of her ambitions was to own a watch on which she could change the time whenever she wanted (which according to her was what Time was meant for in the first place)" (37). In Roy's novel, in one instant, time is treated as unchanging and stationary, that which is alternately not to be trusted, and the accomplice of "history," but in the next, it is also that which is malleable in the service of the mythological narrative from which the twins have been "locked out" (52) as a result of their status as Anglophiles who "adore our conquerors and despise ourselves" (52). History, through the compilation of small instances, has conspired to bring about the various tragedies—Velutha's murder at the hands of the local police, Ammu's subsequent shunning, and the bifurcation of the twins—that ultimately results in another transgression of the love laws, Rahel and Estha's incestuous encounter at the end of the novel.

Recent critics of *Small Things* have examined Roy's unconventional use of language (often comparing her writing style to that of Salman Rushdie), the politics of desire expressed in the work, as well as the novel's aforementioned treatment of time and history as nonlinear constructs. Brinda Bose questions whether a novel that focuses on erotic desire can be politically viable. She states that "Roy's politics exists in an erogenous zone" (61) and that *Small Things* "delineates a politics of desire that is vitally linked with the politics of voice" (67). Anuradha Dingwaney Needham, in a comparative analysis of Roy's novel and Ranajit Guha's "The Small Voice of History," asserts that *Small Things* "presents history . . . as a dominating, oppressive force that saturates virtually all social and cultural space, including familial, intimate, and affective relationships" (372). Murari Prasad defends *Small Things* against C. D. Narasimhaiah's assertion that Roy's work is "pulp" (113) by claiming that Roy's subversion of English allows her to telescope "the signifying events of the past into a simultaneous focus" (118): "Roy's attempt at 'subverting' English is evidenced in her lexical coinages, perhaps in a more belligerent fashion than Rushdie's . . . minting fresh and fetching images, as well as in her sentence-ordering skills where she modifies the given syntactic templates, marshals dazzling protocols of signification, and gives, in effect, a 'sub-version' of the language" (128–29). Of all of the novels examined in this study, *Small Things* has received the most ecocritical attention, despite the fact that the novel is, aside from the two passages about the polluted river that I cited above, only tangentially concerned with environmental issues. The work does, however, critically juxtapose the implementation of "law" against "landscape," and I will examine this juxtaposition in detail throughout the rest of this chapter. It is safe to assume, however, that ecocritical readings of Roy's work are dependent in large part on Roy's subsequent lived experiences in protest of the Narmada dam project and her nonfictional "protest" literature, and, in particular, on her performance in *Dam/Age*.

As Graham Huggan notes in his 2004 essay "'Greening Post-colonialism': Ecocritical Perspectives," Roy's "fulminating essays 'The Greater Common Good' (1999) and 'The End of the Imagination' (1998), capitalizing on the runaway success of her Booker Prize–winning novel *The God of Small Things* (1997), probably represent the most eye-catching ecocritical intervention to date by a recognized postcolonial writer" (705). Roy's lived persona, therefore, makes an ecocritical perspective applicable to her fiction. In terms of this perspective, in his discussion of contemporary writers' tendency to "resist postmodernism's erasure of natural and cultural distinctions" (184), Peter Mortensen argues that *Small Things*'s "1990s episodes describe a 'post-pastoral' India utterly transformed by social, economic and cultural development" (186), and he reads the novel's opening description of the lushness of Ayemenem as a representation of "nature on the rebound" (188). Divya Anand reads the changing landscape and river as metaphors for the changes undergone by the characters, stating that through the eyes of the twins as children, "the landscape is endowed with a pristine purity paralleling the innocence and poignancy of childhood" (3). Further, "the most powerful and pervasive natural entity that maps the changes at the metaphorical and literal plane is the Meenachal River whose ebb and flow mirrors the destinies of the characters" (7). Similarly, Cécile Oumhani reads the river as "part of nature, a hidden force which society fails to master" (89). It is precisely the converse of Oumhani's claim, however, that has proven true in contemporary India, as damming has displaced between 16 and 38 million people (Shiva 66), and deforestation and mining have reduced the ability of water catchments to hold water (2); therefore, according to Shiva, "the water crisis is the most pervasive, most severe, and most invisible dimension of the ecological devastation of the earth" (1). In India, in addition to the damming of rivers, that devastation is exacerbated by climate change and by a green revolution that "is increasingly being watered by plundering the country's underground water" (35), according to Fred Pearse.

In order to examine the performativity of Roy's activism with regard to India's water crisis, it is first necessary to explain what I mean by "performance" in the sense that I will use that term throughout this chapter. According to Marvin Carlson in *Performance: A Critical Introduction*, "the recognition that our lives are structured according to repeated and socially sanctioned modes of behavior raises the possibility that all human activity could potentially be considered as 'performance,' or at least all activity carried out with a consciousness of itself" (4). My claim that Roy's activism is performative is in no way meant to undermine the sincerity and positive significance of that activism, nor is it an attempt to argue for some ulterior motive on Roy's part, but to illustrate Roy's consciousness of the ways that her activism is read as a text and, therefore, her interest in the manipulation of that text. In *Dam/Age*, Roy has claimed that as public figure, she has an ethical obligation to provide social criticism, stating "I have the space to raise a dissenting voice," and it seems clear that Roy's writerly celebrity and upper-caste status allows her this space in which to be heard; her activism does not create her fame, but her fame generates the way in which Roy, as a woman in particular—and she claims also that in India, "every woman is a troublemaker" (*Dam/Age*) —can speak out about environmental and social issues. However, precisely because Roy is a woman and also a famous, "troublemaking" woman, her bodily discourse, particularly as she speaks and "acts" in the film *Dam/Age*, becomes a performative text invested in and acutely aware of the politics of the gaze as explained by Laura Mulvey in her famous 1975 essay "Visual Pleasure and Narrative Cinema": "The determining male gaze projects its phantasy on to the female figure which is styled accordingly. In their traditional exhibitionist role women are simultaneously looked at and displayed, with their appearance coded for strong visual and erotic impact so that they can be said to connote *to-be-looked-at-ness*" (62). To complicate matters further, as Gayatri Spivak has argued, because the voice of the subaltern woman is "deeply in shadow" (83), Roy's activist and personal articulations are in constant danger of being misconstrued and silenced, by both Indian and Western audiences alike, as is illustrated by the Indian

Supreme Court's characterization of and attempt to silence Roy's "vicious stultification," and Huggan's negative reading of Roy's "strategic exoticism" (*Postcolonial Exotic* 77). It becomes necessary then, on some level, for Roy to actively control her image, to construct herself in ways that attempt to defy the negative readings that have arisen as a result of her celebrity status. Conversely, Roy's voice, because it does belong to an upper-caste Indian woman, also presumes to speak for and place "deeply in shadow" the narratives of the lower-caste peoples of the Narmada Valley.

Within *Small Things*, Roy illustrates a keen awareness of the performative nature of caste- and gender-based existence in India while conversely illustrating the lack of artifice inherent in the instances when characters step outside of their proscribed social roles and into the natural world, that which exists in opposition to the various "love laws" the novel critiques. What is natural is represented, within Roy's novel, as Eden run amok, a landscape that is lovely and fecund but also dangerous in its transgression of boundaries: when Sophie Mol's body is pulled into a fisherman's boat, for example, the fisherman "thinks how wrong it is for a fisherman to believe that he knows his river well. *No one* knows the Meenachal. No one knows what it may snatch or suddenly yield. Or when" (245). The first page of the novel is filled with images of this explosive uncertainty of nature, of black crows gorging on mangoes and jackfruits bursting, while "boundaries blur. . . . Brick walls turn mossgreen. Pepper vines snake up electric poles" (3). In Ayemenem, Baby Kochamma gives up care of her garden for the pursuit of cable television, a technological "advance" that ironically allows the ornamental garden to thrive and become "knotted and wild" (27). Throughout the narrative, the natural world—the plants in the garden, the monsoon rains, and, most significantly, the river—push against the constructedness of their confinement and creep into "civilized" spaces. Similarly, love, restricted by both spoken and unarticulated rules, repeatedly pushes at the boundaries of what is acceptable to emerge ultimately, through the corruption of repression—of "civilization's fear of nature, men's fear of women, power's fear of powerlessness" (292)—as incest. At the end of the novel, Baby Kochamma, as history's agent, successfully silences all of the transgressive characters, but the twins silently break the love laws yet again and commit incest as an act of "hideous grief" (311). Their bodies speak a narrative that their voices cannot, a narrative of "quietness" (311) about which "there is very little that anyone could say" (310).

In the context of Ammu and Velutha's relationship, the Meenachal forms a boundary, as Anand claims, "a borderline of water, segregating two different social worlds as well as connecting both the touchable and untouchable worlds" (7). Similarly, Mortensen reads Velutha as "a boundary-figure, a gatekeeper, who mediates between culture and nature" (192). But the Meenachal also functions symbolically as the space in which Velutha can be free to "drift slowly with the current" (*Small Things* 315), unhindered by societal dictates, the space wherein the world of laws ceases to function, the metaphorical "river of life." Being *in* the river, for both Velutha and Roy, allows for a certain amount of mobility, but crossing the river is a transgressive act that requires both character and author to be punished. When Ammu sees Velutha, she is immediately aware that "as he rose from the dark water . . . she saw that the world they stood in was his" (315), and during their sexual encounter, Ammu is "wide and deep as a river in spate" (318). Within the river, the laws that take affect beyond its banks have no sway, but *Small Things* hardly romanticizes the seeming freedom that the river offers. In its rebuke of social order, the river also claims the life of Sophie Mol when the twins feel compelled to cross it to reach the History House after Estha is molested by the Orangedrink Lemondrink Man. Attempts to cross the river, as opposed to simply being in the river—in terms of Roy's rhetoric of swimming in *Dam/Age*—result in Sophie Mol's death and subsequently in Velutha's murder. Velutha crosses the river after his father discovers the affair and prostrates himself before Mammachi. Velutha heads to the History House, the abandoned residence of Kari Saipu, "Ayemenem's own Kurtz. Ayemenem his private Heart of Darkness" (51), the Englishman who goes native and commits suicide prior to the events in the novel. Of the house, the twins' uncle Chacko claims that as Indians, "we've been locked out. And when we look through the windows, all we see are shadows. And when we try and listen, all we hear is whispering. And we cannot understand the whispering because our minds have been invaded by a war. A war we have won and lost. The very worst sort of war. A war that captures dreams and re-dreams them. A war that made us adore our conquerors and despise ourselves" (52). When he crosses the river and hides in the History House, therefore, Velutha once again becomes a character in a staged performance, a scripted and re-dreamed history that views him as dangerous because he has stepped out of nature—or out of what higher-caste Indians view as the "natural" order—and refused to remain inconsequential. Through the discovery of his affair with Ammu, Velutha is forced to leave "his world," the natural world in which he can "float," and is placed within the narrative of history, from which he has been "locked out," and from which he must, therefore, be erased.

Roy explicitly examines the scriptedness of history in chapters 8 and 18 of *Small Things*, "Welcome Home, Our Sophie Mol" and "The History House." In "Welcome Home, Our Sophie Mol," the narrator personifies the Ayemenem House as "an old man with rheumy eyes watching children play" (157). The verandah becomes "a stage and everything that happened there took on the aura and significance of performance" (158). What is performed on this stage is the culmination of the gender-specific, Indian, and Western codes and mores that shape the "Touchable, upper-caste Christian (into whom Christianity had seeped like a tea from a teabag)" (162) family's reception of its English visitors. Throughout this reception, the narrative is focalized through Rahel who, although tangentially aware of her status as a minor actor—"the landscape. A flower perhaps. Or a tree"—"in a Play" (164), remains almost entirely "offstage" where she "watched them perform their elaborate Official Greeting" (166). When Rahel tries to tell Mammachi that Estha vomited at the movie theater, Ammu silences her, and it is this silencing that makes Rahel aware of her status as a performer in the narrative unfolding on the verandah. Rahel's position offstage results from the ways that she (as both child and female), like Velutha (as Paravan), fails to register as historically significant; her exclusion from and simultaneous awareness of the performance arises from her status as outsider and outcast, a girl who "didn't know how to be a girl" (18), one of a pair of "Half-Hindu Hybrids" (44). Furthermore, that which exists offstage, outside of the context of the official version of history, is nature; in that she exists offstage, Rahel aligns herself with the natural world as "the landscape" or a "flower" or a "tree." Ammu's silencing of Rahel by a touch that "meant *Shhhh*" (164), alerts Rahel to her role as a participant in that which is being watched, and her tacit refusal to participate is evidenced by Ammu's awareness, as she watches her daughter interact with Velutha, that Rahel is able to inhabit a "subworld that excluded [Ammu] entirely" (167), a world devoid of the scripted and spoken narrative of history in which Rahel communicates instead via "smiles and laughter" (167). Rahel's position within this world in which "Things lurked unsaid" (165) constitutes a subtle rebuke of the love laws; in her interaction with Velutha, Rahel incurs the wrath of her aunt Baby Kochamma, who demands that Rahel stop being "over-familiar" with the Paravan (175).

It is at this point in the narrative—as well as at this point in the performance that Roy stages in chapter 8—that Baby Kochamma attempts to force Velutha and Rahel to adhere to the script and perform the roles that history requires. In this instant, Velutha "stepped through the trees into the Play" (175) to participate in his role as Mammachi's Paravan employee; he is separated from "the trees," the world of nature, and is forced back into his socially and historically constructed position. Rahel is furious at Velutha's forced expulsion and "looked back into the Play" (176), wanting to slap Sophie Mol, the character around whom this performance is centered. Instead, she takes out her frustration on the natural world, killing a column of red ants, and when Sophie Mol attempts to leave the play to see what Rahel is doing, "the Play went with her. Walked when she walked, stopped when she stopped" (177). Rahel, in turn, runs away from her cousin, and "disappeared into the greenheat" (177), again refusing to participate in the performance. Not only is Rahel's appropriate role within the play determined by her status as a high-caste touchable Indian, it is also determined by her status as female. Because she is a girl—and later, of course, a woman—Rahel is expected to be demurely feminine, to recognize her subordinate position. Of course, Ammu, in that she first marries for love and, when her husband becomes abusive, rather than stay with him, gets a divorce, has hardly provided an "appropriate" feminine role model for her daughter. Femininity, like caste, is revealed as constructed and performative through the narrative's repeated references to femininity as costume, in one instance, drag worn by Estha and Velutha as well as by Rahel.

Judith Butler claims that "drag is a site of a certain ambivalence, one which reflects the more general situation of being implicated in the regimes of power by which one is constituted and hence being implicated in the very regime one opposes" (125). In chapter 9, Rahel, Estha, and Sophie Mol, wearing women's saris, visit Velutha. Rahel remembers how Velutha treated the children: "a grown man entertaining three raccoons, treating them like real ladies. Instinctively colluding in the conspiracy of their fiction" (181). Dressed as "ladies," the children and Velutha participate in a conscious performance of dominance and servitude; Velutha "addressed them all as Kochamma and gave them fresh coconut water to drink" (181), and he lets them paint his nails with red polish. This instance of children's play and mimicry of Indian womanhood is revealed throughout the text to be as performative for Rahel—an Indian woman—as it is for her brother or for her English cousin: the neglect of Rahel after Sophie Mol's death results "in an accidental release of the spirit" (18). As a result, Rahel never learns how to inhabit the role of Indian woman, and, with the exception of her sari-wearing visit to Velutha that takes place three days before Sophie Mol's death, never performs appropriate upper-caste Indian femininity again. Furthermore, for Velutha, this transgression of gender boundaries proves to be as consequential as his transgression of caste. When the Touchable Policemen see Velutha's red nails, they question his sexual orientation: "'What's this?' one had said. 'AC-DC?'" (181), and then the officer "lifted his boot . . . and brought it down with a soft thud" (294) on Velutha's penis. While Velutha allows the children to symbolically emasculate him by letting them paint his nails, the policemen literally emasculate him because of his gender-based transgression. *Small Things* juxtaposes these instances of drag, the children's performative femininity and Velutha's collusion in that performance, with its presentation of the second performative aspect of the text that I want to examine, that of the socially sanctioned drag of the Kathakali Man, the storyteller whose body constitutes another kind of text, that of Malayalam mythology.

The stories that the Kathakali Man tells through his public performances are "the Great Stories" in which members of the audience "know who lives, who dies, who finds love, who doesn't" (218). Kathakali originated in Kerala, and, according to Philli Zarilli, "at the historical moment of its emergence as a distinct genre of performance in the late sixteenth and early seventeenth centuries, *kathakali* was given its present name, which literally means "story-play" and refers to the performance of dramas written by playwright-composers in highly Sanskritized Malayalam" (3). The traditional patrons for these performances were high-caste ruling and land-holding families, and kathakali actors were male. Performances "served as a pleasurable form of education into these well-known stories and their implicit values and meanings" (4). In the 1990s-era India of *Small Things*, however, such performances, which traditionally lasted all night, have become "unviable," and the Kathakali Man, trained in the art of his craft since the age of three, is forced to market "the stories that his body can tell"; as the narrator claims, "he becomes the Regional Flavor" (219). In Roy's novel, Rahel and Estha watch two dancers perform the story of Karna and Kunti, and both actors are drunk or stoned, desperate to escape their status in contemporary Kerala as "impostors" and actors "playing a part" (220). The dancer portraying Kunti, the mother of Karna, is also in drag "a man, but a man grown soft and womanly, a man with breasts, from doing female parts for years" (221), but this gender transgression, unlike Velutha's, is socially sanctioned in that it provides the audience with a lesson about femininity, particularly femininity as viewed by men. The dancer as bearer of social law and custom is not only allowed but required to demonstrate womanhood, in this case a duplicitous femininity that is vain and conniving. Kunti, in "the impudence of youth" calls forth Surya, the God of Day, who impregnates her with Karna (221). Because she is unmarried, she abandons her son and later returns to ask that he not kill her more loved sons, the five Pandavas (222). The desperation of the performers, their frustration at their marginalization and the marginalization of the "traditional values and meanings" of the mythology imparted through their dance, is inherent in the narrator's claim that after the performance, "the Kathakali Men took off their makeup and went home to beat their wives. Even Kunti, the soft one with breasts" (224). As is the case of the cultural villages that function as invented traditions in Ngugi's and Mda's works, the kathakali dancers as cultural relics invent tradition as well, "corrupting their stories" (218) and shortening their night-long performances for audiences with "imported attention spans" (220). While kathakali has always been performative, it becomes, within Roy's narrative, a kind of performance of a performance; within a "town masquerading as a village" (224), the Kathakali Man is "a brilliant clown in a bankrupt circus" (220), hawking a highly contrived Indian "culture" to a largely disinterested and often foreign audience made up of tourists in search of a presumed "authentic" Indian cultural experience.

At the end of chapter 12, after the kathakali performance has ended, Rahel and Estha are aware of how the frenzy at the end of the play, during which Bhima kills Dushasana and devours his body, transcends performance to become the anger and despair of the kathakali performers, and what happens on the stage also becomes a reflection of what the police do to Velutha at the History House: "There was madness there that morning. Under the rose bowl. It was no performance. Esthappen and Rahel recognized it. They had seen its work before. Another morning. Another stage. Another kind of frenzy. . . . The brutal extravagance of this matched by the savage economy of that" (224). The police officers' attack on Velutha, to which the narrator alludes above, takes place in chapter 18, "The History House." Because it is positioned after the preceding performances of the welcome of Sophie Mol and the staging of the Great Stories by the frustrated and culturally anachronistic kathakali dancers, the narrative of "The Terror," as Velutha's beating and subsequent murder are referred to throughout the text, can be read as a performance that answers the preceding two. First, because he is suspected of kidnapping the children and is therefore implicated in the disappearance of Sophie Mol, the beating he receives is to put him back in his place as a Paravan, a place he continually refuses to occupy by stepping out of nature and into history, into "the Play" that Baby Kochamma directs. Velutha is a socially dangerous character who maintains "a lack of hesitation. An unwarranted assurance," an ability to offer "suggestions without being asked," and an ability to

disregard "suggestions without appearing to rebel" (73). The beating is to force Velutha back offstage and to situate the absent Sophie
Mol back in a play that, chapter eight suggests, should be about her.
The irony, of course, is that in Roy's staging of the events that lead
to Velutha's murder, Sophie Mol remains almost entirely offstage
and functions more as the impetus for tragedy than as an actor in
"the Play" that the narrator claims follows her wherever she goes.
Secondly, because Baby Kochamma accuses Velutha of attempting to
rape Ammu, the police act to avenge the wrong done to a touchable
woman by an untouchable man. Just as, in the kathakali performance
witnessed by Rahel and Estha, Bhima avenges the honor of Draupdi,
the wife of the Pandavas who is accosted by Dushasana, the police officers avenge the supposed defilement of Ammu by beating Velutha.[3]
The drama that takes place at the History House, therefore, is a story
that its players have learned by watching other performances, particularly the kathakali dances that, as I mentioned earlier, function
as a form of communal "education" (Zarilli 4). In that "there was
nothing accidental about what happened that morning" and that the
actions of the officers constitute "an era imprinting itself on those
who lived it," the officers' beating of Velutha becomes "History in live
performance" (*Small Things* 293), the scripted enforcement of the
love laws, and another lesson for the community.

The river again functions as the boundary between Velutha's
world and Ammu's after Velutha crosses it to hide in the History
House; at this point in the novel, Velutha actively enters the narrative of history, and is followed by the touchable police officers.
Everyone involved—including, as a result of Roy's circular narrative technique, the audience—knows how this story, like the "Great
Stories" depicted by the kathakali performers, will play out: the love
laws have been broken, and for this transgression, someone must die.
As the officers cross the Meenachal and walk to the History House
at the beginning of chapter 18, the narrator again, as was the case
at the beginning of the novel, walks the reader through the natural
world filled with a verdant and menacing landscape to which Velutha
belongs and that attempts, it appears, to protect him by attaching the
police: "groundcreepers snagged in their dewdamp leghair. Burr and
grass flowers enhanced their dull socks. . . . Rough grass left their leg-

skin raw, crisscrossed with cuts" (289). The landscape surrounding the house is full of birds and insects; egrets, cormorants, storks, sarus, herons, along with beetles, dragonflies, and butterflies move about through giant ferns, flowering plants, and nutmeg trees (289). When the police officers arrive in the house and beat Velutha, their actions are the result of a learned history of oppression, one that characterizes Velutha and those like him as less than human, a being with no biological connection to the touchable posse who come to claim him. Because he is essentially other, an aspect of the natural world that has attempted to enter the realm of culture, the police "had not instruments to calibrate how much punishment he could take" and they beat him out of their fear of him, "civilization's fear of nature, men's fear of women, power's fear of powerlessness" (292). Like all characters who disregard their roles in a play, Velutha is silenced, and Ammu and Estha are silenced along with him. Because of her own fears, Baby Kochamma convinces the twins that they and Ammu are going to prison unless one of the twins "fingers" Velutha as a kidnapper. When Estha then answers the inspector's question with a "yes," "Childhood tiptoed out. Silence slipped in like a bolt" (303) and Estha never speaks again. Furthermore, because Ammu goes to the police station to protest Baby Kochamma's claim that Velutha attempted to rape her, Baby Kochamma convinces Chacko that Ammu and the twins are to blame for his daughter's death; Chacko, in turn sends Ammu and Estha away, and the fractured family members, informed "of their place in the scheme of things" (312), are rendered unable to speak any story that runs counter to the colonial and caste-based "Play" of history.

୨◕

Of course, Roy's novel is the articulation of the history that exists within the realm of nature, and her voice, like the voices of the characters within the story, has also repeatedly been the subject of attempted silencings. In 1997, for example, the final chapter of *Small Things* proved controversial in Kerala, and Roy was charged with "corrupting public morality" (Barsamian 9). The case was later dropped, but as I mentioned at the beginning of this chapter, in 2002 Roy was charged with polluting "the stream of justice" by criticizing the Supreme Court of India, a charge for which she was convicted, fined, and sentenced to a night in jail. At this point in my study, I want to shift my analysis away from the various performances that Roy stages in *Small Things* to focus instead on an analysis of the performative aspects of Roy's social and environmental activism, particularly as that performance is staged in *Dam/Age*, Aradhana Seth's documentary about the Narmada Dam Project in which Roy reads from her essays, particularly from *The Cost of Living*. Roy's position in the film, the subtitle of which is "A Film with Arundhati Roy," situates Roy—not the mass protest of the dam or of the environmental damage the project would engender—as the subject of the film, which ultimately concentrates on the charges brought against Roy and her subsequent trial and conviction. The film situates Roy as activist, champion of the disenfranchised, and, ultimately, self-sacrificing hero. My aim in examining Roy's performance of activism in this film is not to make claims about whether or not this depiction is accurate, but to engage the discourse surrounding Roy's activism in order to illustrate how that discourse and Roy's handling of that discourse generates a mythological narrative about Roy as environmental activist. And that narrative is mediated by Roy's self-conscious and highly effective staging of her activist persona. The honing of Roy's public persona and skills regarding its dissemination, it would seem, is requisite in order for her to negotiate the various aspects of that persona—writer, celebrity, and activist.

There has been considerable criticism of Roy's activism, particularly by literary scholars who feel that her nonfiction writing is often ill informed and self-serving and devalues her status as a writer of serious fiction. Bruce Allen notes that "Roy's progressive involvement in activism and nonfiction . . . has been to the disappointment and scorn of some critics who apparently hoped to see her remain more 'pure' as a literary fiction writer" (157). Julie Mullaney has critically examined Roy's "particular brand of ecofeminism" (63) as it has been constructed by Roy and presented through British print and visual media. This ecofeminism, according to Mullaney, positions Roy as "*the* public voice of India's anti-globalization movement" (57), and such positioning, Mullaney argues, undermines a history of such protest, particularly by such noteworthy activists and scientists as the aforementioned Vandana Shiva.[4] Mullaney examines Roy's collusion in the myth of her singular status and notes the uneasy tension that exists between Roy's critique of the global marketplace and her participation in it. She notes in particular the way that Roy's body becomes a readable text in the discourse of protest: "Roy's body and/or body politics . . . rather than the Narmada Bachao Andolan or the dam project itself, is *the* site where the conflict between private, national and international interests is played out" (63). Graham Huggan criticizes Roy's manipulation of her image through what he describes as her "*strategic* exoticism," her "incorrigibly photogenic" appearance, and her "life story containing almost as many carefully leaked secrets as [*Small Things*]" (*Postcolonial Exotic* 77). Aside from literary critics, Roy has also received negative criticism from environmentalists, particularly Ramachandra Guha, who claimed in a November 26, 2000, editorial in *The Hindu* that Roy's writing about the Narmada Dam Project is "self-indulgent and hyperbolic," her "vanity . . . unreal," her anti-dam essay ("The Greater Common Good") replete with "signs of self-absorption."

These readings of Roy's public persona and body provide an intellectual mirror image, in a sense, to "justice's" — legal, social, historical — treatment of Velutha and Ammu's caste-inappropriate relationship and Rahel and Ammu's various gender-based transgressions. In Roy's case, it seems, her status as a female, Indian writer, specifically of fiction, precludes her ability to be read as a "real" activist. Roy's claim that she has written the novel she wanted to write and is now "swimming in the river of life" can be read as testament to the author's belief that writing and living are two separate entities, but, as is evidenced by the fact that both her writing and her activism have been confronted by the "stream of justice," both writing and living, at least in Roy's case, are transgressive. Furthermore, Roy claims that her shift from writing fiction to writing essays only appears to be a transition; in actuality, she claims, "I've been doing this kind of work since I was twenty-one. . . . I wrote political essays before I wrote the novel" (Barsamian 10). She also claims, very much as South African novelist and essayist Nadine Gordimer did in 1982 when she asserted that "nothing I say here will be as true as my fiction" (264),[5] that "fiction is the truest thing there ever was" (Barsamian 10). Since the 1980s there has been consistent debate in the academy over whether, as Edward W. Said states, "writers and intellectuals can ever be what is called non-political or not" ("Public Role" 20). Roy, as a writer who is also positioned as a public activist, seems to provide a different problem to consider in terms of the role of the public intellectual: as a writer, does Roy have a right to be political in any way other than indirectly through her fiction, and, because of her celebrity, can we read her public activist persona as legitimate despite its potentially contrived status? Instead of arguing that all literary writing is political to some extent, many of Roy's critics seem to assert a kind of contradictory position with regard to Roy, conceding that she can address politics in her fiction, but that to be overtly political in her public life is somehow unacceptable.

In his collection of interviews with Roy, *The Checkbook and the Cruise Missile*, David Barsamian, in an interview conducted in 2001, asks Roy about her involvement with the Indian film industry. She responds, "I worked on a few films that were a part of the lunatic fringe, films that no one really wanted to see. It wasn't at all part of the film industry," and Roy is overtly critical of the documentaries that are produced in India, noting that "few of them transcend the boundaries between activism and art." She goes further to state that she "can't bear the idea of working with a film crew, negotiating with a producer. . . . It's not my thing" (33). In a later interview, however, Barsamian asks Roy about her involvement in *Dam/Age*. She responds, "usually when people ask me to make films with them, I refuse. The request to do *Dam/Age* came just after the final Supreme Court hearing, when it became pretty obvious to me that I was going to be sentenced. . . . I was pretty rattled, and thought that if I was going to be in jail for any length of time, at least my point of view ought to be out in the world" (42). The director of *Dam/Age*, Aradhana Seth, had known Roy since 1987 or so, when the two worked together on Roy's first "fringe" film, *In Which Annie Gives It Those Ones*; Roy wrote the screenplay and was the production designer, while Seth was the assistant director (Chong). While Roy, in her discussion with Barsamian, makes no mention of the fact that she and Seth had been longtime acquaintances, Seth, in an interview with Jennifer Chong, claims that when the BBC approached her about filming *Dam/Age*, she and Roy "didn't immediately say 'yes' because we had become such good friends that that was much more important." Roy agreed to do the film, as she told Barsamian and as Seth asserts, because she wanted to record events "as they happened to her" (qtd. in Chong). While *Dam/Age* is ostensibly about what was happening to the people of the Narmada valley as a result of their potential displacement, the film's interest—as well as Roy's—in terms of what "happened to" Roy indicates two sets of interrelated circumstances around which Seth's narrative is constructed. The story of what happens to displaced persons and to the environment as a result of India's pervasive system of dams becomes the back story for Seth's depiction of what happens to Roy as a result of her vocalization via "The Greater Common Good" of that narrative of devastation and displacement.

Seth notes the power of the corporate-owned media in shaping public understanding of "truth." She claims that if people "pick up the newspaper in the morning, they go, 'Oh, if that's in the newspaper . . . that must be real . . .,'" but she also notes that she does not think "that documentaries are that different, but where it is different is it tells a longer story and in a way, it's not that it doesn't have a point of view, but I think it's a point of view that is as true to yourself as opposed to true to the people you work for" (qtd. in Chong). Because documentary film is not under the purview of "corporate giants" (qtd. in Chong) that control the public media, it is less likely, Seth claims, to be manipulated or censored. She does concede, however, that documentary film does maintain a point of view, and, in the case of *Dam/Age*, that point of view is clearly focused on constructing a narrative of Arundhati Roy, who, as she told Barsamian, believed that "my point of view ought to be out in the world" (42). At the beginning of *Dam/Age*, Roy appears on a boat, literally floating in the Narmada River. In the river, Roy is situated like Velutha, drifting, floating, and the river, in life as in her fiction, functions as the environmentally compromised boundary between nature and culture, between touchable and untouchable worlds: the majority of the people who will be displaced as a result of the dam project are untouchables like Baba Mahaoya who asks, after the river is dammed and the land flooded, "where will we beg?" (*Dam/Age*). Roy, touchable, educated, self-proclaimed "not completely 'traditional' nor wholeheartedly 'modern'" (Barsamian 6), crosses the river in order to see the places that will be submerged should the dams be built and to write about the injustice of the Narmada Dam Project, and she is established through the discourse of the film as champion of the untouchable masses. She, like Ammu, crosses a river and transgresses the social boundaries that are constructed to maintain her supposed purity, in this case, as a writer of fiction. At the beginning of the film, Roy notes this crossing: "I had crossed the Narmada by boat . . . and climbed the headland on the opposite bank, from where I could see . . . the Adivasi hamlets of Sikka, Surung, Neemgavan, and Domkhedi. . . . I knew I was looking at a civilization older than Hinduism, slated — *sanctioned* (by the highest court in the land) to be drowned this monsoon" (*Cost of Living* 7). Conversely, as a result of 3,600 dams that exist in India, the people who have lived in doomed landscapes — some 56 million since 1974, 60 percent of whom are untouchables (*Dam/Age*) — also cross the river to move to urban areas to find work; the film brings to the foreground those people who have traditionally been positioned offstage, those untouchables who "melt into the darkness and disappear" (*Dam/Age*). These crossings result in similar rhetorical outcomes for both displaced persons and for Roy: silencing of any narrative that speaks against the "nation builders." Roy asks, "what has happened to all these millions of people? Where are they now? How do they earn a living?" and responds, "nobody knows" (*Cost of Living* 19); in terms of her research on the subject of displacement, Roy claims, "I feel like someone who's just stumbled on a mass grave" (18). While I have noted that Roy does speak for the untouchable subaltern (in Spivak's sense) masses, and while I also contend that there are various acts of speaking for and silencing inherent in this film — Roy speaks for, while the "nation builders" silence — it is worth acknowledging that this comment about the mass grave points to a lack of recorded discourse surrounding the fate of "millions of people," and Roy is able, because of her upper-caste status, to unearth that discourse. In addition to her concern about the displacement of the human species is a concern about the environmental damage that the project will cause, the destruction of a vast ecosystem — thirty-two thousand acres of forest (Roy, *Power Politics* 72).

As compared to the three performances that I discuss in terms of *Small Things*, Roy's performance in *Dam/Age* and the subsequent construction of her activist identity as a result of that performance can be read as structured in three "acts" within the film. The first is Roy's aforementioned placement on the river at the beginning of the film (a sequence that is repeated again in a flashback forty minutes into the narrative)[6] during which we see her gazing out over the Narmada landscape while, in a voiceover, she reads from her text "The Greater Common Good." The scene shifts to Roy in the present moment as she reads from her essay, periodically making eye contact, via the camera, with the audience. The first part of the film is narrated entirely by Roy and includes information about her relationship with the river, "not as an environmentalist or as an ecologist" but as a friend, about the facts she did and did not uncover when she went looking for statistics about potential displacement, and her drive to tell "the whole story" with "all the connections." The images shift from Roy in the present to Roy attending past protests, situating her as a member of the crowd, listening to Medha Patkar as she speaks to the protesters.[7] Patkar's voice, however, is largely absent from the narrative; we hear her rally the protesters, even as Roy's voiceover again takes precedence. Then the film takes Roy back out of the crowd and places her at the forefront of the narrative as she discusses her role as a writer in terms of speaking about what is happening in the Narmada valley. She pays particular attention to "how power shines a light and what it chooses to illuminate and what it leaves in the darkness," and her role, she asserts, is to widen the scope of what is illuminated. The first line of the film is from "The Greater Common Good," and it is Roy's statement about crossing the river, climbing up the bank and laughing at the seemingly ludicrous nature of the Supreme Court's concern that displaced children have parks in which to play. This narrative of laughter — which Ramachandra Guha attacks as seeming to be "a straight lift from the first lines of that monument to egotism, Ayn Rand's *The Fountainhead*" ("The Arun Shourie") — is meant, Roy claims, not as "disrespect" but as response to an absurdity that displaces, at least for a moment, Roy's anger.

The second "act" is also punctuated by Roy's laughter as she reads the Supreme Court's injunction against her, particularly as she gets to the claim that she has polluted the "stream of justice." The film shifts from the victimization of valley residents as a result of their potential displacement to Roy's victimization by the Supreme Court of India. The film is no longer concerned about the fate of the river and the people who depend on it; the narrative now focuses on the fate of Roy. In this part of the film, Roy discusses the tension that exists in terms of "when to be personal and when to be public" and determines that her fight against the court must take place in the public arena. She also speaks about her persona: "whenever I go abroad, I'm always invited to portray myself as this sort of radical person who's being hunted down by these institutions in this native banana republic." Roy uses her position within the film to square who she wants to be with what those "abroad" want from her; in terms of her relationship with the "institutions" she critiques, Roy claims to want to engage in "conversation" in order to make democracy more sophisticated. Of course, in the third "act" of Seth's film, the impossibility of dialogue or conversation is rendered visible. Laughter, a key thread in the first two parts of the film, is absent from this final sequence; the camera homes in on Roy's eyes as she watches the body of protesters who have gathered in her defense outside the Supreme Court building. She cries, wipes the tears away with her sari, and heads into the building. For the next several minutes of the film, Roy's voice and body are situated offstage, within the Supreme Court building while the camera focuses on the anticipation of the crowd that has gathered outside.

This final sequence is particularly significant in constructing Roy as the voice of a unified front, and the film does this by removing Roy from the story of her persecution and mediating her story through other, less coherent voices. The narrative positions Roy as silenced by the law as it attempts to show Roy her "place in the scheme of things" (*Small Things* 312). That place, the film invites us to see through Roy's missing narration and physical presence, is offstage in the narrative of history; her presence, in that it "pollutes the stream of justice," is displaced from the story, but the film renders her absence visible. During the minutes when Roy is absent, there is no unified narrative voice, and everyone within the narrative frame becomes a member of a seemingly inarticulate crowd. Similarly, the camera seems at a loss, panning across the front of the building, showing protesters lined up on an upstairs balcony, their voices a jumbled and indecipherable cacophony. The camera then lights for a moment on a newscaster talking on his cell phone, discussing his presence at "this Arundhati Roy hearing." Then suddenly, the camera zips to and fro; the person holding the camera is running and capturing shaky glimpses of cars, faces, other camera-people also running. The film feels as if everyone is rushing forward to find out what happened, but Roy is still absent, and the next scene is of the door of the Tihar Jail being closed, another instance of silencing. We then see the inside of that building, and the film's narrative is told through the subtitles that inform the audience of Roy's fate: "Arundhati Roy must decide whether to pay a fine of 2,000 rupees . . . or face a further three months in jail." A woman appears and covers the camera with a piece of paper and, again, the audience is aware of the chaos that exists without Roy's framing discourse.

The next voice is Roy's lawyer, reading Roy's statement: "I stand by what I have said, and I am prepared to suffer the consequences." Immediately thereafter, the crowd is filmed cheering in triumph, arms raised, voices crying out in support of Roy, and Roy steps back into "the Play" in the last minutes of the film, her fist raised, to be received by her supporters after she pays the fine and foregoes the three-month sentence. The voiceover picks up the story again, and Roy asserts that she refuses to martyr herself for a cause that is not hers alone, that "choosing to suffer isn't exactly my style." In the film's final moments Roy claims that "the establishment has always feared writers because they have the weapon of clarity" that, when used effectively, "can be deadly." Roy's writing, both fictional and nonfictional has been deadly to the staging of performative history that her texts reveal, and her works have brought to light the social and environmental injustices that are suffered by a nations' poorest citizens, those who tend to be positioned offstage in the narrative of history. Within the context of both *Small Things* and *Dam/Age*, that narrative is revealed as a carefully scripted performance, and those who are traditionally forced to remain offstage—women, untouchables, and children—are brought to the forefront. While Roy is certainly aware of her position as one of India's most visible social critics, her maintenance of her activist persona is largely influenced by critical response to her as someone who has traded her literary purity for an activism that is ill informed and manipulative. Roy's performance in *Dam/Age* can be read as her attempt to rectify her position as both artist and activist, a writer who is not at the mercy of the various institutions that all of her writing critiques, but a writer who believes that fiction and activism can exist at the same moment, in the same person.

Ecofeminism is a value system, a social movement, and a practice, but it also offers a *political analysis* that explores the links between androcentrism and environmental destruction. It is "an awareness" that begins with the realization that the exploitation of nature is intimately linked to Western Man's attitude toward women.

—JANIS BIRKELAND, "Ecofeminism: Linking Theory and Practice"

Women activists around the world continue to embrace politicized motherhood as an empowering identity. Burning through the mists of biological and emotional essentialism that shroud the reality of motherhood, women are reclaiming and reshaping the role that has so long been used to control them.

—ANNELISE ORLECK, introduction to The Politics of Motherhood: Activist Voices from Left to Right

CHAPTER FOUR

Prophecy, Motherhood, and the Land

An Exploration of Postcolonial Ecofeminism

Ecofeminist philosopher Lori Gruen claims that "woman" and "animal" serve the same symbolic function and render both women and animals items in an exchange economy that places only commodifiable value on the lives of animals (61). For the colonized subject, however, there are additional variables that we must take into account when examining the rhetorical slippage between the binary oppositions of woman/animal and man/culture, a slippage that makes sense in a context where male, female, and animal are considered the criteria that determine an individual's position within a hierarchy dependent primarily on one's species and secondarily on one's sex. In the case of colonized peoples, however, such a hierarchy becomes more nuanced, particularly in terms of the female subject, as explicated by postcolonial feminist theorists. According to Chandra Talpade Mohanty, to ascribe an all-encompassing and Western feminist category of "woman" "to women in the third world colonizes and appropriates the pluralities of the simultaneous location of different groups of women in social class and ethnic frameworks; in doing so, it ultimately robs them of their historical and political agency" (213). Sara Suleri furthers this assertion when she says that "the coupling of postcolonial with woman . . . almost inevitably leads to the simplifications that underlie unthinking celebrations of oppression, elevating the racially female voice into a metaphor for 'the good'" (246). To further complicate matters, along with their rhetorical treatment as children, male colonial subjects were often emasculated—both literally and figuratively—by their colonizers and, therefore, rhetorically constructed as female.[1] While the way that women and nature have been conceptualized in the West has devalued women, nature, animals, and emotion and simultaneously elevated reason, humans, culture, and the mind (Gaard 5), ecofeminist readings of non-Western, postcolonial women's narratives must be informed by an understanding of the double bind that marks their subjects and authors as both female and colonized. As a result of these competing forces, Huey-Li Li claims, "the woman-nature affinity" that is "true of Western cultures, is not a cross cultural phenomenon" (288).

These various binary oppositions—woman/nature, man/culture, animal/human—are complicated in Nigerian novelist Flora Nwapa's *Efuru* (1966), New Zealand novelist Keri Hulme's *the bone people* (1985), and South African novelist Sindiwe Magona's *Mother to Mother* (1998), narratives that depict a pronounced and pervasive absence of the maternal. I argue that this maternal absence occurs in these works in part because colonized female subjects do not have access to the same kinds of "celebrations" of a uniquely (and possibly essentializing) female interiority that ecofeminism traditionally calls for Western women to recognize, embrace, and elevate. All of the aforementioned works contain environmentally significant prophecies that allow the three female protagonists willingly—as opposed to rhetorically—to form a bond with the land from which they have been displaced as a result of colonial history. In this chapter, I connect ecofeminism and postcolonialism through an examination of the trope of the motherless daughters—Efuru, Kerewin, and Mandisa—who serve as protagonists in these texts, and in their contradictory status as childless mothers whose roles, like the authors who write them into being, is to give birth not to human infants, but to narratives that reimagine, hybridize, and revise precolonial, colonial, and postcolonial environmental mythology in order to place women at the forefront of positive social and environmental change.

These reenvisioned narratives result from the female characters' interpretations of environmentally prophetic speeches, orally transmitted to them via male elders. In *Efuru*, it is the dibia, or traditional medicine man, who deciphers Efuru's dream of the goddess of Oguta Lake, Uhamiri, but it is Efuru who interprets how she will worship and who ultimately turns her back on the dibia when he claims that she is ill because she is adulterous. In *the bone people*, one of the kaumatua, or elders, a man referred to as "the last of the cannibals" (335), guards the ancient god whose spirit has withdrawn from a land that bares the scars of "forests burned and cut down; the gouges . . . that dams and roadworks and development schemes had made; the peculiar barren paddocks . . . the erosion, the overfertilization, the pollution" (371). While the kaumatua charges Joe with caring for the god, it is Kerewin who ultimately creates the space in which that god will live after she is saved from cancer by another of the kaumatua, "a small dark person, all etched sharp" (424) of indeterminate gender. In *Mother to Mother*, Mandisa's grandfather tells her the story of the Xhosa Cattle Killing of 1856–57 during which, as I have already discussed in the first chapter of this study, the female prophet Nongqawuse instructed the Xhosa to kill all of their cattle in order to drive the whites to the sea. As is the case with Mda's narrative, which offers a complex view of the killing, in Magona's novel, Mandisa's grandfather tells the story of the killing to correct the story Mandisa learns in school, that Nongqawuse was a "false prophet" who was "superstitious and ignorant" (175). In the grandfather's telling, the cattle slaughter and subsequent starvation of the Xhosa becomes the "noble sacrifice" (176) of a cattle-worshiping nation. Mandisa extends the narrative of sacrifice into the present day, to hint that perhaps a version of Nongqawuse's prophecy may yet come true, but only if the scapegoating that led to and has perpetually resulted from the Xhosa killing is neutralized and replaced with a more holistic nurturance of South Africa's peoples and landscapes. At the end of the novel, such healing has yet to be attained, and Mandisa refers to her son as "the blind but sharpened arrow of the wrath of his race" and to his victim, the white American woman he murders, as "the sacrifice of hers" (210).

In the context of mythological reenvisioning, these characters eschew traditional understandings of motherhood as a biologically determined imperative for women, in favor of a conceptual, self-determined, highly intellectualized notion of motherhood that situates the maternal between various cultural determinants (the colonizing, the colonized, the precolonial, for example) as opposed to outside of the Western, patriarchal narrative of colonial history. While all three protagonists and authors support ecofeminism's "insistence that nonhuman nature and naturism . . . are feminist issues" (Warren, "Taking Empirical Data Seriously" 4) and illustrate the ways that "important connections exist between the treatment of women, people of color, and the underclass on one hand and the treatment of nonhuman nature on the other" (3), all three works subvert essentializing representations of woman as nature. For example, all three female protagonists are both motherless and theoretically or literally childless, and these representations allow for a redefined conception of the maternal that subverts conventional celebratory connections between motherhood, female sexuality, and environmental fecundity: Mandisa is a virgin when she conceives her son, Mxolisi; Kerewin remains a virgin throughout *the bone people*; and Efuru is called to worship the goddess Uhamiri, a deity that denies children to her followers and forbids them from sleeping with their husbands on certain days of the week. Furthermore, Efuru's mother has died "five years" (8) before the narrative begins, and Efuru's only daughter, Ogonium, dies in infancy. In *the bone people*, Kerewin is self-estranged from her mother, but despite her initial characterization of him as an "it" and "ratbag child" (19) she does eventually care for the foundling child Simon Peter Gillayley. Mandisa's mother banishes her to Gungululu "where children are named according to the spaces between years of rain" (99) to live with her maternal grandmother, and Mandisa's own son, Mxolisi, of whom she claims "nothing my son does surprises me anymore. Not after . . . his unreasonably implanting himself inside me . . . totally destroying the me I was" (88)—becomes estranged from her after he commits murder. In turn, Mandisa reaches out to her "Sister-Mother" (198), the mother of the white, American girl—the historical Amy Biehl, who remains unnamed in Magona's narrative—murdered by Mxolisi.

⊰⊚⊱

The various binary oppositions that punctuate the works discussed briefly above—woman/nature, man/culture, animal/human—are complicated in Nigerian novelist Flora Nwapa's *Efuru,* set in the 1940s in the Igbo village of Oguta. The novel centers on the life of a "remarkable" (7) young Igbo woman named Efuru and the implications for her as a motherless and childless woman in a society in which motherhood is the primary goal for women. *Efuru* is significant because, among other things, it is the first novel to have been published in English by an African woman, and initially, Nwapa was accused of imitating the already established style of male West African authors like Chinua Achebe, Elechi Emadi, and Nkem Nwankwo.[2] In actuality, however, Nwapa focuses on the element that her male counterparts have tended to ignore: women's roles in traditional Igbo communal society. In the writing of these men, according to Elleke Boehmer, a type of nationalistic male mythmaking takes place that is absent from Nwapa's more "female" version of reality (7); in addition, male authors like those listed above wrote about male equality, and the women in their texts tended to be largely symbolic. *Efuru* changed the presentation of African nationalism and male domination because it attempted, instead of reinforcing male cultural representations, to repossess, reinscribe, and recreate an African female mythology. According to Susan Z. Andrade, Nwapa's writing has often been dismissed as trivial and "useful only for an understanding of domestic Igbo village life," but Andrade argues that it is precisely because the novel focuses on women's experiences that it is valuable (97). As Gay

Wilentz states in *Binding Cultures*, Nwapa's novel not only focuses on women's positions as wives and mothers, but as instructors of cultural values (10), and unlike her male contemporaries who write about African male unity in the face of Western oppression, Nwapa concentrates on everyday life within women's compounds. The female characters in *Efuru* speak for themselves and "press into Nwapa's narrative as speakers, actors, decision makers, brokers of opinion and market prices and unofficial jurors in their communities" (Boehmer 12). In an agriculturally based society like that of the Igbo, children were considered contributions to the entire community, and women gained status through their ability to have children. According to Wilentz, "the culture says, [marriage] means nothing unless there are children to show for it" (*Binding Cultures* 11); therefore, motherhood was the primary goal for precolonial Igbo women, because the maternal role allotted them the greatest amount of status.

After the death of her daughter, Ogonim—the only child Efuru has over the course of the narrative—Efuru is called to be a devotee of Uhamiri, the goddess of Oguta Lake, and Nwapa presents this honor as a mixed blessing: while Uhamiri gives women wealth and beauty, in Nwapa's novel, she is perceived—at least by Efuru and the village gossip Omirima—as being childless and, therefore, unable to give children to the women who worship her. While colonization had occurred by the time the story takes place, its effects are largely peripheral to the "reality" depicted by Nwapa, and while characters comment on the presence of whites in Nigeria, their statements tend to reflect a sort of curiosity about rather than a need to imitate or be fearful of Western behavior.[3] The one notable exception is Omirima's assertion that "the world is changing. It is now the world of white people" (194), a claim she makes immediately before an extended diatribe about how Western education and religion have undermined the dictates of Uhamiri, the goddess of Oguta Lake, particularly as those dictates affect the natural environment. Omirima criticizes Efuru's mother-in-law, Amede, for allowing Ogea to fish on a day sacred to the goddess: "You allow Ogea to fish on Orie day. The day our Uhamiri says we should keep holy. . . . And your daughter-in-law is an ardent worshipper of the lake? . . . That's why there are no fish in the lake. That's why our Uhamiri is angry with us. The children of these days have polluted the lake. I saw three . . . school girls, on Orie day, going to fish. I scolded them. . . . But did they listen to me? Of course, they did not. . . . That's what they learn in school—to disobey their elders" (195). In addition to blaming Western education for the girls' disobedience and subsequent pollution of the lake—and corruption of the dictates of the goddess that protects it—Omirima also indicts Christianity for undermining Uhamiri's dictates about cultivating the land, rules that require strict observation of the flooding and receding waters of Oguta Lake: "the last flood was no flood at all. And the one before it came too early and damaged the yams, the cassava and other crops. We have these Church-goers to blame" (195). These criticisms point to the importance of both Uhamiri and Oguta Lake in the daily life of the Igbo and to the ways that the West is encroaching upon both Igbo belief and environment.

In their study *Ways of Rivers: Arts and Environment of the Niger Delta*, Martha G. Anderson and Philip M. Peek examine the connections between environment, environmental degradation, and the cultural artifacts of the peoples of the Niger delta. In a foreword to this study, Marla C. Berns and Mary Nooter Roberts assert that "in Nigeria . . . water has always been far more than a simple element of nature. Water is synonymous with life itself, with spiritual sustenance, and wealth and prosperity, and especially with communication and identity" (11). In terms of the profound cultural and social importance of bodies of water in Nigeria, Sabine Jell-Bahlsen notes that the goddess of Oguta Lake "is *the* major reference point in the daily life of Oguta. She is the mythical mother of the Oru people. Their farming cycle and the timing of their cultural activities revolve around the flooding and receding of the lake and its adjacent rivers" ("Flora Nwapa" 254). The goddess requires that her people respect their environment and that they pay attention to the cycles of the natural world as they cultivate both the land and the lake. Jell-Bahlsen points out that Nwapa changes various aspects of the goddess's identity in that, traditionally, worshipers of Uhamiri did not have to be celibate, nor did they have to be childless, and she reads Nwapa's heroines, in *Efuru* and her other works, as empowered by a goddess "who supported her followers beyond—not instead of—childbearing" ("Flora Nwapa" 256). Jell-Bahlsen notes that "in the changing world of contemporary Oguta, the goddess—and by extension (African) woman—is constantly pushed back and encroached upon by alien ideas, problems, and forces. Nwapa accounts for the destructive forces of globalization, the onslaught of foreign powers and their religions attempting to push Uhammiri's [sic] children into the abyss of derangement" (260). Nwapa's alteration of the goddess and her creation of a heroine who exists at the cusp of profound social and environmental upheaval in Nigeria provides an implicit critique of the then-current—1960s—Nigeria during which the novel was written and also depicts Nwapa's ambivalence toward Western ideological conceptions of religion, environmentalism, and gender. But, both in terms of Uhamiri's status as a hybrid deity and in terms of Nwapa's alterations of traditional beliefs and ideas about Uhamiri, the goddess requires that her people also keep an eye on the future and that they be able to change to accommodate the forthcoming environmental and social crises that await Nigeria in the second half of the twentieth century.

I would like to focus more closely on the ways that both Nwapa's and Efuru's reinterpretation of the worship of the goddess of Oguta Lake allows Efuru to function as a postcolonial, ecofeminist prototype, a woman situated at the historical moment when Igbo women's matrilineal power was in decline and environmental devastation, particularly as a result of the discovery of oil in Nigeria, was just beyond the horizon. Efuru is a woman whose childlessness and adherence to the taboos of the goddess Uhamiri—to avoid fishing on Orie day (192) and to discourage others from fishing then as well, to eschew sexual activity during certain times, and to respect the power and sacredness of water—situates her within an historical moment out of which will arise both the rhetoric of population control and the need for conservation of Oguta Lake, the Niger delta, and Nigeria's land and resources. The sets of competing role expectations—the maternal and the conservationist—create conflict within Efuru, however, and she is unable as of the end of the narrative to see fully the value of a nonmaternal position. In order to explore this situation more fully, I want to put forth the dilemma posed by the narrator at the end of the novel: "Efuru slept soundly that night. She dreamt of the woman of the lake, her beauty, her long hair and her riches. She had lived for ages at the bottom of the lake. She was as old as the lake itself. . . . She gave women beauty and wealth but she had no child. She had never experienced the joy of motherhood. Why then did the women worship her?" (221). Efuru questions why women worship Uhamiri,[4] even as her dream seems to be symbolic of her desire to embrace a role other than the one that her culture has chosen for her, that of wife and mother. She cannot, however, understand or see how the role of a childless woman could be valuable, because for Efuru, the roles of women and men in Igbo society are too concrete to be reasonably challenged. Yet, despite her apparent discomfort with her worship of Uhamiri, Efuru does challenge and reinterpret what it means to be a follower of the goddess. As a child, Efuru sees a woman who worships Uhamiri and comments that she seems possessed, rubs white chalk on her body, and chants: "to Efuru now, the figure seemed pathetic though it had amused her years back" (148). Efuru asks herself, "will I rub white chalk, dress in white, sit on the floor and sing swaying from side to side?" and she decides, "no, I am not going to behave like that" (148). Nwapa, according to Sabine Jell-Bahlsen, the preeminent scholar of the water goddess of Oguta Lake, struggled throughout her career with the "mixed blessings of Westernization, positioned, as she was, culturally in Oguta and socially within Nigeria's upper class Christian elite" (*Water Goddess* 285), and this struggle is implicit in Efuru's decision to worship the goddess in her own way, as a childless woman in Oguta who ponders a very Western dilemma, the (im)possibility of having both a career and family.

In terms of colonial, environmental, and historical context, *Efuru* is set in the Igbo village of Oguta in the 1940s, approximately midway between the Igbo Women's War of 1929—during which thousands of Igbo women protested a proposed tax on married women (Egbo 75)—and the discovery of oil in Nigeria in 1956. It is worth noting that Nwapa published *Efuru* in 1966, a year before the outbreak of the Nigerian Civil War, which ranged from 1967 to 1970 and during which southeastern Nigeria—also called Biafra—attempted to secede and take oil revenue with it (McNeill 304). During this conflict, Oguta Lake, located in Nwapa's hometown of Oguta, served as a Biafran army marine base. The political and social events that led to the crisis—particularly the environmental and cultural devastation of the Niger delta as a result of the oil industry—would have been daily realities in Nwapa's life at the time she was writing *Efuru*, yet the novel makes no explicit reference to these events. Implicit references, however, are present in Omirima's aforementioned criticism of the ways that "it is now the world of white people" (194) who "pollute" both the environment and traditional Igbo belief systems. *Efuru* is consciously concerned with personal as opposed to political history, an Igbo woman's history, and, I would argue, an underlying ethos of environmental preservation inherent in the novel's dual focus on the social acceptance of a childless Igbo woman and that woman's specific connection, via her worship of Uhamiri, to Oguta Lake, an ecosystem generally associated with "the spirit of women's collective solidarity" (Amadiume 52) in Igbo culture. In terms of both Nwapa and Efuru's reinterpretations of what it means to worship the goddess, the novel calls for a reconception of Igbo women's roles—one shaped by an awareness of indigenous religious and environmental practices, yet one aware of the impending realities of capitalism, Western education, and Christianity.

Because she is chosen, via a prophetic dream, to be a follower of the goddess of the lake, Efuru is allowed an alternate, socially visible existence as a capitalist; she becomes a trader and farmer, and such a social position, in many ways, runs counter to Igbo cultural expectations. Within communal and matrilineal culture women gained status and property by having children who contributed to the well-being of the entire society and were harshly criticized for not having children. For example, when her only child, a daughter that she has with her shiftless first husband, Adizua, dies early in the novel, Efuru is blamed. One of the village women asks Efuru, "in what ways have you offended our ancestors?" (72). Later, Efuru marries a second husband, Gilbert, but fails to have any more children. The village women again function as her fiercest critics claiming, "a woman, a wife, for that matter, should not look glamorous all the time, and not fulfill the important function she is made to fulfill" (138). Omirima says to Gilbert's mother, "your daughter-in-law is good, but she is childless. She is beautiful but we cannot eat beauty.

She is wealthy, but riches cannot go on errands for us" (163). Such continual use of the pronouns "we" and "our" in the above examples and elsewhere throughout the novel point to the communal nature of Igbo society, a culture in which women—literal mothers as well as what Ifi Amadiume refers to as the "matriarchal umbrella" (43)—at once protect women and girls from patriarchal domination while also enforcing such seemingly sexist practices as "the bath" (female circumcision).

Efuru is considered beautiful, but the village women hold her beauty against her when she does not have children. Not only is Efuru denied certain aspects of personhood because she is unable to fulfill the role of mother, she is also denied her womanhood because to her neighbors, she "was a man since she could not reproduce" (24). While Igbo women are able to exert power in certain situations where their equality is challenged—as in, for example, the effective female uprising that constituted the aforementioned Igbo Women's War—in the novel, with the exception of Efuru, they do not challenge their marital status. According to Nancy Topping Bazin, "those who exert this pressure [to have children as soon as possible] on behalf of the patriarchy are female" (185), and to complicate matters further, Efuru's female peers first criticize her childlessness, but they alternately later feel threatened by her pregnancy: when Efuru is pregnant with Ogonim, "women were jealous of her beauty" (28). Initially Omirima, who laments the current generation's lack of respect for the goddess, scoffs at Efuru's decision to worship her: "'do I hear that [Efuru] now has Uhamiri in her bedroom?' Omirima sneered" (162). But Efuru's subsequent situation as a childless woman is not as bleak as it may appear, because even though she acts contrary to convention in many ways, she is still accepted within the traditional framework of Igbo life as a worshiper of Uhamiri. Women obtain power in Igbo society through a system in which gender is separated from sex roles. For example, as *Efuru* makes clear, women are allowed to worship Uhamiri, a goddess who "blesses the community with fish and fresh water and brings them wealth and beauty" (15) yet requires, at least in Nwapa's interpretation, that her followers be childless. Worshiping Uhamiri allows Efuru to reclaim her femaleness, her beauty, and her very personhood in spite of her childlessness. In a culture where women's roles are defined by their ability to produce children for the community, such an option implies that certain patriarchal dictates can be transcended, at least by certain "remarkable" women.

Efuru's own mother has died prior to the events that take place in the novel, but her rhetorical presence is felt throughout the work. When Efuru tells her father of her dream of Uhamiri, he says to her, "you are like your mother, my daughter, that's why I love you more than all my children" (150), and when Gilbert accuses Efuru of adultery, she replies, "my mother was not an adulterous woman, neither was her mother, why should I be different?" (219). Just as women function as the fiercest critics of other women's childlessness in the novel, mothers, literal and communal, are alternately blamed and revered for the behavior of their own as well as the community's daughters. When a girl is an undesirable bride at one point in the narrative, it is because "her mother is a bad woman" (160); conversely, when "girls gave deaf ears to their mothers' warnings" (106) in a narrative told by the storyteller Eneke, spirits capture them.

But women also act in defense of other women throughout the novel. According to Ifi Amadiume, "in addition to their biological mothers, women were . . . provided with a social mother to support them throughout their adult lives" (46), and such a system of support is apparent particularly in Efuru's relationship with Anjanupu, the sister of Adizua's mother, who defends Efuru throughout the novel, despite Efuru's estrangement from Anjanupu's nephew. In postcolonial Nigeria, however, such a framework of female support, Amadiume's "matriarchal umbrella," was severely compromised because ritual and tradition were banned during the colonial period, and I contend that the pivotal role of Uhamiri, read negatively by Amadiume as "a mirage of modernity," "a postcolonial temptress Goddess, contextualized in capitalist materialism" (49), and "a hybrid, a mulatto, stemming from a colonially derived desire for 'whiteness' by colonized African natives" (53), within the narrative points to the need for a new female identity within the text, particularly a powerful, female protector of a most valuable natural resource, Oguta Lake. At its core, Nwapa's novel is about the quest for the Igbo maternal independent of procreation symbolically manifest in both Efuru and Uhamiri at a time when religious beliefs, the environment, and women's roles were compromised by white influence.

According to J. R. McNeill, "Royal Dutch Shell and British Petroleum (Shell-BP), which had been granted exploration licenses by the British colonial government, struck oil [in the Niger delta] in 1956," and oil production began in the 1960s (301). The water and farmland utilized by fishing and farming inhabitants of the region, particularly the Ogoni people, were polluted and rendered useless, and the Nigerian military government dealt harshly with any complaints from local inhabitants. By the 1990s the government derived 80 to 90 percent of its revenue from oil, and in 1992 the United Nations declared the Niger delta "to be the most ecologically endangered delta" (304) in the world. Furthermore, in the late twentieth and early twenty-first centuries, Nigeria as a whole (and Igboland in particular) has been faced with a variety of environmental stressors. According to the World Igbo Environmental Foundation, "Southeast Nigeria and contiguous territories in the Niger delta . . . are ravaged by the worst combination of environmental degradation known to modern man. The area, which belongs to the equatorial rainforest belt of West Africa, has a population density that is second only to the Nile delta in Egypt. Pressure to procure land for essential human development activities has resulted in deforestation and overcultivation of almost all available land space in the area."[5] As I stated earlier, by setting *Efuru* in the 1940s, Nwapa does not have to engage in any direct way with the environmental implications of the issues cited above, since these circumstances postdate the events in her narrative. However, the novel's focus on the role of Uhamiri points to both the environmental significance that bodies of water serve as well as the way the natural environment, prior to discovery of oil in the Niger delta in 1956, is conceptualized, deified, and sustained in Igbo life.

Even though worshiping Uhamiri allows Efuru to fulfill "an alternative, woman-centered function in the society" (Wilentz, *Binding Cultures* 17), Efuru's desire to be traditional keeps her from coming to terms with her situation. It is this internal conflict between traditional and emergent values that most profoundly affects Efuru's consciousness, despite her inability to articulate the source of her conflict; the narrator notes that, despite her initially happy marriage and success as a trader, "something weighed Efuru down" (19), but the source of this weight remains unstated, either by Efuru or by the narrator. Andrade sees Efuru's desire to be traditional and her reluctance to follow Uhamiri as a threat to "the text's manifest assertion of female independence" (105). It would appear, however, that the very fact that Efuru has the option of worshiping a female deity would argue for a form of female independence that is denied to Western women by virtue of Christianity. Christianity does not abide overt goddess worship and therefore does away with a specific women's outlet: "as history reveals, with the colonization and Christianization of Igboland, women were excluded from participating as priests" (Ezeigbo 157). Efuru's ability to choose to worship Uhamiri is a testament to the degree of independence women enjoy in Igbo society, and without Uhamiri's influence as a valid deity, Efuru's identity crisis as a childless woman would be much more profound. However, as Oladele Taiwo points out, even though Nwapa uses Uhamiri to show that "the happiness of a virtuous woman like Efuru should not depend entirely on her ability to have a child" (52), it is clear that her childlessness is still the cause of most of her grief. Taiwo comments that "Efuru may derive other benefits from her attachment to Uhamiri, but not the kind that can save her marriage from collapse" (51). Furthermore, in spite of the fact that Efuru is able to find an acceptable place in her Igbo society, she is partly able to do so because she has resources that other traditional women are denied. As Theodora Akachi Ezeigbo states, "if a childless woman is wealthy [as is the case with Efuru] her situation is not as tragic or helpless as her other sisters in the traditional society nor in post-colonial and modern society" (157)."

In her first dream of Uhamiri, Efuru claims, "I go to the bottom of the lake and . . . I saw an elegant woman, very beautiful, combing her long black hair with a golden comb. When she saw me, she stopped combing her hair and smiled at me and asked me to come in. I went in. She offered me kola, I refused to take, she laughed and did not persuade me. She beckoned me to follow her. I followed her like a woman possessed" (146). As I stated earlier, the presentation of this deity elicits concern from critics who view Uhamiri as a product of colonial influence. Chimalum Nwankwo, for example, is critical of Nwapa's depiction of the female divinity, claiming that "Uhamiri, the goddess of stability and supposedly unstoppered kindness, is for devotees, like deities everywhere, inexplicably ineffectual" (49). According to Amadiume, this depiction of Uhamiri is "European and not African. She is without family or children and is totally outside any social system" (53); furthermore, "white women, capitalist goods, and Western power become unattainable objects of desire that are represented in [Uhamiri], whose images efface those of indigenous African matriarchs" (63). Such criticism seems in direct conflict with another of Nwankwo's assertions that "the historical markers for [colonial] trauma are unfortunately absent" (49) in Nwapa's narrative, and Susan Z. Andrade's claim that Nwapa's depiction of the water goddess is free from Western influence: "that Efuru's life appears to have no contact with Europe . . . means that the narrative's prototype of female power is Igbo—a powerful statement in the face of a post-world-war feminism that implied the global liberation of women would begin in the 'West'" (98–99). Such contradictory claims point to the difficulty of historians and literary critics alike to adequately position Uhamiri within Igbo culture.

Sabine Jell-Bahlsen, whose 2008 *The Water Goddess in Igbo Cosmology: Ogbuide of Oguta Lake* is perhaps the definitive text on this deity's significance within Igbo culture, reads the goddess as absolutely precolonial in her origins. Jell-Bahlsen's text examines, in great detail, Igbo environmental consciousness as it is dictated by Ogbuide (another name for Uhamiri or Mammy Water)[6] and notes that "recognizing the mother water goddess and her powers" alters our perceptions of "nature, power, and gender" (1). Jell-Bahlsen claims that the prominence of the fluid nature of the goddess provides counterbalance to the static forms of male divinity, and she provides a detailed reading of the ways that, by carefully observing the flooding and receding of the waters of Oguta Lake and as a result of a series of taboos established in conjunction with these natural cycles of ebb and flow, the Igbo "have learned to observe and maintain their vital natural resources through skillful resource management" (49). The Igbo, she asserts, recognize water as both a resource and as a sacred, life-preserving—and life-destroying—entity; they "feel indebted, know how to fear, but also thank and preserve their lake, rivers, and entire environment" (249) through family planning, "sanctions, sanctuaries, and indigenous cultivation techniques" (253). In fact, Jell-Bahlsen links the water goddess to all aspects of environmental conservation practiced by the Igbo, including observation of lake levels in the initiation of annual farming cycles, shifting yam cultivation to ensure a seven-year period to allow farmland to recover, moderation of slash-and-burn land clearance, and the interplanting of different crops as a form of pest control. Furthermore, the Igbo practice strict conservation of medicinal plants and sacred groves, and they protect specific animals sacred to the goddess—the crocodile and turtle, for example—from being hunted (251–54). On the other hand, domestic animals "are slaughtered only in sacrifice, in exchange for a human life, for no life owed to the mother water goddess is to be taken randomly" (260). Finally, in keeping with the dictates of the goddess, Igbo couples space the birth of children at three-year intervals (280), as women are required to abstain from intercourse for two and a half years after the birth of a child. Initiated worshipers of the goddess also abstain from sexual activity on Orie day, the day of the Igbo week devoted to Uhamiri (280).

As a hybrid deity, both Western and African, Uhamiri disrupts readings of Nwapa's novel as unconcerned with Western influence; certainly, the title character of the work, as a motherless and childless woman who is called to worship this deity, to keep a jar of lake water in her room, to help stabilize the fish population by eschewing fishing on certain days, and to prosper through agriculture and trade, represents one option for Igbo women (or at least for a particular and "remarkable" Igbo woman) to maintain a connection to her homeland, even as that land's natural resources in the form of palm oil, zinc, and iron ore, were being depleted through colonial trade. As I stated earlier, bodies of water, in the form of rivers and lakes, play a vital role not only in terms of subsistence but also in terms of Igbo religious beliefs that often associate lakes with goddesses and rivers with gods, and during the time since Nwapa wrote *Efuru*, environmental devastation of such entities as a result of oil drilling has been one of Nigeria's main concerns. Nigerian writers and activists have been at the forefront of the movement to stem the environmental devastation, often suffering horrific consequences. In 1995, for example, Ogoni writer and activist Ken Saro-Wiwa was executed for protesting Shell Oil's environmental devastation of the Niger River Delta. Before he was hanged, Saro-Wiwa stated, "the ecological war that the Company has waged in the Delta will be called to question sooner than later and the crimes of that war be duly punished. The crime of the Company's dirty wars against the Ogoni people will also be punished" (Baxter, Horsman, and Kretzmann). According to the World Lakes Database, Oguta Lake is located within the equatorial rainforest belt, but at the current moment, "most of the rain forest has been replaced by oil palm plantations especially around the lake" (International Lake Environment Committee). The lake continues to function as a major source of drinking water and of fish, but the water and ecosystems within the lake are currently endangered by the fact that the lake is used as a septic pool for domestic sewage and because local people dredge sand from the lake to use in construction. Most significant in terms of this study, however, is the assertion by the International Lake Environment Committee Foundation for Sustainable Management of World Lakes and Reservoirs that despite the implementation of recent environmental protection laws, their enforcement has been a problem because neither the enforcement agents nor the citizens are sufficiently educated with regard to environmental protection of the lake. However, according to the committee, "traditional rules of the local community are concerned with the lake's environment and kept by the residents, particularly by the worshipers of the Lake Goddess and her priests."

Efuru ends with the dilemma that I quoted earlier, and such dilemmas are characteristic of oral African literature.[7] The dilemma is dialogic, inviting the reader to enter the narrative and participate in the debate posed by the narrator. The narrator says of Efuru's final dream of Uhamiri, "she was happy, she was wealthy. She was beautiful. She gave women beauty and wealth but she had no child. She had never experienced the joy of motherhood. Why then did the women worship her?" (221). Many critics have engaged in attempts to answer the narrative's final question. For example, the worship of Uhamiri contradicts the Igbo cosmological belief that, according to Emmanuel Edeh, "the power of production is the only true power a being has. . . . The Earth has her native power of fertility by which she produces. . . . The Earth, because of its fertility, is the archetype of all forms of maternity" (44). To worship Nwapa's reinterpretation of Uhamiri is at once to embrace certain aspects of Western culture but also to be environmentally responsible in ways that allow Nwapa, through the character of Efuru and her counterpart the Lake Goddess, to speak prophetically about Nigerian environmental crises during the twentieth century and beyond. The balance that Uhamiri asks her worshipers to strike between the excesses of capitalism and the religious proscriptions of Igbo culture is mediated by two dictates in Nwapa's novel and in Igbo cosmology: family planning and conservation of resources in the face of colonial environmental exploitation; as I stated earlier, one of Uhamiri's taboos is that her worshipers must not fish on Orie day and must encourage others not to fish on this day as well. Such a policy would certainly have direct implications for reducing overfishing of the lake and would promote the environmental consciousness that the worshipers of Uhamiri—in the present day context—seem, according to the International Lake Environment Committee's report, uniquely inclined to champion. Uhamiri is a hybrid goddess, implicated in capitalist exchange *and* demanding the observance of her taboos, but such hybridity is necessary in terms of female mythmaking, narrative reclamation, and environmental survival.

Late in *the bone people*, New Zealand author Keri Hulme's only novel to date, the Maori elder Tiaki Mira imparts a prophecy that requires that he "wait until the stranger came home or until the digger began planting, or until the broken man was found and healed" (360) before he can die. The fictional fulfillment of this prophecy at the end of the novel is achieved when the three protagonists, Kerewin, Joe, and Simon—previously separated from one another through acts of violence—come together to reinvent and reinterpret the concept of family and, in so doing, generate a multicultural national model for the future of Aotearoa (the most common Maori name for New Zealand, meaning "the land of the long white cloud"). My reading of this familial reconstitution requires an understanding of the ways that

Hulme's narrative problematizes and de-essentializes the ostensibly ecofeminst Kerewin's signification as an "earth mother" figure in order to engage in an act of postcolonial environmental mythmaking. The resultant myth engages traditional Maori legend in a way that heals the cultural "dis-ease" (Wilentz, "Instruments of Change" 127) that has resulted from a history of indigenous cultural repression and environmental destruction, and far from idealizing an assumed inherent Maori environmentalism, Hulme's novel holds Maori and white populations equally responsible for the compromised landscape that they share. The peoples of New Zealand, the narrative suggests, must form a new identity in order to move forward and care for the land and its creatures. In my reading, that care is initially ecofeminist, originating with Kerewin and later influencing Joe, who will, one hopes, pass it along to future Maori and Pakeha (white) generations, starting with the transnational Simon.

According to Janet Wilson, "in New Zealand since the Seventies, writers who have adapted intertextual strategies have focused more on myths and legends of the Maori oral tradition, and those of the Pakeha New Zealand literary tradition than on European texts of the colonial encounter" (271), and Margery Fee claims that the story of the bone people "cannot, ultimately, be told straightforwardly because the text is attempting to rework the old stories that govern the way New Zealanders . . . think about their country" (54). This lack of straightforward narrative is manifest in *the bone people* through the text's layered spiral nature, a narrative strategy that Elizabeth M. DeLoughrey, in *Routes and Roots: Navigating Caribbean and Pacific Island Literatures*, claims is indicative of "a trope that symbolizes dynamic interrelation between the temporal and spatial" (162). In her study, *Decolonizing Cultures in the Pacific: Reading History and Trauma in Contemporary Fiction*, Susan Y. Najita describes the narrative's spiral shape as indicative of Maori conceptions of time: "as in Hawaiian notions of time, the Maori past (*mua*) occurs in front and the future (*muri*) occurs behind" (100). Both Najita and DeLoughrey acknowledge the "layered design of *whakapapa*, Maori genealogy" (Najita 99) as it pertains to the overlapping of past, present, and future in Hulme's novel, and DeLoughrey points to the connection between *whakapapa* and a Maori environmental ethos that emerged in the 1970s: "scholarly interest in *whakapapa* as a methodology and metonym for identity emerged in the late 1970s, in a large part due to Maori land and resource claims against the breached Treaty of Waitangi" (166). The "rhizomorphous system of relation" (164), she claims, establishes relationships between all life forms and inanimate matter.

The novel's engagement with *whakapapa* allows the text to challenge and complicate binary distinctions—Maori or Pakeha, linear or nonlinear—which were still in place as New Zealand moved toward a realization of itself as a bicultural nation, a place shaped by both indigenous and colonial influence, but a place, in the 1980s world of Hulme's narrative, in which the nature of Maori and Pakeha identity were dependent on ancestral, "blood"-based percentages.[8] According to Philippa Mein Smith in her *Concise History of New Zealand*, New Zealand took until the 1990s to consider itself a "multicultural" nation: "the country first had to grow more diverse before acknowledging cultural difference. . . . The multicultural idea transferred belatedly, from the 1980s in law and policy, and effectively from the 1990s" (242). The law and policy of which Mein Smith speaks include the Waitangi Tribunal, which formed in 1975, and the 1985 Treaty of Waitangi Amendment Act, which allowed the tribunal to investigate land claims dating from 1840, when the Treaty of Waitangi was signed (Howard 199).[9] Through the prophecy of the digger, stranger, and broken man, *the bone people* generates a myth that shapes New Zealand's national identity and, perhaps more important to this study, imagines an environmental ethos that benefits both the land and all of its peoples. After Mira's death, the digger, stranger, and broken man are charged with the care of both the contemporary postcolonial landscape and the ancient Maori god who once presided over it, a being whose sensibilities would be in line with Bradley Reed Howard's analysis of the animistic religions of the Maori, which "entail a reverence both for the spirits of natural objects such as rivers, streams, trees, and mountains and for the spirits of the ancestors who coexist with the Maori in daily life" (179). But the caretakers, Kerewin, Simon, and Joe, constitute a combination of races, genders, and nationalities, none of which are easily mapped; Hulme's narrative, therefore, destabilizes rather reductive and stereotypical readings of the Maori as environmentally responsible and the Pakeha as environmentally destructive.

For example, the prophecy imparted by Tiaki Mira provides a postcolonial lesson in the production of a multicultural and nonbinary identity for readers who expect a one-to-one correlation between the terms "digger," "stranger," and "broken man" to Kerewin, Simon, and Joe, since all three characters are, in various ways, at various places in the narrative, and to various extents, diggers, strangers, and broken beings. For example, Kerewin dreams of digging; Simon "digs for most of the afternoon" (202) into a rabbit hole only to find "mummified baby rabbits" (203); and Joe, after Tiaki Mira's death, digs a hole and plants a tiri tree at the foot of Mira's grave (377). All three characters are also broken in various ways, Simon by Joe's abuse, Joe as a result of his suicidal leap from a cliff, and Kerewin as a result of her familial estrangement and supposed stomach cancer. Furthermore, when Tiaki Mira questions Joe early in their acquaintance, he concludes that perhaps Joe is "stranger and digger and broken man all in one" (358). Such lack of one-to-one correspondence between terms destabilizes allegorical readings of the text. According to Antje M. Rauwerda, "Hulme addresses colonialism's legacy by presenting a postcolonial allegory in which Simon stands for all things Pakeha, Joe . . . for all things Maori and Kerewin for something midway between the two" (24). Rauwerda's reading is problematic since Hulme's characters resist allegory, because they can neither be read as one part of a duality nor as a middle variable — "something midway between the two" — that creates the space of taboo, and such a lack of correlation between a prophetic designation and a singular character operates to destabilize binary readings that often inform colonial discourse.

Simon, Joe, and Kerewin, therefore, evoke a mythology that is at once hybridized — influenced by both Maori and Pakeha traditions — and utterly new, ahistorical, and, at points, utterly unreadable. For instance, while Kerewin is a woman, she is continually characterized by particularly masculine behavior — she hunts, fights, drinks — and a tendency to describe herself in gender-neutral terms; she is, in her own estimation, "the neuter human" (96). Furthermore, despite her racialized status as one-eighth Maori, Kerewin defies racial classification and claims to feel all Maori. Similarly, Joe's introspection, bisexuality, and shame over the perceived implications of his tenderness toward Simon are qualities that are at odds with the overt physical violence and alcoholic machismo that characterize his relationships with other characters in the novel; ultimately, Joe's bisexuality, like New Zealand's passing biculturalism, does not fully encompass the range of human experience that defines either him or his country. At the end of the novel, in front of Luce, Joe tenderly touches Simon, stirring "the silvergold hair with one cool finger. Not deep enough to touch the skull, enough to make his cool cool point" (444). Finally, despite the narrative's extensive focus on his whiteness, Simon's similarities to the Maori god Maui, his androgyny, and his inexplicable ability to see auras blur the boundaries of Maori/Pakeha, man/woman, and human/god. Maui, the demigod of Polynesian legend responsible for, among other things, pulling New Zealand's North Island from the sea, is recast in part as the Christlike Simon, but ultimately, Simon is neither Christ nor Maui.

Simon, like the other characters in the novel, constitutes something alternately hybrid and new, a being shaped by colonial history who nonetheless demands to be read beyond the parameters of one particular narrative of colonization, one particular set of racial determinants, and one gender. Simon is multifaceted, multicultural, and, as the child of French parents, transnational. In fact, there are no easy readings of any of Hulme's characters; they signify at once a myriad of possible meanings, as indicated by Tiaki's inability to ascribe a singular, prophetic identity to Joe. Furthermore, each of the three main characters is unable to maintain a constant picture of the other two. For example, after talking with Joe about his family, Kerewin "stays up arranging the picture she had built in her mind of what Joe is, until it is daylight" (231); similarly, after Tiaki Mira dies, Joe thinks of Kerewin, "I was trying to make her fit my idea of what a friend, a partner was. I could only see one way . . . whatever she thought she was, bend her to the idea of what lovers are, marriage is, the only sanity. Don't accept merely what she can offer, make her give and take more . . . now I can see other possibilities, and there is still a hope" (381). Joe's thoughts about Kerewin point to three realizations that are necessary in the process of healing New Zealand's colonial and environmental wounds: the realization that identity, in the shifting context of the postcolonial environment, is never a fixed entity, the ability to imagine alternate possibilities, and the understanding that one must accept gifts when they are given and, alternately, that one must give without hope of reciprocity.

The god at the heart of *the bone people*, Maui, is marked in Hulme's ambiguous depiction of him as androgynous, silenced by Pakeha influence, and further damaged by Maori neglect. Hulme creates an image of Maui that is at once multicultural and multifaceted, by transposing many of his characteristics onto the excessively white Pakeha character of Simon, a being whose characterization is also replete with Christian iconography and, I would argue, environmental signification in this connection to the sea. According to Rauwerda, "Maui is cast into the sea, as is Simon. Both are orphans who wash up on shore and find alternate homes. . . . Joe thinks that Simon is a tangle of seaweed like . . . the seaweed that wraps around Maui. He sees Simon's long hair, an image echoing Taranga's [Maui's mother's] top-knot and the hair in which she wraps Maui. He thinks Simon, again like Maui, must be dead. Both Simon and Maui, however, are unexpectedly alive (this makes them both seem divine and invincible)" (32). Simon, like the sleeping god in the stone in Tiaki Mira's phosphorescent pool, also slumbers, comatose, awakening after the prophecy is fulfilled. Kerewin, like Simon, maintains a kind of kinship with and responsibility for water; she says, "I am . . . a tidal child stranded on land" (89); she fishes and depends on the sea for survival, and she is a childless conservationist. But despite Kerewin's childlessness, Simon's "birth" from the sea is later mirrored in the rebirth of the little god—possibly Maui—during an earthquake. After the quake, Joe finds the god in the stone, "a hump in the dusk, a disk . . . settled on a broken-backed rock. . . . It looks very black or very green, and from the piercing, the hole in the center, light like a glow worm, aboriginal light" (384). Furthermore, the earthquake that Joe fears will kill the god coincides with the miraculous disappearance of Kerewin's "false pregnancy" (Fox 416) in the form of stomach cancer, and Simon's emergence from his coma.

The fact that Kerewin's biological pregnancy is "false" posits a new reading of *whakapapa*, one that is not dependent on biology but is instead determined by one's creation of a nonbiological family, and in terms of the ways in which Hulme problematizes aforementioned earth mother iconography, *the bone people* depicts a pronounced and pervasive absence of biological mothers—Kerewin's and Simon's, for example—as well as a female protagonist who balks at the conception of herself as maternal, claiming that "to care for anything deeply is to invite disaster" (34). Such sentiment about motherhood appears to be in stark opposition to the reality of motherhood in contemporary Maori women's lives: "in 1995, the fertility rate of Maori women . . . was twice that of non-Maori women," and Maori women tend to have children at younger ages than their non-Maori counterparts (Ministry of Women's Affairs 6).

the bone people presents Kerewin as a kind of composite and subversive maternal figure whose identity is informed in part by her semblance to both the Virgin Mary (Kerewin remains a virgin throughout the novel) and the Maori Papatuanuku, the "goddess of the whenua/ land . . . widely understood to symbolize the necessity for holistic and ecologically aware national policies" (Wood 107). As a woman who eschews biological motherhood, Kerewin nonetheless emerges as a maternal figure who adopts Simon (and Joe) and who embodies, at least by the end of the novel, a holistic and inclusive ecofeminist ethos.

Through the fulfillment of Mira's prophecy, Hulme's protagonists willingly—as opposed to rhetorically, as symbolic manifestations of the components of Mira's prophecy—form a bond with the land from which they have been displaced as a result of colonization. In *the bone people*, Tiaki Mira, a kaumatua or Maori elder who is referred to as "the last of the cannibals" (335), guards the ancient god whose spirit has withdrawn from a land that bares the scars of "forests burned and cut down; the gouges . . . that dams and roadworks and development schemes had made; the peculiar barren paddocks . . . the erosion, the overfertilisation, the pollution" (371). While the kaumatua charges Joe with caring for the god, it is Kerewin who ultimately creates the space in which that god will live after she is saved from cancer by another of the kaumatua, "a small dark person, all etched sharp" (424) of indeterminate gender. In the context of mythological reenvisioning, Kerewin eschews traditional understandings of motherhood as a biologically determined imperative for women, in favor of a conceptual, self-determined, highly intellectualized notion of motherhood that situates the maternal role between various cultural determinants (the colonizing, the colonized, the precolonial, for example) as opposed to outside of the Western, patriarchal narrative of colonial history.

In terms of *the bone people*, the character of Kerewin Holmes illustrates the double bind of colonized womanhood not as an indigenous Maori woman, but through her conflicted status, as she claims, as predominantly ancestrally white but spiritually Maori. Kerewin's need to make these distinctions points to her own, as well as her nation's, sense of fractured identity, as does the novel's focus of fractures of various kinds, particularly in terms of the scarred flesh and broken bones of its protagonists. Kerewin is wealthy but alone, an unproductive artist alienated from both her biological family—as the result of an unexplained estrangement—and from her spiritual center—as the result of self-imposed alienation. Kerewin may bear the trappings of eccentricity, artistic ability, and monetary comfort, and she may *appear* to be a Pakeha woman who is a firm believer in the Western notion of individualism to the point of isolation. But she claims to "feel all Maori" (62), a statement that seems to indicate a desire for a communal and family-centric lifestyle. However, Kerewin lives alone and wants nothing to do with her extended family or with motherhood. Kerewin's status as both motherless and biologically childless allows Hulme's depiction of Kerewin to break celebratory connections between motherhood, female sexuality, and environmental fecundity: Kerewin remains a virgin throughout *the bone people*, and her refusal to become romantically involved with Joe functions, in Najita's reading, as a "symptom of history" and "a symptom of colonial contact, in particular the exchange [beginning in 1769] in Maori women" (101) for commodities. Despite her initial characterization of him as an "it" and "ratbag child" (19), however, Kerewin eventually does care for and ultimately adopts Simon Peter Gillayley. Through Kerewin, Hulme provides a maternal model that follows some Maori traditions—adopting an outsider child into her "tribe," for example—but who also maintains her individual identity.

As I mentioned earlier, *the bone people* is nonlinear, a spiral narrative that begins with "the end at the beginning" (3) and ends with the Maori phrase, "te mutunga — ranei te take," or, "the end — or the beginning" (445). The spiral, or koru, is a traditional Maori symbol associated with the fern and used in bone carvings and in Maori tattoo, and in 1983, Austrian artist Friedensreich Hundertwasser designed a koru flag as New Zealand's second flag, "which represents an unmistakable identity that combines New Zealand's age old heritage of nature and the heritage of Maori history with the growing future of a new nation" and symbolizes "nature's organic power, quietly reassuring that its bearers elect to be the custodians of the forces of Life on this planet" ("The Koru Flag"). Similarly, it is possible to read the spiral shape of Hulme's narrative as underlying the development of an environmental consciousness that infuses the simultaneous multicultural development of an unlikely family from three disparate characters, the auspiciously named Kerewin Holmes, who feels "all Maori" despite the fact that "by blood, flesh and inheritance, [she is] but an eighth Maori" (62); the Maori Joe Gillayley; and his foundling son, the mute, silver-haired, blue-green-eyed and otherworldly Simon P. All three characters carry physical and emotional scars of various kinds, and all three are estranged, either through death or self-imposed separation, from their "real" families, particularly from their mothers. Simon's biological mother drowns, and his stepmother, Joe's wife Hana, dies as well. For reasons that are never revealed to the reader, Kerewin has been estranged from her mother for six years, and when Joe is afflicted with polio as a child, his mother gives him to her parents to raise.

The turning point of the novel occurs when Joe viciously and irreparably beats Simon, and Kerewin sets fire to her tower home. Joe's abuse results in Simon's comatose state and extended hospital stay thereafter, Joe's arrest and subsequent suicide attempt, and Kerewin's self-imposed exile as she waits to die from supposed stomach cancer that she refuses to treat with Western medicine. Separated from one another, all three characters are healed — Joe and Kerewin by Maori elders and Simon (although he never fully regains his hearing) after a lengthy hospital stay — and they come back together to form a different version of themselves as family at the end of the novel. Tiaki Mira, the "old one" or kaumatua who saves Joe, tells him the aforementioned prophecy; Mira must "wait until the stranger came home, or until the digger began planting, or until the broken man was found and healed" (360) before he can die. On the surface, this prophecy appears to refer to a specific trinity, that of Kerewin (the digger who gardens), Simon (the stranger of unknown origin), and Joe (the man whose bones are broken during his suicide attempt), but it also identifies three destructive facets of New Zealand's colonial history: first, invasion by "strangers"—the British, French, and North American whalers of the late eighteenth century and later British colonizers from 1840 to 1907—second, the "breaking" of Maori tribal connections, beliefs, and traditions as a result of colonization, and third the environmental impact of deforestation, gold mining, whaling, and alien species introduction that may possibly be rectified by people who "dig," plant, and care for the land. Ultimately, in Hulme's novel care for the land constitutes a first step toward the creation of a new Aotearoa in which characters learn to give and receive without thought for reciprocity, and such care creates a space for the awakening of the "little god that was brought on one of the great canoes" (363)—possibly Maui—guarded by Tiaki Mira and, after Tiaki's death, by Joe.

The land for which the characters in *the bone people* must care is a land shaped by a colonial history of environmental exploitation, nonnative species introduction and subsequent indigenous species decimation. Rampant whaling and sealing by the British, American, and French in New Zealand during the late eighteenth century and the extinction of two of New Zealand's indigenous birds, the moa and the harpagornis, by the nineteenth, are illustrative of the environmental impact of resource-based colonization. Even before the signing of the Treaty of Waitangi in 1840, the Maori population had been decimated by tribal wars and the introduction of unfamiliar diseases, particularly influenza, and by the beginning of the twentieth century the Maori had lost the majority of their land. This loss came about, according to Stephen D. Fox, because "the Maori see themselves as one with the land, and, until the British arrived, they had no concept of land as commodity" (416). The discovery of another imperial commodity, gold, on the South Island of New Zealand in 1861 and that island's subsequently bolstered economy further divided the white settler population from the indigenous Maori, particularly since the majority of white settlers—who outnumbered the Maori by 1850—inhabited the South Island. Urban development in the nineteenth and twentieth centuries has also had an impact on traditional Maori social structures and relationships with the land. As Hulme states in "Mauri: An Introduction to Bicultural Poetry in New Zealand," "in the cities [the Maori] are cut off from the life of the land, the sea, [their] family marae" (293).

Such readings as Fox's and Hulme's of the Maori as seemingly inherently connected to the land are problematic if one considers the colonial rhetoric of the noble savage as a being somehow at once pure and uncivilized, more connected to nature—and therefore averse to civilization—than the colonial invaders. Such depictions clearly indicate a romanticized view of the precolonial landscape and its inhabitants, and such a view was championed in New Zealand during the 1980s as the Waitangi Tribunal sought to redress tribal land claims. According to Mein Smith, the tribunal "suggested that the Maori were more ecologically minded than Pakeha and, significantly, had suffered for that outlook." Furthermore, the tribunal claimed that the Maori saw themselves as "guardians who held resources in trust as taonga (treasures) for future generations. They had to guard and protect the land, lakes, rivers and the sea as gifts from their ancestors" (13–14). Roger Wilson's 1982 study, *From Manapouri to Aramoana: The Battle for New Zealand's Environment*, chronicles significant environmental battles of the 1960s and 1970s, from the proposed raising of the level of Lake Manapouri in order to generate energy for aluminum smelting to the battle against nuclear testing off the coast of New Zealand. The first paragraph of his work clearly illustrates a romanticized view of the Maori: "the first arrivals in New Zealand found Aotearoa to be a land of plenty. . . . The Maori learnt to care well for the environment; indeed they revered the trees and mountains and formed a bond with the land quite alien to the European view that the land was there to be exploited" (9). According to Mein Smith, however, such a view is factually inaccurate. Ecologists have demonstrated that the Polynesian settlers brought rats on their boats as early as 2000 BP, and these rats—as well as the dogs they brought later—were responsible for the extinction of the moa and other animal species long before Europeans arrived in the eighteenth century. Furthermore, these settlers, the ancestors of the Maori, exploited the land, decimated marine life, and did not practice environmental conservation (Mein Smith 15).

One factor to consider in the mythology of the ecoconscious Maori (or Native American, or South African Khoikhoi and San, or whatever indigenous population one might choose to examine) is the reality that environmental conservation is a rather recent phenomenon, predicated by not only increased global population but by the perception that the earth's resources are in limited supply, as well as by the advances of the information age that allow media watchers to see images of global environmental devastation. Therefore, it is not unrealistic to suggest that for the precolonial Maori, the development of an environmental conscience would have been neither possible nor relevant. I raise the issue of the spurious environmentally conscious status of the Maori not to undermine the historical ways that that people has been dispossessed as a result of colonization or to imply that traditional Maori relationships with the environment underlie New Zealand's current environmental issues, but to posit that the belief in an inherently conservationist Maori population is a myth dependent on the co-opting of a particular narrative of New Zealand's colonial history in order to further current environmental agendas. However admirable the impetus behind the embellishments of indigenous environmentalism — Wilson, for example, obviously believes that the Maori model is one that can be resurrected in the service of current environmental damage — such a narrative nonetheless perpetuates the myth of the Maori as noble savage as compared to their European corruptors. Such a framework again establishes a problematic binary that promotes an impossible solution to New Zealand's environmental woes: a return to an imagined precolonial Eden.

Conversely, Hulme's novel refuses to advocate this imaginary return but instead borrows aspects of both Maori and Pakeha mythology to posit a contemporary model of environmental and social responsibility. Of the many environmental issues that affect contemporary New Zealand — whaling, rainforest decimation, foreign species introduction, and land development for tourism — in *the bone people* several are explicitly championed by Kerewin, whose environmental consciousness is fully formed before she ever meets the other two characters. When she, Joe, and Simon go to Moerangi, for example, Kerewin refers to the transplanted pines that border the road as "immigrants" unsuitable for the New Zealand topography. They are preferred to the native kahikatea, she claims, because "pines grow faster, when they grow. The poor old kahikatea takes two or three hundred years to get to its best, and that's not fast enough for the moneyminded" (157). Such sentiment is a response to the advent of industrial forestry in New Zealand: "mass plantings of *pinus radiata* began in 1925 and continued through to 1937" (R. Wilson 128). Kerewin also comments on the sale of sea stones, particularly greenstone and jade: "Ah, they'll be selling the air we breathe next . . . first gold, then coal, then all the bush they could axe, and all the fish they could can. And now the very beach" (284). This sentiment foreshadows a contemporary political and environmental controversy regarding the ownership status of the New Zealand coast. According to Mein Smith, "focus on the foreshore reflected global as well as local tides. Struggles for land moved to the foreshore and seabed as the global economy sought fish and energy resources, and the beach as real estate to develop" (253). In 2003 the Labor government introduced the Foreshore and Seabed Bill in order to assert that the shore and seabed belong to the Crown. Because of mass Maori denunciation of the bill, this legislation prompted the formation of the Maori Party, which opposed the bill, in 2004.[10]

With the continual reinterpretation of the Treaty of Waitangi and the various translations and linguistic differences in the English and Maori versions of the document that the British say effectively colonized the Maori, much historical revision has taken place, particularly during the 1980s and especially with regard to the depiction of the Maori, as I mentioned above, as environmentally conscious in the precolonial milieu. Again, while such mythology functions as an effort to restore land that was seized by the British from the Maori, such revisionism simultaneously serves to further problematic Manichean oppositions. Hulme's text, conversely, in that it situates the land as gift from Tiaki Mira to Joe, ultimately leaves the question of the land's inherent value—and Joe's "inherent" Maori environmentalism—open to interpretation.[11] Joe's nascent environ-mental consciousness is clearly shaped by Kerewin's conservationist rhetoric. Initially, Joe does not understand why the immigrant pines make Kerewin so angry and asks Simon "what's she in a bad mood over?" (158). But later, when Tiaki Mira asks Joe if he can imagine the slumbering little god waking in the context of contemporary New Zealand, given the "mess the Pakeha have made" (371), Joe thinks "of the forests burned and cut down; the gouges and scars that dams and roadworks and development schemes had made . . . the erosion, the overfertilisation, the pollution" (371), and decides that the god will most likely remain sleeping. It is not until, in his will, Tiaki Mira gives Joe "796 acres of pakihi and private sea beaches," land that is, according to a tongue-in-cheek analysis by Tiaki's so-licitor, "nearly worthless unless you care to develop it" (376), that Joe must confront the environmental devastation that he chronicles earlier. Tiaki's land, covered with indigenous trees, untouched and unconquered by developers, is bequeathed in the spirit of giving and evokes the principle that land cannot be owned. The concepts of "usefulness" and "uselessness," in the context of this land, allude to the terms of the Land Claims Ordinance of 1841, which stated that "all 'unappropriated' or 'waste land' beyond what was necessary for the 'rightful and necessary occupation of the aboriginal inhabit-ants of the said Colony' to be in possession of the Crown" (Howard 188). What will become of the land remains unknown at the end of the novel, but underlying the rhetoric of the solicitor's speech is the possibility for the land to be converted to commercial "worth" by developing it. At the point in the narrative when Tiaki gives Joe the land, the little god wakes during an earthquake and leads Joe back to Kerewin's newly constituted, spiral Maori hall at Moerangi. The spi-ral, filled with family, replaces the solitude represented by Kerewin's tower home and alludes to a more inclusive sense of *whakapapa*. Such a scenario indicates the possibility of salvation for the land, even as it positions such salvation beyond the scope of the narrative, at some point in the future.

At the end of the novel, the god in the stone in Joe's pack becomes heavy, and Joe fears that he may not be able to carry it. He says, "I was sure I would drop. But I have grown strong. I got out of sight, and the mauri, set down, sunk itself into the hard ground. Or maybe the earth turned willing water beneath its touch. It vanished completely. But we all came back to it, after the hoha died down, and each of us can feel where it is resting" (445). The god embraces the land and the land embraces the god because the prophecy of the stranger, digger, and broken man has been fulfilled, and the narrow classifications of Maori, Pakeha, masculine, feminine, nature and civilization have been recombined in the creation of the new people who are charged with the care of the land and of one another. Families are likewise reconstituted and redefined; Kerewin receives a "long wordless embrace" from her mother (443), and she extends to Joe and Simon "that unlikely gift, her name. As umbrella, as shelter, not as binding" (444). The woman's name, "Holmes," becomes "home" for Joe and Simon, just as her literal house, "holds them all in its spiraling embrace" (442). It seems apparent, as Fox claims, that Kerewin is connected to "the Earth Mother" (416) who recognizes an imperative to care for the land, its people, and its gods. This Earth Mother, however, is not the beneficent, hyper-feminine, and excessively fertile mother of Western imagination; she is something new, the postcolonial female archetype that is just coming into existence. While comparisons to the mother of Christ, the Virgin Mary, are inescapable and thus invoke an earth-centric hybrid deified human female, Kerewin does not give birth to a male savior. Her childlessness is an affront to both that Christian myth and to Maori conceptions of *whakapapa*, just as her virginity is an affront to an essentializing Earth Mother archetype. Instead, Kerewin gives birth to the story and asserts that the woman's role in the invention of the new Aotearoa's mythology will be that of writer/speaker and environmental caretaker.

❧

Because the Xhosa character of Mandisa, the narrator of Sindiwe Magona's *Mother to Mother*, refuses to have sexual intercourse with China and is a virgin when she conceives her son Mxolisi—she is examined by the village midwife who proclaims, "*Utakelwe!* She has been jumped into!" by her lover's sperm (112)—Mandisa, like Kerewin, evokes comparisons to the Christian icon of the Virgin

Mary. Mandisa claims, "my virginity was rent not by a lover or husband, even. No, but by my son" (156), and as Meg Samuelson asserts, "Magona's greatest innovation [in *Mother to Mother*] lies in her
recreation of the killer [Mxolisi] as a Christ figure" (237). But by
virtue of the fact that Mandisa is a sexual being and because her ability to function as a "good" mother (in the white, middle-class sense)
is denied to her as a result of her status as black in apartheid-era
South Africa, a position that requires her to care for the children of
a white woman who calls her "Mandy," Magona also challenges the
virgin mother archetype. Despite the fact that Mandisa's mother routinely checks her daughter's hymen and fiercely protects her virgin
status early in the text, going so far as to "banish" her to Gungululu
to live with her grandparents, her body—like the land from which
her family is displaced during a forced removal from Blouvlei to
Guguletu in 1968—is ultimately not hers to control. In the context
of South Africa, Mandisa's body, labor, and children do not belong
to her, and the protection offered by another possible "matriarchal
umbrella"—Mandisa's mother, her grandmother Makhulu, and her
friend Nono—is oppressive, ineffectual, and utterly doomed to failure. As a result, Mandisa forms a bond, albeit one-sided, with another mother, a white American woman whose daughter Mandisa's
son murders.[12]

Samuelson claims that through her writing, Magona longs for the
"freedom from being a mother" (231) that is often denied to literal
black South African women as well as to female characters in South
African women's fiction. Because of the ambivalence and even anger
with which Mandisa characterizes her status as a mother, going so far
as to blame Mxolisi for "implanting" himself in her, Magona's narrative, like Nwapa's, challenges readings of motherhood as the sole
desirable role for African women. Furthermore, Samuelson claims
that such ambivalence allows for "movement away from an idealized
and pure African past, which is fundamentally linked to the Mother
Africa figure and all her suggestions of purity and origin" (236).
For Mandisa, motherhood is inflicted upon her, and her lack of reproductive freedom is mirrored by Magona's depiction of Mother
Africa as a captive culture and site of both environmental and human destruction. In this section, I argue that Magona's incorpora-

tion of a historical and unfulfilled prophecy that led to the Xhosa Cattle Killing of 1856–57 — the only prophecy detailed in this chapter that does not come to fruition — functions to illustrate the ineffectuality of destruction and scapegoating as means to bring about positive change in South Africa. Furthermore, Magona makes clear that there can be no return to the environmentally "pristine" South Africa promised by the prophecy, just as there can be no return to a time before white settlers displaced indigenous peoples; the concept of a pristine past is mythical, based on the stereotype that the Xhosa were innately environmentally conscious, and the destruction of the environment called for by the Xhosa prophet Nongqawuse in order to drive white settlers into the sea results instead in a cycle of retributive scapegoating that ends, in Magona's narrative, with the murder of American Fulbright scholar Amy Biehl. If there is a solution to this cycle of racially motivated retributive justice, Magona seems to imply, it is through the maternal and through the cultivation of both children and the land, a claim that she makes more explicit through the parable of "Mama Afrika," a story that she wrote for *The New Internationalist*'s "Red and Green: Eco-Socialism Comes of Age" issue. The story, which appeared immediately after the publication of *Mother to Mother*, implores all Africans to recognize that "life is a chain" and to realize the interconnectedness between all beings. The solution to Africa's problems, Mama Afrika claims, is to "celebrate life" instead of participating in cyclical destruction: "when a child is born, plant a tree to mark the event. Help both grow strong and healthy. Let the child know the tree that is her life." The need for a recognition of the connections between various types of human and nonhuman life is Magona's plea, and the prophecy offered by Magona's fictional "Mama Afrika" becomes the mythical revision of the prophecy put forth by the historical Nongqawuse.

At the heart of *Mother to Mother*, a fictionalized series of letters from Mandisa, the mother of a black South African murderer, to the mother of the white American woman he kills, is an attempt to resurrect and reposition the historical and environmentally devastating Xhosa Cattle Killing of 1856–57 during which a young Xhosa girl named Nongqawuse prophesied the end of colonial rule and a return to a precolonial utopia, if the Xhosa slaughtered all of their animals. As I discussed in chapter 1, after over four hundred thousand cattle were slaughtered and the prophecies remained unfulfilled, mass starvation resulted. Like Mda's *Heart of Redness*, Magona's work is testament to the power of the prophecy and the significance of the land in Xhosa society, but it also illustrates the lack of retributive productivity inherent in acts of destruction—of animals, humans, or the land. Magona explicitly states her disdain for the belief in destruction as solution in an interview with David Attwell and Barbara Harlow: "a prophet or prophets, a voice, a movement, a feeling . . . says—destroy everything and your lot will be improved. . . . You cannot advance by destroying everything. I don't believe in that" (290). The narrative also contains two other prominent threads, the first of which is Mandisa's story of her life, her unplanned pregnancy, the mistreatment she experiences while living with China's family, and the impact of her son's violent act on her life. Mandisa's first-person narration requires the reader to position herself as the mother of the murdered girl and to empathize not only with the murderer but also with his mother and their ancestors. Interspersed among the events of Mandisa's life is the second thread, Magona's imagined chronicling of the events of Wednesday, August 25, 1993, in the lives of both Mxolisi and Amy Biehl who, despite Magona's identification of her in the preface to the book, remains nameless throughout the work. Despite its dependence on an historical event, Magona's narrative is a work of fiction that conflates the four men charged in Biehl's killing into one character and that speculates about Biehl's actual thoughts and actions: "what thoughts filled her mind as she woke! What dreams were hers the night just past!" (5). The novel paints a scathing portrait of the mob mentality that leads to Biehl's murder as well as to the black-on-black killings that take place daily in Guguletu. Within this mob, Mxolisi "is lost. You couldn't tell him from the others" (11). The crowd itself is described throughout the text as a "gigantic, many-limbed millipede" (11) devoid of consciousness, acting out of anger for a past and present history of police torture, racial injustice, and utter alienation. The narrative culminates with the loss of motherhood for both women, one of whom is rendered childless through murder and the other through her son's imprisonment as a result of that murder.

Unlike Nwapa's Efuru, who exists prior to—or perhaps outside of—major colonially imposed disruption of Igbo sociocultural practice, particularly with regard to Igbo women's roles, and Hulme's Kerewin, whose apparent position of privilege allows her to transcend gender norms without social retribution, Magona's Mandisa is a working-class black South African woman living in abject poverty in 1993 during the final days of apartheid. Also unlike her aforementioned literary predecessors whose status as mothers is more symbolic than literal, Mandisa has given birth to children who are alive throughout the narrative. She claims, "three children have come from my womb. Three claim me as mother. Three" (115). The oldest of these children is Mxolisi, whose name ironically means "peace bringer." Within this particular context, it is worth examining the role of the mother, particularly the poor black mother, and the general nature of women's work for both black and white women during the 1980s and 1990s in South Africa. In "Why Are You Carrying Books? Don't You Have Children?" an examination of motherhood in Magona's autobiographical works *To My Children's Children* (1990) and *Forced to Grow* (1992), Siphokazi Koyana differentiates between the meaning of the concept of "good mother" for black and white South African women: for white mothers, the good mother is "someone who cares physically and emotionally for her children (even if she leaves most of the grueling work of physical care to her black domestic worker . . .)"; for black working class mothers, on the other hand, the good mother "is the one who provides financial support and discipline, even if she is not there for the day-to-day care of the child" (46). Such sentiment is reflected in the epistolary questions Mandisa rhetorically asks of Linda Biehl after Mxolisi's arrest: "where was the government the day my son stole my neighbor's hen; wrung her neck and cooked it—feathers and all, because there was no food in the house and I was away, minding the children of the white family I worked for? Asked to stay for the week-end—they had their emergency . . . mine was just not being able to tell my children beforehand that they would be alone . . . not being able to leave them enough food for the time I was away . . . not being able to phone them and tell them of the change of plans" (3). Even as she is forced into motherhood, in South Africa, Mandisa is also denied a role as "good" mother, and this is one of Magona's most poignant criticisms of apartheid. In an interview with Siphokazi Koyana and Rosemary Gray, Magona claims that "good mothering entails ensuring it of others—i.e. working to see that it is possible and available to all mothers: that nurturing is available to all children" (2). As a result of her position in the apartheid hierarchy, however, Mandisa's ability to function as mother is abbreviated by the fact that she must work to care for a white woman's children. The government that houses and feeds Mxolisi after he is arrested—but that never gives him anything beforehand—Mandisa's above questions suggest, is now his paternal caretaker, providing for him in ways that she cannot, but also denying him the things that she alone can but is environmentally unable to ensure: understanding, forgiveness, nurturance, and love.

Furthermore, in addition to the fact that apartheid white supremacy dictates that in order for Mandisa to care for her children she must work away from home in the service of a white woman, within her own culture, Mandisa is also situated in a markedly subordinate position as a Xhosa woman. Whereas the traditional Igbo culture depicted in *Efuru* is matrilineal—a paradigm that helped alleviate some effects of the double bind of the colonized female position in that women could own and inherit land, and within which women had access to their own institutions of justice, commerce, and public position—traditional sex role proscriptions for black South African women are considerably less egalitarian, pronouncedly more patriarchal, and historically more oppressive. Koyana argues that women like Mandisa—as well as Magona, whose life in some ways mirrors her protagonist's—experience the "triple jeopardy of the black working mother" ("Why Are You Carrying" 51) who first cannot, by virtue of her race and social position, attain the standard of white, nuclear family; second, must conform to the "Eurocentric legal system" (51) that privileges the work of men; and third, is expected to conform to "traditional black patriarchy" (51). The power of this black South African male dominance over women is apparent in the current political and social milieu, shaped as it is by the specter of both pervasive rape and subsequent AIDS, the discourse of which haunts Magona's novel, particularly with regard to Mandisa's protection of her own daughter, Siziwe, from assaults that can result not only in pregnancy but in death. When Mandisa returns to Guguletu after hearing that there has been trouble in the township, she comments on her concern for her daughter, a concern that is nonetheless overshadowed by her worry over the whereabouts of her sons, Mxolisi and Lunga: "a girl-child, she is more vulnerable than the other two children. However . . . deep down in my heart, I knew I was more worried about Mxolisi" (40).

In a recent *New York Times Magazine* article, Tina Rosenberg writes about the dangers that black South African women face not only with regard to AIDS, but also of the dangers inherent in admitting to one's male partner that one has tested positive for HIV. Despite the fact that the antiviral medication Nevirapine is available to pregnant women for free, many black South African women deny their status as HIV positive. The reasons for the denial, for placing one's fetus at risk, have everything to do with the often violent response of the father to the news that the mother of his child is infected. According to Rosenberg, women fail to be tested or refuse to admit to a positive test out of fear that their partners might inflict physical harm upon them:

> At the Alexandra clinic, I listened to a tall young man named Vernon as he gave pretest group counseling to about two dozen pregnant women. "Think about your baby before you think about yourself," he urged them. He assured them the results of their H.I.V. tests would be confidential but encouraged the women to tell their families and partners. "Don't hide it. Don't use the phone — tell him face to face. You use the phone, he will hunt you down. Try to prepare him. Some people are very violent. He will beat you. But when he's alone, he will think about it. If anything happens to you, your family knows you went to tell him your H.I.V. status and never came home." This speech seemed unlikely to encourage many women to be tested. But it obviously reflected reality.

The threat of violence against women and the reality that men perceive women to be to blame for their infection with HIV/AIDS is based in the notion that South African women are responsible for the virtue of other South African women, a reality that is illustrated by Mandisa's mother's fierce attempts to preserve her daughter's virginity. The theory that "God put mothers on this earth to ensure the health of their daughters" (Magona, *Mother to Mother* 95) is further reinforced by men who refuse to acknowledge that through culturally accepted male promiscuity, they play the major part in the production and transmission of the disease. Such circumstances are made worse for Mandisa, who becomes pregnant at the age of thirteen. AIDS was not the looming specter in South African culture during the 1970s when Mandisa conceives, but she is nonetheless shunned by the baby's father, China, who refuses, given the strange circumstances of her virgin pregnancy, to believe that he is the baby's father. He tells her to "go and find whoever did this to you" (122), that he is going away to school, and that he will claim no responsibility for her pregnancy. Magona has said that because Mandisa is a teenage mother, her "potential is lost to the world, which will never benefit from whatever talent she was to have brought to it. Also lost to the world is the potential of her child" (Koyana and Gray 2). In this sense, according to Magona, Mandisa, who is depicted as hard working and academically gifted before she is forced to drop out of school, illustrates the success of apartheid as systemic and self-perpetuating, passed from generation to generation, and, in the case of *Mother to Mother*, from mother to son.

Of central importance to breaking this pattern is another kind of transmission in the form of oral narrative that is also passed from one generation to the next. Mandisa describes how her knowledge that the whites stole the land from black South Africans seems to be "knowledge with which [she was] born" (173). This knowledge results from the pervasive presence of Xhosa oral history as it is told to Mandisa by her grandfather Tatomkhulu, who provides her with a series of narratives that often contradict the "official" history Mandisa is taught in school, particularly the narrative of the Xhosa Cattle Killing of 1856–57. A young girl named Nongqawuse prophesied the end of colonial rule and a return to a precolonial utopia, "as they had been Embo, in the very beginning" (180), if the Xhosa slaughtered all of their animals. According to Peires, Nongqawuse claimed that "on the great day, two suns would rise red in the sky over the mountain of Ntaba kaNdoda where they would collide and darkness would cover the earth. . . . Then the righteous dead . . .

and the new cattle would rise. . . . The English . . . would retreat into the sea, which would rise up in two walls to engulf them and open a road for them" (98). After over four hundred thousand cattle were slaughtered and the prophecies unfulfilled, mass starvation resulted, causing the Xhosa population to drop from 105,000 in January of 1857 to 25,916 a year later (319). Subsequently, over six hundred thousand acres of Xhosa land was lost to whites. In *Mother to Mother,* Mandisa's grandfather describes the deep resentment that must have driven the Xhosa to kill their cattle, a resentment that in his retelling of Xhosa history marks the Cattle Killing as an act of extreme bravery as opposed to the act of ignorance and superstition described by Mandisa's white teachers.

Magona has said that there are two versions of the story of the killing: "there's one version that we were taught in school, there's another version that we African people believe" (Attwell and Harlow 289), and in Magona's narrative, the incident of the killing and its presentation within the context of codified, white-authored South African history provides an example of the ways that whites, both historically and in the current moment, manipulate colonial history at the expense of indigenous oral narrative. Magona's novel, in an ironic turn, transcribes the oral history of the Cattle Killing in an attempt to voice the Xhosa side of a story about a people's connection to their land and animals, their conservationist mentality prior to colonization, and the bravery required of them to turn against these things in the hope that whites might leave their land. The historical impact of the killing—the destruction of cattle and crops by the Xhosa, the subsequent starvation, death, and ultimate abdication of the land in order to survive—has resulted in a cycle of blame and retributive justice, scapegoating and division, that has further alienated South Africans from one another. In retelling the story of the killing, Magona works to undermine the power of such divisiveness and to recreate a narrative of hope and unity. Mandisa's grandfather tells her that cattle are not merely food but serve a much more foundational and holistic function in Xhosa culture as the source of milk, dung, and clothing, and that to kill such an esteemed creature was a hugely significant phenomenon. He says that the sacrifice of the cattle and crops "was to drive abelungu [whites] to the sea, where, so the seer had said, they would all drown. . . . Such noble sacrifice. But then, the more terrible the abomination, the greater the sacrifice called for" (178).

The scapegoat myth underlies the historical narrative of the Xhosa Cattle Killing in South Africa, an event that has had a profound effect on both subsequent literature and life in South Africa and abroad. But the historical and symbolic role of cattle in South African culture is not limited to the Xhosa Cattle Killing; it is omnipresent, from the time that the Khoikhoi people broke with the hunter San, for whom "control over hunting for the distribution of meat, and particularly trade in ivory, were mechanisms for asserting power, stamping territorial authority, and defining gender roles" (Beinart and Coates 19). Sometime before the fifteenth century, the Khoikhoi began to cultivate livestock, and in their communal culture, "livestock was by far the most valued form of private property in a society where land was never divided among individuals" (Elphick 59). Despite the value placed on livestock, according to Richard Elphick, "neither sheep nor cattle were regularly slaughtered. Slaughter was undertaken chiefly to celebrate special occasions . . . or as a sacrifice to combat illness among humans or stock" (60); milk was a much more valued nutritional source, because it did not require depletion of an owner's livestock population. Furthermore, the fact that animal sacrifice was practiced to save livestock as well as humans clearly indicates the value the Khoikhoi placed on livestock animals, a value that, while it may have been predicated on the need for the subsistence that animals allotted, is at least structured on a sense of respect for the inherent value of the animal.

By the late 1600s, however, the Khoikhoi lost their livestock in large part because of the Dutch East India Company's policies of robbery and military action, as well as by virtue of the Dutch colonizers' "spread of new diseases, interdiction of chiefly aggrandizement, expropriation of pastures, [and] demand for Khoikhoi labor" (Elphick 174). As the Cape settlers moved inland, they appropriated not only large tracts of land, but also any livestock that was on that land (Ohlson and Stedman 21). The contested role of cattle in South Africa was still apparent well into the twentieth century, when "voluntary" removals, like the Mogopa removal of 1984, for example, forced black South Africans to leave their farms and sell their cattle for mere pittance to Boer farmers. Because "cattle are a measure of a man's success in the villages" (Goodman 325), the loss of cattle that one had cared for and seen increase over generations was not only a devastating financial blow, but was also akin to the loss of a kind of ancestral memory, the loss of a history dependent on human and animal codependency and interaction. For a people like the Xhosa, that ancestral memory is tainted by such a loss, but a loss of much more devastating proportions. During the Cattle Killing, the cattle became the scapegoat of the Xhosa people, who felt that butchering their animals and destroying their crops would guarantee the disappearance of the white settlers from South Africa.

Within the context of Magona's novel, the narrative of the killing is juxtaposed against the murder of a white American woman by a black South African man. The act is retributive justice, a way for Mxolisi to symbolically claim a life in return for having witnessed a specific incident, the killing of two of his friends by police when he is a young boy. When the police come to his house in search of the boys, who are hiding in the wardrobe, a four-year-old Mxolisi, thinking he is playing a game, tells the officers where his friends are hiding. After the officers shoot the two boys, Mxolisi "zipped his mouth and would not say one word. Not one word more — for the next two years" (148). But the murder is also an act of symbolic retribution for the more generalized killings — by both black and white perpetrators — that surrounds Mxolisi, his family, and the rest of Guguletu. Finally, Nongqawuse's failed prophecy of 1856, which stated that after the Xhosa killed their cattle "the people with hair like the silken threads of corn would be no more" (180), is replaced with another prophecy in the form of a communal chant uttered by the township South Africans in 1993: "one settler, one bullet" (182), the call that drives the angry mob in *Mother to Mother* to kill the golden-haired Amy Biehl. While the nature of this scapegoat mentality is not dependent on a colonial infrastructure, it is impossible to read the scapegoat narrative of the Cattle Killing outside of the colonial situation imposed on the Xhosa. The destruction of crops and animals is clearly indicative of mentalities in transition; physically powerless against the British colonizers, the Xhosa displaced their aggression onto entities that they constructed as other for perhaps the first time in their history: animals and the land. The fact that the death of the cattle and destruction of the crops was intended to bring about the regeneration of plants, animals, *and* humans points to an attempt to restore a more interdependent and holistic order while abolishing the colonial imperative toward dualistic thinking. The Cattle Killing was an effort to preempt colonial rule, returning the Xhosa to their state of existence as "unspoiled" (180), instead of seeking to progress by colonial standards and engaging in the capitalist exchange of currency, the "button without a hole" (182) described by Mandisa's grandfather. As such, and because Xhosa action was displaced onto the animal body as symbolic sacrifice, just as the anger of the mob is displaced onto the body of Amy Biehl, the goal of the movement, to drive the whites from South Africa, failed.

Tatomkhulu's retelling of the killing spans ten pages of the text, and his story imparts to a young Mandisa the reality that what is true in any narrative may depend on who is telling that narrative and who is listening. Furthermore, he provides her with a portrait of the Xhosa, their lifestyle, and their relationship to their land that differs markedly from Mandisa's description of life in 1993 for the people of Guguletu, a "congested" place where "the streets are narrow, debris-filed, full of gullies alive with flies, mosquitoes, and sundry vermin thriving in pools of stagnant water" (27) in which children play. Furthermore, the land is not arable but sandy, unable to "hold down anything, not even wild grass. . . . It would take a hundred years of people living on it to ground the sand and trample some life into it so that it would support plant and animal" (28). This description of Guguletu as a congested, dirty, miserable wasteland serves to illustrate the historical result of the Xhosa Cattle Killing; when the killing did not drive whites into the sea as Nongqawuse had predicted, the Xhosa were forced to give up and exploit the land by working in diamond mines and participating in the white capitalist commerce that later supported the creation of townships like Guguletu. Magona's extensive inclusion of Tatomkhulu's contrasting oral history lesson clearly indicates an authorial desire to set the record straight with regard to the killing, but her strategy in this regard perpetuates, at least as an aside, a somewhat problematic myth concerning indigenous South African people's relationships with their environment. Tatomkhulu's story is replete with conservationist and environmentalist rhetoric, from his oratory reference to his ancestors as "Readers of Nature's Signs" who "allowed themselves fallacious belief" (176), to his statement that "cattle are not for food," that "when one is hungry, there is corn in the field" (177). Every part of the cattle was used by the Xhosa, Mandisa's grandfather claims, from the milk to the dung to the skin and bones. Nothing was wasted by Mandisa's Xhosa ancestors, who also "diligently tended their fields" (178). The implications of killing cattle by the Xhosa, a "cattle-worshipping nation" (176), and razing tenderly nurtured crops, therefore, is all the more profound. While much of this sentiment is true—as Beinart and Coates claim, while animals were killed for consumption in precolonial South Africa, "indigenous peoples actively fattened the land," practicing ecological conservatism, "rather than live off its fat" (52)—there emerges the familiar danger of equating environmental consciousness with an indigenous group, in this case the precolonial Xhosa.

The current environmental situation in South Africa according to Patrick Bond in *Unsustainable South Africa* is dire: as a result of its continued dependence on coal, South Africa maintains "one of the world's worst global greenhouse gas emissions, corrected for population size and income" (10); furthermore, water, at least for the poor, is scarce and often contaminated with pollutants. In a narrative that mirrors Mandisa's earlier account of living conditions in Guguletu, Guguletu resident Caroline Nongauza, who spoke to Bond in 2001, claims "there are about four or five taps of water providing the whole area [of Tambo Square with water]. I have to walk fifteen minutes from my shack to the tap. . . . We are still using the bucket system of toilets, which is disgusting. Our children are always sick as a result" (qtd. in Bond 186). As a result of such factors, cholera broke out in KwaZulu-Natal in 2002 (16), and cholera continues to persist in South Africa. As we have seen to be the case in India, in South Africa, damming, as a remedy to the water situation, has resulted in environmental activist uproar over the destruction of ecosystems—as was the case with the Katse-Mohale Dams that destroyed the habitats of the endangered Mulati Minnow, bearded vulture, and four other "globally threatened" species (145). Dam building projects also further displace various groups whose land must be flooded in the damming process. In terms of arable land for farming, the Land Act of 1913 left 87 percent of the land to white farmers and displaced millions of blacks into overcrowded Bantustans. Over time, these areas have been vastly overgrazed and inefficiently farmed, and the result has been degradation of wetlands (41). While all of these circumstances — overcrowded living conditions, overgrazed land, greenhouse gasses, and inadequate or stagnant water — as well as others, including deforestation, industrial development, and pollution from mining and aluminum smelting, have become markedly detrimental in the period after colonization, particularly after the implementation of apartheid, we cannot assume that there has ever been a pristine (or in Mandisa's grandfather's words, "unspoiled") South African environment, at least not since the arrival of humans.

In *The Rise of Conservation in South Africa: Settlers, Livestock, and the Environment*, William Beinart debunks the myth of an Edenic and unspoiled South African past: "Human survival necessitates environmental disturbance, nor is nature in itself static. There is no possibility of restoring a pristine environment in South Africa — or anywhere else — short of the complete abandonment of farming. . . . In this context, a concept of environmental transformation should be set beside that of degradation" (390).

During the nineteenth century, according to Beinart, settlers and missionaries made note of "the environmental profligacy of African farmers and their apparent propensity for cutting down trees" (335– 36). Furthermore, indigenous South Africans prior to white intrusion, like the indigenous New Zealanders I discussed earlier in this chapter, were not inherently environmentalists and often established a pattern of environmental degradation that was exacerbated by white settlers. According to Patrick Bond, "the conquest of nature dates to the Bantu people." But, he claims, "the most disastrous . . . moments were reserved for white traders, bureaucrats, farmers, bankers, miners, industrialists, tourist-industry moguls, road and dam builders, even nuclear engineers" (8). Therefore, attempts to divide people of different races and historical periods in South Africa into groups of either environmentalist or environmentally destructive results in the creation of a mythology that fails to accomplish any real work in the way of offering solutions to South Africa's current environmental crisis.

Such a point is apparent in Magona's rendering of Nongqawuse's prophecy's focus on the restoration of a precolonial environmental purity as a prophecy based on another myth, one that has contributed to the cyclical violence responsible for the death of Amy Biehl. Instead of the divisiveness generated and perpetuated by the prophecy that led to the killing, Magona advocates, through her telling of the story of Mama Afrika—and in *Mother to Mother* as well—for a reevaluation of the maternal, one that is positioned in the rhetoric of eco-socialism, a movement that calls for popular mobilization that is inclusive rather than divisive. According to Bond, in the eco-socialist sense, "the issues associated with the survival of society's oppressed communities can only be understood and tackled through an increasing convergence of green, brown, feminist, racial/ethnic justice" (422). Magona's Mama Afrika calls for this recognition: "Sibanye! We are one. All nature is linked. What happens to any part of that chain cannot but affect when happens to another. People and forests, rivers, seas, mountains, deserts and wetlands; beasts of the forest and those of the home . . . everything is one—connected, mutually dependent." At the end of *Mother to Mother* however, Mandisa, despite her desire to move beyond the model of retributive violence, is unable to escape the desire to return to a better past, no matter how mythic that past may be. Like her ancestors who wanted to believe Nongqawuse's prophecy that the killing of cattle would return them to a precolonial idealized existence, Mandisa also tries to position herself within an impossible moment *before*, in this case, the moment prior to the murder, the moment marked by "the resentment of three hundred years" (210). She says, "my son, perhaps not a murderer. Perhaps, not yet" (210).

The horses didn't want it—they swerved apart; the earth
didn't want it . . . the temples, the tank, the jail, the
palace, the birds, the carrion, the Guest House . . . : they
didn't want it, they said in their hundred voices, "No,
not yet," and the sky said, "No, not there."
—E. M. FORSTER, *A Passage to India*

"Tomorrow . . . tomorrow . . ." he murmured to himself.
—NGUGI WA THIONG'O, *Petals of Blood*

She turned to say it once again: "*Naaley.*" Tomorrow.
—ARUNDHATI ROY, *The God of Small Things*

My son, perhaps not a murderer. Perhaps, not yet.
—SINDIWE MAGONA, *Mother to Mother*

Conclusion

Writing and Theorizing the
Environmental Interregnum

At the end of *The Future of Environmental Criticism*, Lawrence Buell
says, "I hate conclusions. A good book, essay, course, or lecture
should open up its subject, not shut it down. Conclusions are chrono-
logically hamstrung by the temptations to reach closure or attempt
prophecy in the narrow sense of prediction" (128). What makes
conclusions about ecocriticism particularly difficult to make, Buell
asserts, is that field's nature as a "fast-burgeoning movement" (128)
still in the process of becoming. At this point in my study, I find it
necessary to assert a similar sensibility with regard to the even newer
field of postcolonial ecocriticism. If the field of ecocritical inquiry is

still in a state of development and invention, then the convergent field of postcolonial ecocriticism is even more nascent and less codified. If ecocriticism attempts to strike a workable balance between the study of literature, the application of science, and the role of social activism, then postcolonial ecocriticism—particularly in its current manifestation as a white and, more often than not, Western academic discourse—is further complicated by its need to maintain rigorous and sustained literary and social critique while simultaneously working to avoid speaking for the environmental needs of non-Western peoples and landscapes. In the current moment, when many of the postcolonial loci discussed herein are characterized by a social uncertainty often marked by violence,[1] the future of various postcolonies, like the environmental future of planet Earth, is unknowable. Therefore, to conclude anything about the field of postcolonial ecocriticism seems premature at best, so I will end this study with a brief examination of the ways that the texts examined here gesture toward the future and call on readers to expand their geographical and cultural imaginations in the service of both peoples and environments in the global twenty-first century.

In the epigraph from E. M. Forster's 1924 novel *A Passage to India* that appears at the beginning of this chapter, Fielding receives the answer to his question of why he and Aziz cannot be friends in the here and now of colonial India. The final lines of Forster's narrative present the answer as not coming from Aziz, but from the juxtaposition of culture and nature. The laboring animals—the horses beneath Fielding and Aziz—and the land beneath the horses' hooves establish a hierarchy that extends upward to include the dualism of self and other inherent in the colonial relationship between the English Fielding and the Indian Aziz. Furthermore, the human-made symbols of religion and empire—the temples, the jail, the palace—stand incongruously beside one another, unable to reconcile their existence with the absolute alterity of the nonhuman natural world represented by the birds above and the ground below. The space depicted in this instant is the space of the Gramscian interregnum during which "the old is dying, and the new cannot be born; in this interregnum there arises a great diversity of morbid symptoms."[2] As this moment is depicted in Forster's India, binary oppositions step to the forefront, bookending a historical moment of betweenness, illuminated beneath an unyielding sky, forced further apart by rocks jutting from a seemingly divisive Earth. In the mythical "now" of the interregnum, the "voices" that resonate the loudest are not those of extant humanity; they are instead the dead, the landscape, and the animals depicted therein. As Fielding and Aziz realize, they, as representatives of the colonizing and colonized factions depicted in Forster's text, cannot "yet" engage in a discourse of friendship, a discourse that would require a measure of equality that is impossible in the present moment of the narrative. The ending of Forster's novel situates the space for friendship beyond the realm of the narrative and suggests, through the narrative assertions of "not now" and "not yet" (362), that such a space may open up at some unforeseen future moment.

Similarly, every work that I examine in this study either positions the "conclusion" of various environmental and postcolonial scenarios beyond the scope of the narrative, in some fictive future moment, or raises a dilemma that asks the audience to participate in the social and environmental issues raised within the text. These works define the space for both social and environmental change as existing beyond the interregnum moment defined within the parameters of the narrative. For example, Flora Nwapa's *Efuru* ends with a dialogic question about why the women worship "her"—either Uhamiri or Efuru—despite the fact that she does not have children. The answer, in my reading, has positive resonances for both the Igbo environment and for Igbo women in the 1940s-era Nigeria depicted in the book. In Yann Martel's *Life of Pi*, the question posed to the Japanese officers by Pi as to which is the better story, the one with animals or the one without, is on the one hand about the nature of belief, but on the other can be read as a metaphor for environmental depletion and subsequent species extinction. Pi's question and defense of zoos raise another question about what constitutes the better world, the one with nonhuman animals or the one that we come ever closer to day by day, the world without. J. M. Coetzee's *Disgrace* does not end with a dilemma; indeed, it ends with David's sacrificial giving up of the dog he has grown to love. However, the novel situates at its end a place of beginning, however bleak that beginning may be. Lucy states that her status as raped, pregnant, and ready to marry Petrus is "perhaps . . . a going point to start from again," a point at which, David claims, she becomes "like a dog" (205). At the end of the Coetzee's novel, the future is unknowable just as Lucy's baby remains unborn, and the landscape on which Lucy lives and works will be shaped by a new set of unforeseeable circumstances. Similarly, at the end of Sindiwe Magona's *Mother to Mother*, Amy Biehl's murder has not yet occurred, and Mandisa imagines her son "perhaps not yet" (210) a murderer and the prophecy made during the Cattle Killing, for the restoration of the land to the Xhosa people, perhaps not yet nullified.

Both Ngugi wa Thiong'o's *Petals of Blood* and Arundhati Roy's *The God of Small Things* also look beyond the present moment to some point beyond the "not yet" depicted in the works. The final word uttered by both Karega and Ammu is, in fact, "tomorrow" (Thiong'o 345, Roy 321). The tomorrow that fills Karega with hope for a new Africa, a place where he and his fellow Kenyans can obtain equality through socialism, and a place devoid of environmental pollution and degradation is a space imagined by Ngugi when he wrote the novel in the 1970s. Sadly, in the present moment of the twenty-first century, that tomorrow has not yet arrived, as is evidenced by Kenya's political turmoil and environmental crises. Conversely, the reader realizes, because of the circular structure of the narrative, that the tomorrow that Ammu promises to Velutha will never arrive. The river that defines both Ayemenem and Velutha serves as the boundary between touchable and untouchable Indian woman and man that cannot be transgressed without violent consequences for the transgressors. Velutha's presumed "pollution" of Ammu when the twins are eight is later mirrored by the literal decimation and pollution of the river as a result of pesticides, feces, and damming. Joy Williams's *The Quick & the Dead* is similarly nonlinear. Just as Roy's novel blurs the line between past and present by presenting time as circular, Williams's novel blurs the distinction between life and death, and, through its presentation of the decimation of African animal species as a result of safaris, demonstrates the danger, both to the environment and to the psyche, of losing a connection to one's ancestral past. The novel ends in an enigmatic place in which this connection to the past has been severed, and the narrator speaks directly to the reader: "you have never seen such animals as these. . . . In their jaws you are carried so effortlessly . . . that you think it will never end, you long for it never to end, and then you wake and know that, indeed, they have not brought you back" (307). A return to the past, in Williams's novel as elsewhere in this study, is impossible, but *The Quick & the Dead* presents a connection to the past as absolutely necessary if we are to salvage what is left of both our humanity and the natural world in order to move forward into the future.

The tentative hope that is present at the end of Zakes Mda's *The Heart of Redness,* inherent in the fact that the building of the casino is averted and an ecotourist backpacker hostel is built instead, is pessimistic, as Camagu realizes that greed and environmental disregard in South Africa will eventually allow the casino to come into being. Mda's narrative places responsibility for the preservation of South Africa's natural spaces on the younger generation, as is evidenced by another dialogic question, this one about Heitsi: "how will he carry out the business of saving his people?" (277). While Mda's narrative presents an ecotourist model that may work for the time being, the narrative's skepticism of the permanence of that model is evident. The one unequivocally hopeful ending that appears in any of the works in this study takes place at the end of Keri Hulme's *the bone people,* but getting to a place of genuine hope for Kerewin, Joe, and Simon is a painful process. Hulme's novel presents a New Zealand where the Maori and Pakeha must alternately destroy one another and their environment before they can begin to work together to build a more sustainable, multicultural future. The optimism that characterizes Hulme's "end at the beginning" is dependent on the disparate populations of New Zealanders coming together in a new configuration to take care of one another and of the land. The vision imparted in Hulme's novel, both with regard to the environment and to the creation of a multicultural Aotearoa, may be utopian, but it is dependent on a recognition, by both Maori and Pakeha, of the ways that the environment has been compromised throughout the history of both New Zealand and Aotearoa. To remedy the situation, the novel suggests, both factions must work together to overcome a precolonial and colonial history of environmental devastation.

Deane Curtin asserts that "in an increasingly interconnected world, we need to recognize that [our Western] understanding of nature's zones is distinctively American, and it results from a kind of cultural amnesia. This cognitive and emotional lapse in the ways we think of people in relation to place continues to affect our conception of the American past, as well as the ways we think of ourselves today and into the future" (3). In all of the works examined in this study, a sense of ambivalence is pervasive; even Hulme's novel ends with the Maori phrase "TE MUTUNGA — RANEI TE TAKE" (445), which means "the end — or the beginning" (450). The environmental future of New Zealand, the text suggests, is as nascent and unformed as its multicultural identity was in the 1980s era it depicts. Similarly, all of the environmental and social futures of the postcolonial loci that I examine here are unknown and unknowable, in a continual process of being shaped alternately by histories of indigenous cultural eradication and subsequent postcolonial invention and by the exploitation of natural resources, by both colonists and indigenous peoples alike. In the contemporary moment, the twenty-first-century world is increasingly shaped by a global consciousness that, in its best manifestations, abandons a nation-based worldview in favor of a more holistic model in which cultures are interconnected and interdependent. The first step in moving beyond the present moments depicted in the narratives included in this study, whether they be 1970s era Kenya, the 1990s of the United States and India, or South Africa in the twenty-first century, the texts suggests, is the ability to imagine — for both indigenous and settler populations — a future in which this global conception of cultures extends into the realm of the noncultural, into the sphere of the environmental. In terms of the postcolonial environment, as in terms of all forms of creation and invention, imagination is at the forefront of change and is the impetus for possibility.

NOTES

INTRODUCTION

1. Harrison is, of course, speaking about Achebe's lecture entitled "An Image of Africa," a text that is now widely anthologized.

2. Benita Parry echoes a similar assertion when she notes that "those who have been or are still engaged in colonial struggles against contemporary forms of neo-colonialism could well read the theorizing of discourse analysts [like Homi K. Bhabha and Gayatri Spivak] with considerable disbelief at the construction this puts on the situation they are fighting against" (26).

3. Cheryll Glotfelty maintains that there is a strong connection between changes in the profession and changes in the "real world," and she claims that "we have witnessed the feminist and multi-ethnic critical movements radically transform the profession, the job market, and the canon. And because they have transformed the profession, they are helping to transform the world" (xxiv). The very real sense of this discourse is that it arises from a lived ethic that informs life and scholarship alike.

4. Buell asserts in his 2005 text *The Future of Environmental Criticism,* "the environmental turn in literary and cultural studies emerged as a self-conscious movement little more than a dozen years ago. Since then it has burgeoned, however. A tell tale index is the growth within the last decade of the Association for the Study of Literature and the Environment" (1).

5. Furthermore, unlike Head, who reads ecocriticsm as potentially confined within the academy, Buell sees environmental criticism as engaging beyond academia in ways that provoke a "self-examination of premises that has intensified the movement beyond an initial concentration on nature-oriented literature . . . to take into account urban as well as rural loci and environmental justice concerns as well as nature preservation" (*Future* 7).

6. Anthony Vital echoes these sentiments in his discussion of an emergent South African ecocriticism in an article published the same year as Nixon's. He discusses "two sources of tension which can be considered definitive of any postcolonial understanding of ecology and crucial to any ecocriticism alert to postcolonial conditions" ("Situating Ecology" 298–99). These are

the fact that notions of conservation historically have been linked to empire, and the fact that postcolonial environmentalism will be "unrepentantly anthropocentric," a condition that will "generate inevitable friction between the tendency to value human need and the recognition (supplied by ecology) that the natural world has its own value" (299).

7. Soper comments on the connection between the nature/human divide and Western notions of cultural superiority: "what is deployed, as if it were a universal concept, carries with it traces of a semantic history that has always defined what is more properly 'human' on the model of Western culture, and selected in favor of that in its very disposition to think of other societies as 'primitive,' 'closer to nature' or less alienated from it" (61).

8. Mazel's work, both in this essay and elsewhere, focuses on American literature and takes the position that "no matter how it is defined, ecocriticism seems less a singular approach or method than a constellation of approaches, having little more in common than a shared concern with the environment" (*Century* 2), and he has critiqued the concept of "nature" as "universal," arguing that "any politically actionable environment . . . rests upon two creations of difference: an initial discrimination of an inside from an outside, and a secondary marking off and foregrounding of some targeted portion of the remaining totality" (*American Literary* 2). Mazel compares choices about which "remaining totality" is preserved with choices about which literary texts make up the American literary canon, and he concludes that Frederick Law Olmstead's comparison of the United States parks movement to England's early literary movement points to the way that "the most spectacular New World landscapes were to be transformed into a canon of Great Texts that would discipline an entire society" (*American Literary* 4). The result, of course, is a fictitious narrative of universality, both in terms of the literature that makes up the canon as well as in terms of what Mazel calls "ecological literacy." These points are significant in that they speak to—without explicitly stating—the way that the canon is challenged by the project of postcolonial studies and the way that a universal understanding of "nature" can be challenged by studies that extend ecocritical analysis beyond the realm of the West.

9. According to Lawrence Buell, "the term 'ecocriticism' was coined in the late 1970s . . . but its antecedents stretch back much further" (13).

10. Said's work "relentlessly unmasks the ideological disguises of imperialism" (Gandhi 67) that are present in imaginative works of art. Said takes the late eighteenth century as his starting point and notes that in literary, artistic, and scholarly representations, the Muslim world was "viewed as if

framed by the classroom, the criminal court, the prison, the illustrated manual" (41), an ordering that situates the "Orient," not as a place, but as "a *topos*, a set of references, a congeries of characteristics, that seems to have its origin in a quotation, or a fragment of a text, or a citation from someone's work on the Orient, or some bit of previous imagining, or an amalgam of all these" (177).

11. Garrard states very explicitly that "I will be dealing principally with British and North American literature and culture, although the principles of ecocriticism would of course admit of more general application" (5).

12. Guha discusses such entities as the Narmada Bachao Andolan and Kenya's Green Belt movement, headed by Waangari Matthai, as well as Nigerian opposition to oil drilling as manifest in the activism and death of Ken Saro-Wiwa.

13. According to Joy Williams, wildlife protection areas generate the illusion that "you have entered a portion of the earth that wild animals have retained possession of. The illusion here is that wild animals exist" ("Safariland" 27).

14. According to Negative Population Growth's Web page "Fast Facts about U.S. Population Growth," "over four million babies are born each year in the United States. The U.S. population is growing by about 2.5 million people each year. Of that, immigration contributes over one million people to the U.S. population annually. The U.S. fertility rate is currently 2.0 births per woman, an increase from 1.8 in 1988. The United States has one of the highest natural growth rates (0.7%) of any industrialized country in the world. For comparison, the United Kingdom's natural increase is one quarter the rate of the U.S. at 0.2%, while Germany's natural increase is 0. Using the Census Bureau's medium projections, U.S. population will grow to 394 million by the year 2050" (11 August 2009, http://www.npg.org/facts/uspopfax.htm).

15. There has also been an international explosion of conferences and conference panels interested in submissions from literary scholars who work in the area of environmental postcolonial study. In addition to ASLE's annual conference, some of the more recent include a panel at the annual British Commonwealth and Postcolonial Studies Conference entitled "Convergent Evolution: The Continuing Development of Postcolonial Ecocriticism" (February 15 and 16, 2008, in Savannah, Ga.) and the third annual South African Literature and Ecology Colloquium (October 6–8, 2006, at Rhodes University, Grahamstown, South Africa). Another conference, Re-Routing the Postcolonial, at the University of Northampton, UK,

November 4–5, 2006, submitted a call for papers that engaged with the ways that "global capitalism . . . which redefines culture as both production and commodification, helps reroute the debate on eco-environmental issues through a new model of geopolitics." Finally, there was a panel titled "Postcolonial Environments" at the Modern Language Association's annual convention in December 2007.

CHAPTER ONE. Inventing Tradition and Colonizing the Plants

1. In his 1882 lecture "What is a Nation?" Renan claims that "forgetfulness, and I shall even say historical error, form an essential factor in the creation of a nation; and thus it is that the progress of historical studies may often be dangerous to the nationality" (66).

2. Hobsbawm's and Anderson's studies, both published in 1983, fall approximately midway between the post-independence 1960s Kenya depicted by Ngugi and the late 1990s South Africa of Mda's novel; Renan's 1882 lecture was delivered one year after Boer forces defeated the British in South Africa in 1881 in the first Anglo-Boer war, and three years before the scramble for Africa incited the Berlin Conference of 1884–85, during which Britain staked its claim over what is present-day Kenya (Gatheru 7).

3. In terms of invention and imagination with regard to the nation, Arnove argues that Kenya itself is a fiction, a colonial construct (278).

4. In *The Location of Culture*, Bhabha asserts that "Mimicry is . . . the sign of a double articulation; a complex strategy of reform, regulation and discipline, which 'appropriates' the Other as it visualizes power. Mimicry is also the sign of the inappropriate, however, a difference or recalcitrance which coheres the dominant strategic function of colonial power, intensifies surveillance, and poses an immanent threat to both 'normalized' knowledges and disciplinary powers" (86).

5. "Gikuyu" and "Kikuyu" are both acceptable spellings. I use "Gikuyu" in my study; authors that I quote may use "Kikuyu."

6. See, in particular, Simon Gikandi, *Ngugi wa Thiong'o* (Cambridge: Cambridge UP, 2001), and his "Traveling Theory: Ngugi's Return to English," *Research in African Literatures* 31.2 (2000): 194–209; and Ângela Lamas Rodrigues, "Beyond Nativism: An Interview with Ngugi wa Thiong'o," *Research in African Literatures* 35.3 (2004): 161–67.

7. Ngugi was charged by Vice President Daniel arap Moi under the Public Security Act and imprisoned in Mamiti Maximum Security Prison in

December of 1977. He was detained for a year without trial because of the uncensored political message inherent in his 1977 play *Ngaahika Ndeenda* (*I Will Marry When I Want*) (Gikandi, *Ngugi* 186).

8. Such passages as "our present day historians . . . insist we only arrived here yesterday. Where went all the Kenyan people who used to trade with China, India, Arabia long before Vasco da Gama came to the scene and on the strength of gunpowder ushered in an era of blood and terror and instability—an era that climaxed in the reign of imperialism over Kenya?" (67) seem particularly invested with Ngugi's need to retell Kenyan history. The text is filled with similar examples.

9. According to Chris McGreal's article in the *Guardian*, "the Kenyan Human Rights commission . . . says about 160,000 people were held in dire conditions and tens of thousands were tortured to get them to renounce their oath to the Mau Mau." Furthermore, "after the emergency was lifted in 1961 an official report determined that 32 whites were killed while more than 11,000 Africans died, many of them civilians."

10. According to Gatheru, women were excluded from minor and major oath taking, but they could oath against wrongdoings, particularly of a sexual or marital nature (149).

11. For more on this discussion, see chapter 4 of this study, in particular my analysis of Flora Nwapa's *Efuru*.

12. In his dedication, Mda writes "I am grateful . . . to Jeff Peires, whose research—wonderfully recorded in *The Dead Will Arise* . . .—informed the historical events in my fiction." It is as if Mda takes Peires's suggestion in that aforementioned work: "even if no further information can be obtained, it must be possible to write histories of Nongqawuse from other perspectives than mine" (322).

13. In "Duplicity and Plagiarism in Zakes Mda's *Heart of Redness*," Andrew Offenburger has claimed that Mda's novel plagiarizes Peires's work.

14. According to Robert Ross, "so effectively did [Sir George Grey, Governor of the Cape Colony] exploit the Cattle-Killing that many Xhosa today are convinced that Grey himself was hiding in the reeds by the Gxarha, whispering to Nongqawuse" (53).

15. I have read the literal Cattle Killing and fictional representations of it as a form of scapegoating. See *Writing "Out of All the Camps": J. M. Coetzee's Narratives of Displacement*, particularly chapter 5, for this analysis.

16. See, in particular, Sindiwe Magona's *Mother to Mother*, a text that I examine in detail in chapter 4 of this study, and African American author John Edgar Wideman's *The Cattle Killing* (Boston: Houghton Mifflin, 1996).

CHAPTER TWO. Safari, Zoo, and Dog Pound

1. For example, according to McNeill, between 1890 and 1990, there was a 406 percent increase in the number of cattle, a 951 percent increase in the number of pigs, and a 1,525 percent increase in the number of poultry (264).

2. It seems appropriate, given my reading of the environmentally destructive nature of various traditions invented in postcolonial societies to note that Makah whaling in the twenty-first century provides another such example.

3. In a February 20, 2003, story in the *New York Times*, Keith Bradsher states, "the city has never had a zoo, at least not as far as anyone here can remember. So in a case of life imitating art, officials have set out to build a zoo" in the hope of increasing tourism to the area, particularly after all the publicity generated for the area when *Life of Pi* won the Booker Award.

4. See, for example, Marc Maufort and Franca Bellarsi, eds., *Reconfigurations: Canadian Literatures and Postcolonial Identities* (Brussels: Peter Lang, 2002); Laura Moss, ed., *Is Canada Postcolonial?: Unsettling Canadian Literature* (Waterloo, Ont.: Wilfred Laurier UP, 2003); Diana Brydon, "Global Designs, Postcolonial Critiques: Rethinking Canada in Dialogue with Diaspora," *Ilha do Desterro: A Journal of Language and Literature* 40 (2001): 61–84; and Donna Bennett, "English Canada's Postcolonial Complexities," *Essays on Canadian Writing* 51–52 (1993–94): 164–210.

5. This information can be found on her author biographical information on her Random House author page, 17 Aug. 2009, http://www.randomhouse.com/author/results.pperl?authorid=33270.

6. A May 21, 2007, search of the MLA bibliography pulls up only one hit, an essay in the *Journal of Translations Studies* on Williams's short story "Harmony" (Yakin Orhun, "Ingilizceden Türkçe'ye Üç Çok Kisa Öykü Çevirisi," *Çeviribilim ve Uygulamalari Dergisi/Journal of Translation Studies/Revue de Traduction et d'Interprétation* 10 [2000]: 125–30).

7. Carter even thinks at one point, "didn't three symbolize spiritual synthesis? Didn't it solve the problem posed by that infernal dualism?" (257).

8. Honey provides statistics for several such ventures that indicate that "the involvement of and benefits to the local community have so far been fairly minimal" (368). For more information, see chapter 10, "South Africa: People and Parks under Majority Rule" in Honey.

9. Honey says that "a hunter brings in 100 times more revenue than a nonhunting tourist; the Wildlife Conservation Society of Tanzania estimates it is 55 times more. Either way, the difference is enormous" (245).

10. The animal-welfare movement in South Africa is an incredibly recent phenomenon. Michelè Pickover claims that "since 1990 the effects of the animal rights movement have begun to be felt in South Africa" (13).

11. Numerous critics—like Teresa Dovey and Derek Attridge—have commented on Coetzee's refusal to ascribe to a "master narrative" of history. In an interview with Tony Morphet, Coetzee himself has claimed that he will not "produce a master narrative for a set of texts that claim to deny all master narratives" (464).

12. For information about rape statistics in South Africa, see "Rape Statistics: South Africa and Worldwide," *Rape Survivor Journey*, 9 Jan. 2008, 5 Sept. 2009, http://www.rape.co.za/index2.php?option=com_content&do_pdf=1&id=875.

13. Coetzee writes dialogically in the Bakhtinian sense, as one who refuses to claim the narrative position of the monologic insider, the textual presence that has access to the answers, or access to contested notions of the truth. According to Bakhtin, "the word in living conversation is directly, blatantly, oriented toward a future answer-word: it provokes an answer, anticipates it and structures itself in the answer's direction. Forming itself in an atmosphere of the already spoken, the word is at the same time determined by that which has not yet been said but which is needed and in fact anticipated by the answering word. Such is the situation in any living dialogue" (280). For a fuller explanation of "dialogic drag," see Wright, particularly chapter 5.

14. Personal email, 29 Jan. 2007.

15. For *Life & Times of Michael K* in 1983 and for *Disgrace* in 1999. Coetzee was the first author to win the prize twice.

16. See in particular Derek Attridge, "Age of Bronze, State of Grace: Music and Dogs in Coetzee's *Disgrace*," *Novel: A Forum on Fiction* 34.1 (2000): 98–121; Lucy Graham, "'Yes, I am giving him up': Sacrificial Responsibility and Likeness with Dogs in J. M. Coetzee's Recent Fiction," *Scrutiny2: Issues in English Studies in Southern Africa* 7.1 (2000): 4–15; Herron; and Jolly.

CHAPTER THREE. "Swimming in the River of Life" but Caught in "the Stream of Justice"

1. It is worth noting that Mukherjee has been criticized for her unrealistic portrait of a poor Indian woman, who would have not had the resources to travel to the United States after her husband is murdered (see Gurleen Grewal, "Born Again American: The Immigrant Consciousness in Jasmine,"

in *Bharati Mukherjee: Critical Perspectives,* ed. Emmanuel S. Nelson [New York: Garland, 1993], 181–96).

2. Roy has published several volumes of essays since the publication of *The God of Small Things,* including *The Cost of Living* (1999), *Power Politics* (2002), *The Algebra of Infinite Justice* (2002), *War Talk* (2003), and *The Ordinary Person's Guide to Empire* (2004). Of this proliferation of work, much of which appeared initially as singular essays in British and American news magazines, Julie Mullaney says, "the ubiquity of this work and its creative recycling by a number of publishers and journalists suggests, significantly, that in their lexicon, at the very least, the name of Roy is a byword for protest" (58).

3. Just as King Pandu has six sons, the five legitimate princes the Pandavas and their abandoned brother Karna, there are also six police officers whom the narrator describes as "New-Age princes in funny pointed helmets. Cardboard lined with cotton. Hairoil stained. Their shabby khaki crowns" (288).

4. Shiva has been a champion of the Indian environment since the 1970s and has written prolifically on environmental issues, women's rights, and globalization.

5. Gordimer made this claim in her now famous 1982 essay "Living in the Interregnum," during which she spoke about the black state that was coming into being in South Africa. Interestingly, Gordimer's status as overtly and legitimately political has not been called into question in the way that Roy's has.

6. We can tell that this second appearance is a flashback because in both instances when Roy appears on the river, her hair is long. In the current context of waiting for her date with the Supreme Court, her hair is short.

7. Medha Patkar is the founder of the Narmada Bachao Andolan.

CHAPTER FOUR. Prophecy, Motherhood, and the Land

1. We see literary representations of this phenomenon often enough in male-authored texts, for example, in Ngugi wa Thiong'o's *Weep Not, Child* (1964) when Njoroge's father is castrated, and in J. M. Coetzee's *Waiting for the Barbarians* (1980) when the Magistrate, who has disobeyed the colonial imperative to torture and to confess, is dressed in women's clothing and hung from a tree.

2. In Marie Umeh's interview with Flora Nwapa, "The Poetics of Economic Independence for Female Empowerment" (*Research in African Literatures* 26

[1995]: 22–30), the following exchange takes place that highlight's Nwapa's correcting—as opposed to merely imitating—the style of established male authors:

UMEH: The critic Katherine Frank, in an article entitled "Women Without Men: The Feminist Novel in Africa," describes you as a radical feminist. What is your opinion of this assessment?

NWAPA: I don't think that I'm a radical feminist. I don't even accept that I'm a feminist. I accept that I'm an ordinary woman who is writing about what she knows. I try to project the image of women positively. I attempt to correct our men-folks when they started writing, when they wrote little or less about women, where their female characters are prostitutes and ne'er-do-wells. I started writing to tell them that this is not so. When I do write about women in Nigeria, in Africa, I try to paint a positive picture about women because there are many women who are very, very positive in their thinking, who are very, very independent, and very, very industrious.

UMEH: What do you perceive to be the major ideological difference between male and female writing in Nigeria?

NWAPA: The male writers have disappointed us a great deal by not painting the female character as they should paint them. I have to say that there's been a kind of an ideological change. I think male writers are now presenting women as they are. They are not only mothers; they are not only palm collectors; they are not only traders; but they are also wealthy people. Women can stand on their own. (27)

3. In fact, *Efuru* even indicts Igbo complicity with the slave trade and colonization. The narrator notes that the cannon that announces Efuru's father's death commemorates "the departure of a great son, the last of a generation that had direct contact with the white people who exchanged their cannons, hot drinks and cheap ornaments for black slaves" (203).

4. It is equally possible to argue that the question is not Efuru's question about why women worship Uhamiri but is instead the narrator's question about why the women worship Efuru, who over the course of the novel becomes the goddess incarnate.

5. For more information, go to the Web site of the World Igbo Environmental Foundation, Inc., http://www.wief.net/index.htm.

6. The goddess has various names. "Mammy Water" is, according to Jell-Bahlsen, "a Pidgin English name with different spellings — *Mami Wata, Mammywater, Mami Wota* — in West African coastal areas and near major bodies of water like rivers, lakes, and lagoons. There, the people refer to their highly localized divine waters as *Mammy Water* when addressing audiences beyond their local communities" (345).

7. See, for example, William Russell Bascom's *African Dilemma Tales* (Berlin: Walter de Gruyter Inc., 1975).

8. This idea is apparent in the fact that, according to DeLoughrey, "Hulme [who has one Maori grandparent] became a magnet for criticism for those who felt that her *whakapapa* was not substantial enough to justify her novel being awarded the Pegasus Prize for Maori Fiction in 1984" (187).

9. The terms of the Treaty of Waitangi have been debated since its inception in 1840, and the conflict surrounding the treaty is based primarily on two factors, first, the existence of two versions of the treaty, one in English and one in Maori, and second, that the terms of the Maori version of the treaty were never honored by the British. According to Bradley Reed Howard, "according to the Maori version of the text, and as Maori-speaking missionaries explained to the Maori, Britain recognized Maori independence and sovereignty, and in exchange the Maori granted the British the exclusive right to purchase their lands and recognized the British Crown as the source of ultimate justice and resolution of disputes, like a court of the international law of nations" (177).

10. But despite the fact that the bill went into full effect in 2005 ("Foreshore and Seabed"), declaring the state the owner of the coast, since Hulme wrote *the bone people*, the people of New Zealand have altered the course of some negative environmental policy, particularly with regard to rainforest logging. In 2000, for example, according to Bob Burton, the government of New Zealand introduced legislation that began to "bring to an end a 30-year campaign by environmentalists to stop the logging of publicly owned temperate rainforests" ("New Zealand"). While concessions were made to continue logging the five-hundred-year-old rimu trees until 2002, rainforest logging has finally been phased out. Other environmental debates, however, particularly over the protection of whales, have spilt the Maori, some of whom believe, as does Sir Tipene O'Regan, former chairman of the Ngai Tahu tribe, that environmentalists have taken whale protection to the extreme and "that conservation regulations greatly restricted the

ability of the Maori to access bone from whales that beached themselves on New Zealand's shores" (Burton, "Maori"). Others like Sandra Lee, also of the Ngai Tahu tribe, feel that "we must balance our customary use of material from stranded whales against our relationship with them. Some 'iwi' [tribes] regard the whale as an ancestor. My own 'iwi' holds to the tradition that we were guided here by one" (qtd. in Burton, "New Zealand").

11. Hulme herself has become publicly involved in the environmental debate in New Zealand, and regards herself as a "kaitiaki (guardian) of Okarito's lagoon, wetlands, and special character" (Newth). Hulme is one of only a handful of permanent residents of the West Coast settlement of Okarito, which is home to kahikatea and rimu rainforests as well as New Zealand's largest tract of unmodified wetland. She has been a pronounced voice in the fight against the development of the area as a tourist attraction. She claims that "there are plenty of dear little tourist traps up and down the coast. I think—and will fight to the utmost over this—that Okarito, as it currently is, is an iconic place, a place that many New Zealanders—and people from overseas—draw sustenance from" (qtd. in Newth). Inherent in such a philosophy is the belief that the land has intrinsic value, that one can gain strength from a relationship with the land as land as opposed to land as commodity, and such a philosophy, it would seem, has no historical grounding in either Maori or Pakeha tradition in New Zealand. The question of where such a philosophy originates, then, becomes as important as the philosophy itself.

12. Magona's novel is a fictionalization of the murder of Fulbright scholar Amy Biehl, who, as Magona claims in her author's preface to *Mother to Mother*, was killed "by a mob of black youth in Guguletu, South Africa in August of 1993" (v). Furthermore, Magona claims to have written the novel to answer some pertinent questions, particularly "what was the world of this young woman's killers, the world of those, young as she was young, whose environment failed to nurture them in the higher ideals of humanity and who, instead, became lost creatures of malice and destruction?" (v).

CONCLUSION

1. At the time of this writing, Alexander G. Higgins reports that "in a report released Wednesday [March 20, 2008], United Nations officials urged Kenya to prosecute 'gross human-rights violations,' including those perpetrated by police. The report said there was evidence that police were responsible for most of the gun deaths after the country's disputed vote. Kenyan

opposition leader Raila Odinga and President Mwai Kibaki both claimed victory in a Dec. 27 presidential election, unleashing weeks of bloodshed. More than 1,000 people were killed in the ensuing violence, which took on an ethnic dimension and exposed divisions over land and economic inequality."

2. Nadine Gordimer uses this quote from Gramsci as the epigraph to *July's People*. In a note in Gordimer's essay "Living in the Interregnum," Stephen Clingman notes that the quote appears in a slightly different translation in *Selections from the Prison Notebooks of Antonio Gramsci*, ed. and trans. Quintin Hoare and Geoffrey Nowell Smith (London: Lawrence & Wishart, 1971).

WORKS CITED

Adams, Carol J. *The Sexual Politics of Meat: A Feminist-Vegetarian Critical Theory.* New York: Continuum, 1996.

Allen, Bruce. "Facing the True Costs of Living: Arundhati Roy and Ishimure Michiko on Dams and Writing." *Coming into Contact: Explorations in Ecocritical Theory and Practice.* Ed. Annie Merrill, Ian Marshall, Daniel J. Philippon, and Adam W. Sweeting. Athens: U of Georgia P, 2007. 154–67.

Amadiume, Ifi. "Bodies, Choices, Globalizing National Enchantments: African Matriarchs and Mammy Water." *Meridians* 2.2 (2002): 41–66.

Anand, Divya. "Inhabiting the Space of Literature: An Ecocritical Study of Arundhati Roy's *God of Small Things* and O. V. Vijanyan's *The Legends of Khasak.*" *ISLE* 12.2 (2005): 95–108.

Anderson, Benedict. *Imagined Communities: Reflections on the Origins and Spread of Nationalism.* London: Verso, 1983.

Anderson, Martha G., and Philip M. Peek, eds. *Ways of the Rivers: Arts and Environment of the Niger Delta.* Los Angeles: UCLA Fowler Museum of Cultural History, 2002.

Andrade, Susan Z. "Rewriting History, Motherhood and Rebellion: Naming an African Women's Literary Tradition." *Research in African Literatures* 21.1 (1990): 91–110.

Armstrong, Timothy. "Wildlife Conservation in Kenya." *Modern Kenya: Social Issues and Perspectives.* Ed. Mary Ann Watson. Lanham, Md.: UP of America, 2000. 89–117.

Arnove, Anthony. "Pierre Bourdieu, the Sociology of Intellectuals, and the Language of African Literature." *Novel: A Forum on Fiction* 26.3 (1993): 278–96.

Ashcroft, W. D. "Intersecting Marginalities: Post-Colonialism and Feminism." *Kunapipi* 11.2 (1989): 23–35.

Atieno-Odhiambo, E. S. "The Formative Years: 1945–55." *Decolonizing and Independence in Kenya; 1940–93.* Ed. B. A. Ogot and W. R. Ochieng'. London: James Currey, 1995. 25–47.

Attridge, Derek. *J. M. Coetzee and the Ethics of Reading: Literature in the Event.* Chicago: U of Chicago P, 2004.

Attwell, David, and Barbara Harlow. "Interview with Sindiwe Magona." *Modern Fiction Studies* 46.1 (2000): 282–95.

Bakhtin, Mikhail. *The Dialogic Imagination: Four Essays.* Trans. Caryl Emerson and Michael Holquist. Ed. Michael Holquist. Austin: U of Texas P, 1981.

Barsamian, David. *The Checkbook and the Cruise Missile: Conversations with Arundhati Roy.* Cambridge, Mass.: South End P, 2004.

Baxter, Cindy, Paul Horsman, and Steve Kretzmann. "Ken Saro-Wiwa and Eight Ogoni People Executed: Blood on Shell's Hands." 10 Nov. 1995. Greenpeace Archive. 9 Mar. 2006, http://archive.greenpeace.org/comms/ken/murder.html.

Bazin, Nancy Topping. "Weight of Custom, Signs of Change: Feminism in the Literature of African Women." *World Literature Written in English* 25.2 (1985): 183–97.

Beinart, William. *The Rise of Conservation in South Africa: Settlers, Livestock, and the Environment, 1770–1950.* Oxford: Oxford UP, 2003.

Beinart, William, and Peter Coates. *Environment and History: The Taming of Nature in the usa and South Africa.* London: Routledge, 1995.

Benoit, Madhu. "Circular Time: A Study of Narrative Techniques in Arundhati Roy's *The God of Small Things.*" *World Literature Written in English* 38.2 (1998): 98–106.

Bhabha, Homi. *The Location of Culture.* London: Routledge, 1994.

Birbalsingh, Frank. *Novels and the Nation: Essays in Canadian Literature.* Toronto: tsar, 1995.

Birkeland, Janis. "Ecofeminism: Linking Theory and Practice." *Ecofeminism: Women, Animals, Nature.* Ed. Greta Gaard. Philadelphia: Temple UP, 1993. 13–59.

Boehmer, Elleke. "Stories of Women and Mothers: Gender and Nationalism in the Early Fiction of Flora Nwapa." *Motherlands: Black Women's Writing From Africa, the Caribbean and South Asia.* Ed. Susheila Nasta. London: The Women's P, 1991. 3–23.

Bond, Peter. *Unsustainable South Africa: Environment, Development, and Social Protest.* Pietermaritzburg: U of Natal P, 2002.

Bose, Brinda. "In Desire and Death: Eroticism as Politics in Arundhati Roy's *The God of Small Things.*" *ARIEL* 29.2 (1998): 59–72.

Bradsher, Keith. "Pondicherry Journal; The Zoo Is Fiction, but It Just Might Spring to Life." *New York Times* 20 Feb. 2003. 26 Aug. 2009, http://query.nytimes.com/gst/fullpage.html?res=9407E6D8143DF933A15751C0A9659C8B63&sec=travel.

Brown, Carson. "Life and Death Rituals." Review of Joy Williams's *The Quick & the Dead. January Magazine* Mar. 2001. 17 Aug. 2009, http://januarymagazine.com/fiction/quickanddead.html.

Buell, Lawrence. *The Future of Environmental Criticism: Environmental Crisis and Literary Imagination.* Oxford: Blackwell, 2005.

———. *Writing for an Endangered World: Literature, Culture, and Environment in the U.S. and Beyond.* Cambridge: Harvard UP, 2001.

Burton, Bob. "Maori People Split on Whaling." *Monitor* 4 Dec. 2000. 4 Sept. 2009, http://www.albionmonitor.com/0012a/copyright/maori-whale.html.

———. "New Zealand Bars Rainforest Logging." *Asia Times Online* 20 May 2000. 4 Sept. 2009, http://www.atimes.com/oceania/BE20Aho2.html.

Butler, Judith. *Bodies That Matter: On the Discursive Limits of "Sex."* New York: Routledge, 1993.

Caldwell, Gail. "Motherless Girls." Review of Joy Williams's *The Quick & the Dead. Boston Globe* 1 Oct. 2000. 17 Aug. 2009, http://www.pulitzer.org/archives/6425.

Carlson, Marvin. *Performance: A Critical Introduction.* London: Routledge, 2003.

Carson, Rachel. *Silent Spring.* New York: Mariner, 2002.

Chong, Jennifer. "Interview with Aradhana Seth." *Asia Pacific Arts* 1 Oct. 2004. ucla Asia Institute. 7 Jan. 2008, http://www.asiaarts.ucla.edu/article.asp?parentid=15190.

Coetzee, J. M. *Disgrace.* New York: Viking, 1999.

———. *The Lives of Animals.* Princeton: Princeton UP, 1999.

Cole, Stewart. "Believing in Tigers: Anthropomorphism and Incredulity in Yann Martel's *Life of Pi." Studies in Canadian Literature* 29.2 (2004): 22–36.

Curtin, Deane. *Environmental Ethics for a Postcolonial World.* Lanham, Md.: Rowman and Littlefield, 2005.

DeLoughrey, Elizabeth M. *Routes and Roots: Navigating Caribbean and Pacific Island Literatures.* Honolulu: U of Hawai'i P, 2007.

Duffy, Rosaleen. *A Trip Too Far: Eoctourism, Politics, and Exploitation.* London: Earthscan, 2002.

Dunlap, Thomas R. *Nature and the English Diaspora: Environment and History in the United States, Canada, Australia, and New Zealand.* Cambridge: Cambridge UP, 1999.

Dwyer, June. "Yann Martel's *Life of Pi* and the Evolution of the Shipwreck Narrative." *Modern Language Studies* 35.2 (2005): 9–21.

Dyson, Tim, Robert Cassen, and Leela Visaria, eds. *Twenty-First Century India: Population, Economy, Human Development, and the Environment.* Oxford: Oxford UP, 2004.

Edeh, Emmanuel M. P. *Towards an Igbo Metaphysics.* New Orleans: Loyola UP, 1985.

Egbo, Benedicta. *Gender, Literacy and Life Chances in Sub-Saharan Africa.* Bristol, Pa.: Multilingual Matters, 2000.

Elphick, Richard. *Kraal and Castle: The Founding of White South Africa.* New Haven: Yale UP, 1977.

Ezeibgo, Theodora Akachi. "Traditional Women's Institutions in Igbo Society: Implications for the Igbo Female Writer." *African Languages and Cultures* 3.2 (1990): 149–65.

Fee, Margery. "Inventing New Ancestors for Aotearoa." *International Literature in English: Essays on the Major Writers.* Ed. Robert L. Ross. New York: Garland, 1991. 53–62.

"Foreshore and Seabed Act 2004." *New Zealand Legislation: Acts.* 1 Jan. 2009, http://www.legislation.govt.nz/act/public/2004/0093/latest/DLM319839.html.

Forster, E. M. *A Passage to India.* New York: Harcourt Brace, 1924.

Fox, Stephen D. "Barbara Kingsolver and Keri Hulme: Disability, Family, and Culture." *Critique* 45.4 (2004): 405–60.

Friedrich, Bruce. "Vegetarianism in a Nutshell: The Environment." *Vegetarian 101* 13 May 2007. 22 Aug. 2009, http://goveg.com/veganism_environment.asp.

Gaard, Greta. "Living Interconnections with Animals and Nature." *Ecofeminism: Women, Animals, Nature.* Ed. Greta Gaard. Philadelphia: Temple UP, 1993. 1–12.

Gandhi, Leela. *Postcolonial Theory: A Critical Introduction.* New York: Columbia UP, 1998.

Garrard, Greg. *Ecocriticism: The New Critical Idiom.* London: Routledge, 2004.

Gatheru, R. Mugo. *Kenya: From Colonization to Independence, 1888–1970.* Jefferson, N.C.: McFarland, 2005.

Gerhardt, Christine. "The Greening of African-American Landscapes: Where Ecocriticism Meets Post-Colonial Theory." *Mississippi Quarterly* 55.4 (2002): 515–33.

Gikandi, Simon. *Ngugi wa Thiong'o.* Cambridge: Cambridge UP, 2001.

———. "Traveling Theory: Ngugi's Return to English." *Research in African Literatures* 31.2 (2000): 194–209.

Glotfelty, Cheryll. *The Ecocriticism Reader: Landmarks in Literary Ecology.*
    Athens: U of Georgia P, 1996.

Goodman, David. *Fault Lines: Journeys into the New South Africa.* Berkeley:
    U of California P, 1999.

Gordimer, Nadine. "Living in the Interregnum." *The Essential Gesture:
    Writing, Politics and Places.* Ed. Stephen Clingman. New York: Penguin,
    1989. 261–84.

Gruen, Lori. "Dismantling Oppression: An Analysis of the Connection
    Between Women and Animals." *Ecofeminism: Women, Animals, Nature.* Ed.
    Greta Gaard. Philadelphia: Temple UP, 1993. 60–90.

Guha, Ramachandra. "The Arun Shourie of the Left." *The Hindu* 26 Nov.
    2000. 7 Jan. 2008, http://www.hindu.com/2000/11/26/stories
    /13260411.htm.

———. *Environmentalism: A Global History.* New York: Longman, 2000.

Hall, Cheryl Jackson. "Racial and Ethnic Antagonism in Kenya." *Modern
    Kenya: Social Issues and Perspectives.* Ed. Mary Ann Watson. Lanham, Md.:
    UP of America. 275–301.

Hancocks, David. *A Different Nature: The Paradoxical World of Zoos and Their
    Uncertain Future.* Berkeley: U of California P, 2001.

Haraway, Donna. *The Companion Species Manifesto: Dogs, People, and
    Significant Otherness.* Chicago: Prickly Paradigm P, 2003.

Harrison, Nicholas. *Postcolonial Criticism: History, Theory and the Work of
    Fiction.* Cambridge: Polity, 2003.

Hartmann, Betsy. *Reproductive Rights and Wrongs: The Global Politics of
    Population Control.* Boston: South End P, 1995.

Head, Dominic. "The (Im)Possibility of Ecocriticism." *Writing the
    Environment: Ecocriticism and Literature* Ed. Richard Kerridge and Neil
    Sammells. London: Zed Books, 1998. 27–39.

Herne, Brian. *White Hunters: The Golden Age of African Safaris.* New York:
    Holt, 2001.

Herron, Tim. "The Dog Man: Becoming Animal in Coetzee's *Disgrace.*"
    Twentieth-Century Literature 51.4 (2005): 467–90.

Higgins, Alexander G. "un: No Amnesty for Kenyan Vote Violence."
    Associated Press 20 Mar. 2008. 13 May 2008, http://ap.google.com
    /article/ALeqM5hzqHtJ5ifJWY5AeQ87G2iTSDOfgwD8VHoTC00.

Hobsbawm, Eric, and Terence Ranger. *The Invention of Tradition.*
    Cambridge: Cambridge UP, 1983.

Honey, Martha. *Ecotourism and Sustainable Development: Who Owns Paradise?*
    Washington, D.C.: Island P, 1999.

Hooper, Glenn. "History, Historiography and Self in Ngugi's *Petals of Blood*." *Journal of Commonwealth Literature* 33.1 (1998): 47–62.

Howard, Bradley Reed. *Indigenous Peoples and the State: The Struggle for Native Rights*. DeKalb: Northern Illinois UP, 2003.

Huggan, Graham. "'Greening' Postcolonialism: Ecocritical Perspectives." *Modern Fiction Studies* 50.3 (2004): 701–33.

———. *The Postcolonial Exotic: Marketing the Margins*. London: Routledge, 2001.

Hulme, Keri. *the bone people*. New York: Penguin, 1986.

———. "Mauri: An Introduction to Bicultural Poetry in New Zealand." *Only Connect*. Ed. Guy Amirthanayagam and S. C. Harrex. Adelaide: Centre for Research in the New Literatures in English and East-West Center, 1981. 290–310.

International Lake Environment Committee Foundation for Sustainable Management of World Lakes and Reservoirs. "Oguta Lake." *World Lakes Database*. 12 Dec. 2005. 21 Jan. 2006, http://www.ilec.or.jp/database /afr/afr-18.html.

Jacobs, J. U. "Zakes Mda's *The Heart of Redness*: The Novel as *Umngqokolo*." *Kunapipi* 24.1–2 (2002): 224–36.

Jell-Bahlsen, Sabine. "Flora Nwapa and Oguta's Lake Goddess." *Dialectical Anthropology* 31.1–3 (2007): 253–62.

———. *The Water Goddess in Igbo Cosmology: Ogbuide of Oguta Lake*. Trenton, N.J.: Africa World P, 2008.

Johnson, Joyce. "A Note on 'Theng'eta' in Ngugi wa Thiong'o's *Petals of Blood*." *World Literature Written in English* 28 (1988): 12–15.

Jolly, Rosemary. "Going to the Dogs: Humanity in J. M. Coetzee's *Disgrace, The Lives of Animals*, and South Africa's Truth and Reconciliation Commission." *J. M. Coetzee and the Idea of the Public Intellectual*. Ed. Jane Poyner. Athens: Ohio UP, 2006. 148–71.

Kauer, Ute. "Nation and Gender: Female Identity in Contemporary South African Writing." *Current Writing* 15.2 (2003): 106–17.

"The Koru Flag." No date. 12 July 2006, http://www.liong-faye.org.nz /koru-flag/.

Koyana, Siphokazi. "Qolorha and the Dialogism of Place in Zakes Mda's *The Heart of Redness*." *Current Writing* 15.1 (2003): 51–62.

———. "'Why Are You Carrying Books? Don't You Have Children?': Revisiting Motherhood in Sindiwe Magona's Autobiographies." *English Studies in Africa* 45.1 (2002): 45–55.

Koyana, Siphokazi, and Rosemary Gray. "An Electronic Interview with Sindiwe Magona." *English in Africa* 29.1 (2002): 99–107.

Li, Huey-Li. "A Cross-Cultural Critique of Ecofeminism." *Ecofeminism: Women, Animals, Nature.* Ed. Greta Gaard. Philadelphia: Temple UP, 1993. 272–94.

Lloyd, David. "The Modernization of Redness." *Scrutiny2* 6.2 (2001): 34–39.

MacDonald, Michael. *Why Race Matters in South Africa.* Cambridge, Mass.: Harvard UP, 2006.

Magona, Sindiwe. "Mama Africa: A Parable." *The New Internationalist* 307 (1998). 10 July 2006, http://www.newint.org/issue307/mama.htm.

———. *Mother to Mother.* Boston: Beacon, 1998.

Marais, Mike. "J. M. Coetzee's *Disgrace* and the Task of Imagination." *Journal of Modern Literature* 29.2 (2006): 75–93.

Martel, Yann. *Life of Pi.* New York: Harcourt, 2001.

Martinez-Alier, Juan. *The Environmentalism of the Poor: A Study in Ecological Conflicts and Valuation.* Northampton, Mass.: Edward Elgar Publications, 2003.

Mazel, David. *American Literary Environmentalism.* Athens: U of Georgia P, 2000.

———. "American Literary Environmentalism as Domestic Orientalism." *The Ecocriticism Reader: Landmarks in Literary Ecology.* Ed. Cheryll Glotfelty and Harold Fromm. Athens: U of Georgia P, 1996. 137–46.

———, ed. *A Century of Early Ecocriticism.* Athens: U of Georgia P, 2001.

McGreal, Chris. "Mau Mau Veterans to Sue Britain over Torture and Illegal Killings in Kenya." *The Guardian* 6 Oct. 2006. 20 Mar. 2008, http://www.guardian.co.uk/world/2006/oct/06/kenya.topstories3.

McNeill, J. R. *Something New under the Sun: An Environmental History of the Twentieth-Century World.* New York: Norton, 2000.

Mda, Zakes. *The Heart of Redness.* New York: Picador, 2000.

———. Interview. *Africultures* 40 (9 Jan. 2001). 31 Mar. 2009, http://www.africultures.com/anglais/articles_anglais/40mda.htm.

Meffan, James, and Kim L. Worthington. "Ethics before Politics: J. M. Coetzee's *Disgrace.*" *Mapping the Ethical Turn: A Reader in Ethics, Culture, and Literary Theory.* Ed. Todd F. Davis and Kenneth Womack. Charlottesville: UP of Virginia, 2001. 131–50.

Mein Smith, Phillipa. *A Concise History of New Zealand.* Cambridge: Cambridge UP, 2005.

Ministry of Women's Affairs. "Maori Women in Focus: Families and Households." April 1999. 25 Aug. 2009, http://www.mwa.govt.nz /news-and-pubs/publications/maori/maori-women-in-focus.html /families-and-households.html.

Mohanty, Chandra Talpade. "Under Western Eyes: Feminist Scholarship and Colonial Discourse." *Colonial Discourse and Postcolonial Theory: A Reader.* Ed. Patrick Williams and Laura Chrisman. New York: Columbia UP, 1994. 196–220.

Morphet, Tony. "Two Interviews with J. M. Coetzee, 1983 and 1987." *TriQuarterly* 68/69 (1987): 454–464.

Mortensen, Peter. "'Civilization's Fear of Nature': Postmodernity, Culture, and Environment in *The God of Small Things*." *Beyond Postmodernism: Reassessments in Literature, Theory, and Culture.* Ed. Klaus Stierstorfer. Berlin: de Gruyter, 2003. 179–95.

Moss, Laura. "Is Canada Postcolonial? Introducing the Question." *Is Canada Postcolonial: Unsettling Canadian Literature.* Ed. Laura Moss. Waterloo, Ont.: Wilfrid Laurier UP, 2003. 1–23.

Mukherjee, Bharati. *Jasmine.* New York: Grove P, 1989.

Mullaney, Julie. "'Globalizing Dissent?' Arundhati Roy, Local and Postcolonial Feminisms in the Transnational Economy." *World Literature Written in English* 40.1 (2002–03): 56–70.

Mulvey, Laura. "Visual Pleasure and Narrative Cinema." *Feminism and Film Theory.* Ed. Constance Penley, New York: Routledge, 1988. 59–78.

Mwangi, Evan. "The Gendered Politics of Untranslated Language and Aporia in Ngugi wa Thiong'o's *Petals of Blood*." *Research in African Literatures* 35.4 (2004): 66–74.

Nadakavukaren, Anne. *Our Global Environment: A Health Perspective.* 6th ed. Long Grove, Ill.: Waveland P, 1984.

Najita, Susan Y. *Decolonizing Cultures in the Pacific: Reading History and Trauma in Contemporary Fiction.* New York: Routledge, 2006.

Needham, Anuradha Dingwaney. "'The Small Voice of History' in Arundhati Roy's *The God of Small Things*." *Inverventions* 7.3 (2005): 369–91.

Newth, Kim. "Celebrated Writer Keri Hulme Wants the Government to Give Special Environmental Protection to the Tiny West Coast Settlement of Okarito." *Sunday Times* 13 May 2001. 14 Aug. 2006, http://www.okarito.net/page/sunday_times_may_2001.html.

Ngugi wa Thiong'o. *Decolonising the Mind: The Politics of Language in African Literature.* Portsmouth, N.H.: Heinemann, 1986.

————. "Europhonism, Universities, and the Magic Fountain: The Future of African Literature and Scholarship." *Research in African Literatures* 31.1 (2000): 1–11.

————. *Petals of Blood.* New York: Penguin, 1977.

Nicholls, Brendon. "The Landscape of Insurgency: Mau Mau, Ngugi wa Thiong'o and Gender." *Landscape and Empire, 1770–2000.* Ed. Glenn Hooper. Aldershot, U.K.: Ashgate, 2000. 177–94.

Nixon, Rob. "Environmentalism and Postcolonialism." *African Literature: An Anthology of Criticism and Theory.* Ed. Tejumola Olaniyan and Ato Quayson. Malden, Mass.: Blackwell, 2007. 715–23.

Nwankwo, Chimalum. "The Igbo Word in Flora Nwapa's Craft." *Research in African Literatures* 26.2 (1995): 42–52.

Nwapa, Flora. *Efuru.* Oxford: Heinemann, 1966.

O'Brien, Susie. "'Back to the World': Reading Ecocriticism in a Postcolonial Context." *Five Emus to the King of Siam: Environment and Empire.* Ed. Helen Tiffin. Amsterdam: Rodopi, 2007. 177–99.

Ochieng', W. R., and E. S. Atieno-Odhiambo. "Prologue on Decolonization." In *Decolonization and Independence in Kenya: 1940–93.* Ed. B. A. Ogot and W. R. Ochieng'. London: James Currey, 1995. xi–xviii.

Offenburger, Andrew. "Duplicity and Plagiarism in Zakes Mda's *Heart of Redness.*" *Research in African Literatures* 39.3 (2008): 164–99.

Ogude, James A. "Imagining the Oppressed in Conditions of Marginality and Displacement: Ngugi's Portrayal of Heroes, Workers, and Peasants." *Wasafari* 28 (1998): 3–9.

————. *Ngugi's Novels and African History: Narrating the Nation.* London: Pluto P, 1999.

Ohlson, Thomas, and Stephen John Stedman. *The New Is Not Yet Born: Conflict Resolution in Southern Africa.* Washington, D.C.: Brookings Institution, 1994.

Oumhani, Cécile. "Hybridity and Transgression in Arundhati Roy's *The God of Small Things.*" *Commonwealth Essays and Studies* 22.2 (2000): 85–91.

Parry, Benita. *Postcolonial Studies: A Materialist Critique.* London: Routledge, 2004.

Pearse, Fred. *When Rivers Run Dry: Water— The Defining Crisis of the Twenty-First Century.* Boston: Beacon, 2006.

Peires, J. B. *The Dead Will Arise: Nongqawuse and the Great Xhosa Cattle-Killing Movement of 1856–7.* Johannesburg: Ravan, 1989.

Pickover, Michelè. *Animal Rights in South Africa.* Cape Town: Double Storey P, 2005.

Platz, Norbert H. "Rediscovering the Forgotten Space of Nature: A Plea for Ecocriticism in the New Literatures in English." *Borderlands: Negotiating Boundaries in Post-Colonial Writing.* Ed. Monika Reif-Hülser. Amsterdam: Rodopi, 1999. 175–88.

Plumwood, Val. *Environmental Culture: The Ecological Crisis of Reason.* London: Routledge, 2002.

———. *Feminism and the Mastery of Nature.* London: Routledge, 1993.

Prasad, Murari. "The Issue of Linguistic Competence: Arundhati Roy's *The God of Small Things.*" *CIEFL Bulletin* 14.1–2 (2004): 113–35.

Rauwerda, Antje M. "The White Whipping Boy: Simon in Keri Hulme's *The bone people.*" *Journal of Commonwealth Literature* 40.2 (2005): 23–42.

Renan, Ernest. "What Is a Nation?" *Poetry of the Celtic Races and Other Studies.* Port Washington, N.Y.: Kennikat, 1970. 61–83.

Rodrigues, Ângela Lamas. "Beyond Nativism: An Interview with Ngugi wa Thiong'o." *Research in African Literatures* 35.3 (2004): 161–67.

Roos, Bonnie. "Re-Historicizing the Conflicted Figure of Woman in Ngugi's Petals of Blood." *Research in African Literatures* 33.2 (2002): 154–70.

Rosenberg, Tina. "When a Pill Is Not Enough." *New York Times Magazine* 6 Aug. 2006. 15 Aug. 2006, http://www.nytimes.com/2006/08/06 /magazine/06aids.html?ei=5087%0A&en=773789c9aecf8065&ex=115 5096000&pagewanted=all.

Ross, Robert. *A Concise History of South Africa.* Cambridge: Cambridge UP, 1999.

Rothfels, Nigel. *Savages and Beasts: The Birth of the Modern Zoo.* Baltimore: Johns Hopkins UP, 2002.

Roy, Arundhati. *The Cost of Living.* New York: Random House, 1999.

———. *The God of Small Things.* New York: Harper, 1997.

———. *Power Politics.* Cambridge, Mass.: South End P, 2001.

———. *War Talk.* Cambridge, Mass.: South End P, 2003.

Rueckert, William. "Literature and Ecology: An Experiment in Ecocriticism." *Iowa Review* 9.1 (Winter 1978): 71–86.

Said, Edward W. *Orientalism.* New York: Vintage, 1978.

———. "The Public Role of Writers and Intellectuals." *The Public Intellectual* Ed. Helen Small. Oxford: Blackwell, 2002. 19–39.

Sallis, John. *Force of Imagination: The Sense of the Elemental.* Bloomington: Indiana UP, 2000.

Samuelson, Meg. "Reading the Maternal Voice in Sindiwe Magona's *To My Children's Children* and *Mother to Mother*." *Modern Fiction Studies* 46.1 (2000): 227–45.

Schuessler, Jennifer. "Virtue Is Its Own Punishment." Review of Joy Williams's *The Quick & the Dead*. *New York Times* 22 Oct. 2000. 17 Aug. 2009, http://www.nytimes.com/books/00/10/22/reviews/001022 .22schuest.html?_r=1&oref=slogin.

Seth, Aradhana, dir. *Dam/Age: A Film with Arundhati Roy*. 2002. 26 Aug. 2009, http://www.weroy.org/video_damage.shtml.

Shiva, Vandana. *Water Wars: Privatization, Pollution, and Profit*. Cambridge, Mass.: South End P, 2002.

Shulevitz, Judith. "Author Tour." Rev. of *Elizabeth Costello*, by J. M. Coetzee. *New York Times Book Review* 26 Oct. 2003: 15–16.

Sielke, Sabine. "The Empathetic Imagination: An Interview with Yann Martel." *Canadian Literature* 177 (2003): 12–32.

Slaymaker, William. "Ecoing the Other(s): The Call of Global Green and Black African Responses." *PMLA* 116.1 (2001): 129–44.

Soper, Kate. *What Is Nature? Culture, Politics and the Non-Human*. Oxford: Blackwell, 1995.

Spivak, Gayatri. "Can the Subaltern Speak?" *Colonial Discourse and Post-Colonial Theory: A Reader*. Ed. Patrick Williams and Laura Chrisman. New York: Columbia UP, 1994. 66–111.

Steinhart, Edward I. *Black Poachers, White Hunters: A Social History of Hunting in Colonial Kenya*. Athens: Ohio UP, 2006.

Stratton, Florence. "'Hollow at the Core': Deconstructing Yann Martel's *Life of Pi*." *Studies in Canadian Literature* 29.2 (2004): 5–21.

Suleri, Sara. "Woman Skin Deep: Feminism and the Postcolonial Condition." *Colonial Discourse and Postcolonial Theory: A Reader*. Ed. Patrick Williams and Laura Chrisman. New York: Columbia UP, 1994. 244–56.

Taiwo, Oladele. *Female Novelists of Modern Africa*. New York: St. Martin's, 1984.

Vital, Anthony. "Situating Ecology in Recent South African Fiction: J. M. Coetzee's *The Lives of Animals* and Zakes Mda's *The Heart of Redness*." *Journal of Southern African Studies* 31.2 (2005): 297–313.

———. "Toward an African Ecocriticism: Postcolonialism, Ecology and *Life & Times of Michael K*." *Research in African Literatures* 39.1 (2008): 88–106.

Waggoner, Gloria. "The Environment: What Is Kenya Doing?" *Modern*

Kenya: Social Issues and Perspectives. Ed. Mary Ann Watson. Lanham, Md.: UP of America, 2000. 75–88.

Warren, Karen. *Ecofeminist Philosophy: A Western Perspective on What It Is and Why It Matters.* Lanham, Md.: Rowman and Littlefield, 2000.

———. "Taking Empirical Data Seriously: An Ecofeminist Philosophical Perspective." *Ecofeminism: Women, Culture, Nature.* Ed. Karen Warren and Nisvan Erkal. Bloomington: Indiana UP, 1997. 3–20.

Whitty, Julia. "Gone: Mass Extinction and the Hazards of the Earth's Vanishing Biodiversity." *Mother Jones* May/June 2007. 26 Aug. 2009, http://www.motherjones.com/news/feature/2007/05/gone.html.

Wilentz, Gay. *Binding Cultures: Black Women Writers in Africa and the Diaspora.* Bloomington: Indiana UP, 1992.

———. "Instruments of Change: Healing the Cultural Dis-Ease in Keri Hulme's *the bone people.*" *Literature and Medicine* 14.1 (1995): 127–45.

Williams, Elly. "An Interview with Zakes Mda." *Missouri Review* 28.2 (2005): 62–79.

Williams, Joy. *Ill Nature.* New York: Vintage, 2001.

———. *The Quick & the Dead.* New York: Knopf, 2000.

Wilson, Janet. "Reinventing New Myths of Aotearoa in Contemporary New Zealand Fiction." *Across the Lines: Intertextuality and Transcultural Communication in the New Literatures in English.* Ed. Wolfgang Klooss. Amsterdam: Rodopi, 1998. 271–90.

Wilson, Roger. *From Manapouri to Aramoana: The Battle for New Zealand's Environment.* Waiwera, N.Z.: Earthworks, 1982.

Wood, Briar. "Mana Wahine and Ecocriticism in Some Post-80s Writing by Maori Women." *ISLE: Interdisciplinary Studies in Literature and the Environment* 14.1 (2007): 107–24.

Woodward, Wendy. "Postcolonial Ecologies and the Gaze of Animals: Reading Some Contemporary Southern African Narratives." *JLS/TLW* 19.3–4 (2003): 290–315.

Wright, Laura. *Writing "Out of All the Camps": J. M. Coetzee's Narratives of Displacement.* New York: Routledge, 2006.

Zarrilli, Philli. *Kathakali Dance-Drama: Where Gods and Demons Come to Play.* London: Routledge, 1999.

cholera: and South Africa 171

coal, South African dependence on, 171

Coetzee, J. M., 13, 15, 16, 21, 56–57, 185n15, 187n11, 187n13, 187n16, 188n1; *Disgrace*, 15–16, 90–96, 176–77; *Elizabeth Costello*, 94; and *In the Heart of the Country*, 93; *The Lives of Animals*, 13, 94; *Waiting for the Barbarians*, 188n1

communalism. *See under* Igbo culture

confession, in *Disgrace*, 90

Conrad, Joseph: and Achebe, 2, 181n1; and intertexts in *The God of Small Things*, 111; and intertexts in *The Heart of Redness*, 43

contextual moral vegetarianism, 62, 100. *See also* Curtin, Deane; vegetarianism

Cost of Living, The (Roy), 104, 119, 123

Cunninghame, R. J. *See under* safari

Curtin, Deane, 10–12, 13, 56, 61–62, 179. *See also* contextual moral vegetarianism

Dam/Age motion picture (Seth), 16, 104–5, 109, 111, 119, 121–27

damming: environmental damage of, 104, 124, 130, 151, 158, 171; and displacement of human populations 108, 123, 172

D.D.T., 8–9

Decolonising the Mind (Ngugi), 24, 26

Defoe, Daniel, *Robinson Crusoe*, 73

deforestation: in Kenya, 36, 38; in India, 108; in New Zealand, 154; in Nigeria, 140; in South Africa, 22, 98, 172

dialogic drag, 94

dialogism, 94, 144, 176–78. *See also* Bakhtin, Mikhail

dilemma: in *Efuru*, 135–36, 144, 176. *See also* dilemma tale

dilemma tale, 190n7. *See also* dilemma

Disgrace (Coetzee), 15–16, 90–96, 176–77

dogs, 95, 155; in *Disgrace*, 16, 90–92, 95–97, 100–101, 187n16

Dutch East India Company, 98, 168

ecocriticism, 174–75, 182, 182n11; as political, 2; history of, 3–4, 8; intersections with postcolonialism, 9–13, 175, 181

ecofeminism, 128–29, 131; and Arundhati Roy, 119; intersections with postcolonialism, 130; Western conceptions of, 129. *See also* feminism

ecological literacy, 182n8

ecotourism, 1, 22, 54, 82; connection to hunting, 83–85; environmental impact of, 53, 85. *See also* Ecotourism Society

Ecotourism Society, 82. *See also* ecotourism

education: and alienation from traditional culture, 47; as colonizing agent, 23, 28, 36, 68, 133–34, 137; in the "New" South Africa, 97

Igbo culture: communalism in, 132; childlessness in, 138–39; environmental issues of, 140, 142–44, 190n5; and female circumcision, 138; matrilineality in, 135, 137, 164; religion in, 145; role of women, 133, 135–42, 163–4, 176; and slave trade, 189n3. *See also* Uhamiri

Igbo Women's War (1929), 136, 138

Ill Nature (Williams), 77

Ilmorog: in *Petals of Blood*, 22–23, 27–28, 34–38, 53. *See also* Trans-Africa highway

Indian Supreme Court, 103, 105. *See also* Roy, Arundhati

International Lake Environmental Committee Foundation for Sustainable Management of World Lakes and Reservoirs, 144

interregnum, 174–66, 188n5, 192n2. *See also* Gramsci, Antonio

In the Heart of the Country (Coetzee), 93

In Which Annie Gives It Those Ones (Roy), 121

Jasmine (Mukherjee), 103–4

Jell-Bahlsen, Sabine, 134–36, 142–43, 190n6. *See also* Uhamiri

Judd, Bill. *See under* safari

kathakali dancers, 105, 114–17; and Bhima and Dushasana, 116; and the "Great Stories," 117; and Karna and Kunti, 115. *See also* Kerala

Katse-Mohale Dams, 171

kaumatua: in *the bone people*, 130, 151, 153

Kerala, 115, 119. *See also* kathakali dancers

Khoikhoi, 98–99, 156, 168; and San 98, 168

Kibaki, Mwai, 192n1

Kikuyu, 184n5. *See also* Gikuyu

"Killing Game, The" (Williams), 86–87

koru flag, 153. *See also* Hundertwasser, Friedensreich

Lake Manapouri, 155

Land Act (1913), 172

Land Claims Ordinance (1841), 158

Lee, Sandra, 191n10

Life of Pi (Martel), 62–63, 66–69, 73, 75–76, 80, 92, 176

Lives of Animals, The (Coetzee), 13, 94

Lugard, Frederick, 30

Maathai, Wangari, 33–34. *See also* Green Belt Movement

magical realism. *See under* Mda, Zakes

Magona, Sindiwe: *Forced to Grow*, 163; "Mama Afrika," 161, 173; and motherhood, 160, 164; *Mother to Mother*, 17, 129–30, 132, 159–64, 166–67, 169–70, 173–74, 177, 185n16, 191n12; on prophecy, 162; *To My Children's Children*, 163

Mahaoya, Baba, 122

Makah Nation, 62, 186n2

"Mama Afrika" (Magona), 161, 173

"Maori: An Introduction to Bicultural Poetry in New Zealand" (Hulme), 155

Maori culture: and Aotearoa, 145; and conceptions of time, 146; and environmentalism, 146, 148, 154–57, 178, 191n11; and Keri Hulme, 190n8; and Papatuanuku, 151; and religion, 147, 149–50; and spiral, 153, 158; and *whakapapa*, 146–47; and women, 151–52. *See also* kaumatua; Maui; Treaty of Waitangi

Martel, Yann, 14–16, 56–57; and animals, 76; and *Life of Pi*, 62–63, 66–69, 73, 75–76, 80, 92, 176; and national identification, 66–67, 69, 72; and postcolonialism, 93. *See also* metafiction

matrilineality. *See under* Igbo culture

Maui, 149–50, 154

Mau Mau: emergency period, 1952–1956, 21, 30; insurgency, 30, 32; in *Petals of Blood*, 27, 29, 37; relationship to the environment, 32, 38

Mazel, David, 6–7, 182n8

McNeill, J. R., 33; on extinction, 58–60; on oil in Nigeria, 136, 140; on South Africa, 42. *See also* minion biota

Mda, Zakes, 15, 19–20; on apartheid and writing, 20–21; and doubling, 43–44; *The Heart of Redness*, 39–54, 178; and magical realism, 40; and plagiarism of Peires, 185n13; and postmodern pastoralism, 40;

and satire, 48; and Xhosa cattle killing, 21, 40–42, 49, 130, 162, 185n12. *See also* Black Economic Empowerment (BEE)

Meenachal River, 104–5, 108, 110–11, 117

metafiction: and *Life of Pi*, 63, 65, 93; and *The Quick & the Dead*, 93

mimicry, 22, 30, 114, 184n4. *See also* Bhabha, Homi K.

minion biota, 59–60, 91. *See also* McNeill, J. R.

Modern Language Association (MLA), 184n15

Mogopa removal (1984), 99, 168

Moi, Daniel arap, and Ngugi wa Thiong'o, 184n7

monsoons: and environment, 10; and *The God of Small Things*, 110; and the Narmada dam project, 123

Mother to Mother (Magona), 17, 129–30, 132, 159–164, 166–17, 169–70, 173–4, 177, 185n16, 191n12

Mukherjee, Bharati, *Jasmine*, 103–4

Narmada Bachao Andolan, 120, 183n12, 188n7. *See also* Patkar, Medha

Narmada dam project, 16, 104–5, 108, 119–20, 123

Narmada Valley, 110, 122, 124

National Book Critics Circle Award: Joy Williams, finalist for, 77

nativism: and Ngugi wa Thiong'o, 23–25, 184n6

Ndumo Game Reserve, 84

New literatures in English, 9

ern peoples, 11; rhetoric of, 12,
135; and Western peoples, 59
population growth, 11–12, 183n14
Power Politics (Roy), 124
public intellectual: Ngugi as, 25;
Roy as, 121
Pulitzer Prize: Joy Williams, finalist
for, 77

Qolorha, 39–41, 43–51, 54
Quick & the Dead, The (Williams),
77–90, 92–3, 95–6, 177–78

rape: and *Disgrace*, 90, 93, 94, 100–
101, 174; and *The God of Small
Things*, 117–18; and *Jasmine* 104;
and South Africa, 93, 95, 164,
187n12
Robinson Crusoe (Defoe), 73
Roy, Arundhati, 12, 16, 103–13,
115–127, 177, 188n2, 188n5,
188n6; *The Cost of Living*, 104,
119, 123; in *Dam/Age*, 16,
104–5, 109, 111, 119, 121–27;
"The End of the Imagination,"
108; *The God of Small Things*,
103–20, 125, 127; "The Greater
Common Good," 108, 122, 124;
*In Which Annie Gives It Those
Ones*, 121; and Narmada dam
project, 16; *Power Politics*, 124.
See also Indian Supreme Court
Royal Dutch Shell and British
Petroleum (Shell-BP), 140
Rueckert, William, 6
Rushdie, Salman, 107

safari, 15, 57, 82; and R. J.
Cunninghame, Bill Judd, George

Outram, and Leslie Tarston, 83;
and decimation of animal species, 177; and hunting, 82–85;
and photography, 83–86, 90;
and *The Quick & the Dead*, 82;
and "Safariland," 86–88,
183n13
"Safariland" (Williams), 85–86, 88,
99, 183n13
Said, Edward, *Orientalism*, 2, 6, 121
Saro-Wiwa, Ken, 144, 183n12. *See
also* Niger delta; Ogoni people
Seth, Aradhana, *Dam/Age*, 16–17,
104–5, 109, 111, 119, 121–24,
127
Shiva, Vandana, 16, 103, 104, 108,
120, 188n4
slave trade. *See under* Igbo culture
Smith, Sir Harry, 41–42
South Africa, 1, 13, 15, 20; and
apartheid, 20–21, 43, 46, 48,
97, 100–101, 163–64, 166;
and Coetzee, 13, 15, 16; and
Magona, 17; and Mda, 15,
20–23, 39–44, 46, 48–49, 51;
and the environment, 13, 42.
See also New South Africa; rape;
Xhosa cattle killing.
spiral. *See under* Maori culture
Spivak, Gayatri, 109, 123, 181n2
Subaltern Studies Group, 2. *See also*
Guha, Ranajit

Tanzania, 82–85; Wildlife
Conservation Society of, 186n9
Tarstan, Leslie. *See under* safari
Tarzan of the Apes (Burroughs), 77
Theng'eta, in *Petals of Blood*, 15, 21,
24, 26–29, 31–33, 36–39

58–60; and Nonkosi, 45; and
Nongqawuse, 17, 21, 40–42,
44–45, 48–52, 54, 130–31, 161,
166, 169–70, 173

Zimbabwe, 84
zoos: arguments for and against,
74; and *Life of Pi*, 16, 63–64, 66,
70–71, 74–77, 176, 186n3

Lightning Source UK Ltd.
Milton Keynes UK
UKOW040819131112

202105UK00003B/59/P